# THEORY OF
# PROSE

VIKTOR
SHKLOVSKY

# THEORY OF PROSE

TRANSLATED BY
BENJAMIN SHER

INTRODUCTION BY
GERALD L. BRUNS

DALKEY
ARCHIVE
PRESS

First paperback edition, 1991
Second printing, 1991
Third printing, 1998

Library of Congress Cataloging-in-Publication Data:

Shklovskiĭ, Viktor Borisovich, 1893-1984
    [O teorii prozy. English]
    Theory of prose / Viktor Shklovsky; introduction by Gerald L.
Bruns; translated with an introduction by Benjamin Sher.
    Translation of: O teorii prozy, 2n ed. (Moscow, 1929).
    Includes bibliographical references.
    1. Prose literature—History and criticism. 2. Prose literature—
Technique. I. Sher, Benjamin. II. Title.
PN3457.S4913     1990
809.3—dc20                         90-2714
                                        CIP

ISBN: 0-916583-54-6 (cloth)
ISBN: 0-916583-64-3 (paper)

Partially funded by grants from the National Endowment for the Arts, a
federal agency, and the Illinois Arts Council, a state agency.

Dalkey Archive Press
Illinois State University
Campus Box 4241
Normal, IL 61790-4241

*website: www.cas.ilstu.edu/english/dalkey/dalkey.html*

Printed on permanent/durable acid-free paper and bound in the United
States of America.

# Contents

# Preface

It is perfectly clear that language is influenced by socioeconomic conditions.

There is an essay by Gleb Uspensky in which he shows how a fishing crew creates its own reality by inventing names for a constellation of stars which guides them in their nightly "search for the white salmon."

In the language of cattle breeders you will find numerous words designating such peculiarities as the coat colors of cows and bulls. These do not lend themselves easily to translation.

Nevertheless, the word is not a shadow.

The word is a thing. It changes in accordance with the linguistic laws that govern the physiology of speech and so on.

If in some language the name of a breastplate becomes the name of the breast of a human being, then, of course, this can be understood historically. But the changes of words do not necessarily correspond to the changes in the form of the breastplate, and, besides, the word may survive the phenomenon that had given rise to it in the first place.

As a literary critic, I've been engaged in the study of the internal laws that govern literature. If I may bring up the analogy of a factory, then I would say that neither the current state of the world cotton market nor the politics of cotton trusts interests me. One thing alone concerns me: the number of strands that make up the cotton plant and the different ways of weaving them. For that reason, this book is devoted in its entirety to a study of the changes in literary form.

VIKTOR SHKLOVSKY

# Introduction

# Toward a Random Theory of Prose
## Gerald L. Bruns

I have a taste for reading even torn papers
lying in the streets.
—Don Quixote

Modernity begins with the recognition that the object before me is not a sign but a random particle. And it is all there is; nothing is behind or beyond it, nor is anything underneath. It is opaque and irreducible, one singularity among others multiplied excessively in every direction. The universe is made of such things. The historic task of modernity, starting in the seventeenth century and continuing to this day, has been to develop a theory of rationality adequate to a universe of randomness—and not only a theory but a program of strategic operations capable of entering into the heterogeneity of things and bringing it under control. One could say that with modernity the task of reason was no longer to interpret the world but rather to overcome it—to reduce it conceptually, to grasp and contain it within an order of general laws and technological systems, finally to intervene in its operations and to turn it to productive account. To make sense of the world, we must penetrate its incoherent surface and lay bare its deep structures; we must grasp not its hidden meanings but its inner workings. Grammar is mastery. And with this idea comes the invention of politics, whose task is to produce a cultural system free from internal contradiction, social fragmentation, and endless crises of legitimacy.

Another way to put this might be to say that modernity begins with the discovery that the book of the world is written in prose. A poetic universe is, philosophically speaking, a universe of correspondences. In a poetic universe, every fragment is a luminous detail. It resonates with the supersensuous. It is in perpetual transport from the everydayness of its material appearance to the sphere of the transcendental where it is really located, and its impact upon consciousness constitutes a moment of vision or the sense of embracing the totality of all that is. There are overarchings everywhere. But a prose universe is just one damn thing after another, like an attic or junkyard or side of the road. Shklovsky says that Cervantes began his great book by organizing it as a dinner table, but almost at once things got away from him. *Don Quixote,* as Shklovsky emphasizes, is a narrative whose parts are out of place; and so is the world it mirrors, in which (in Ortega y Gasset's phrase) the poetic has collapsed, leaving only leftovers like the books Don Quixote reads. The prose world is a place of violent interruption; it is the nonlinear region of pure historicality that can only be described by means of chaos theories and models of catastrophe, or perhaps not so much catastrophe as the slow breaking down of entities piece by piece. It is an unpredictable and dangerous world in which everyone is someone's victim. We are liable to a beating at every intersection, because the adversary no longer dwells at the mouth of the cave or the depths of the fen but is going by in every direction, no more in place than we are. No quest is needed to take us to him; he is always at our blind side, the roving bandit or lurking street thug, but of course he might just as easily be the local innkeeper or a member of the family. The world of prose is bourgeois all the way down.

The task of reason in the world of prose is to bring things under control— not, however, by poeticizing them, not by allegorizing events into semantic superstructures (theories of chivalry, for example, or of culture), but rather by the construction of plots, that is, by means of deep syntactic structures whose operations do not so much abolish randomness as justify it, rather the way linguistics tries to justify the arbitrariness of words by appeals to internal necessity. Syntax, so to speak, replaces semantics. The effect of such justification would not be to transform the singular particle into something else but, on the contrary, to hold its singularity in place, fixing its difference as such. In this way the allegory of love gives way to structuralist poetics. The random particle is not to be interpreted as an element in a symbolic order that subsumes it and renders it transparent; the particle remains refractory and dense, nothing in itself but only a combinatory potential. Enclosed in a purely relational environment of codes, networks, and total systems, the particle gains in power what it loses in meaning; or rather its meaning is now its relationality as such rather than its correspondence to something external to itself. So Don Quixote is always out of place; he is not a character in a romance but at best a character exiled from romance, a character turned to prose, wandering in a world that takes him apart piece by piece and spreads him along a plane of random intersections. The task of reason is to connect him up with Sancho Panza. Here is a random encounter with binary consequences, the beginnings of a new system (call it the novel, or the discourse of everyday life). The difference between Sancho and Don Quixote has a point to it (it inscribes everyday-ness as the collapse of the poetic). Sancho meanwhile, like the comic figures in Shakespeare, is a prose character who understands that the world is best served by getting out of its way. Falstaff is likewise only Falstaff; the classical typology to which his sort once belonged has been swallowed up in a prosaic theory of the world, along with all thoughts of hierarchic grandeur. The honor ethic has given way to the ethic of ordinary life. The task of reason in the world of prose is to articulate this ethical framework, which does not seek to endow the ordinary with any transcendental sublimity but simply seeks to preserve it as the untranscendable horizon of the singular. Shklovsky's way of putting this is to say that the task of art is to make the stone stony, that is, to keep us from experiencing an object as something other than it is; as if the task of art were to free us from allegory or the semantic transparency of particulars.

It is obvious at once, however, that the world of prose is irreducible even to a structuralist poetics. Prose is by nature unstable and self-interfering; it is refractory and uncontainable. Prose does not so much flow as overflow. Sancho Panza's storytelling in chapter 20 of part 1, which is more like counting than recounting, preserves exactly the nonlinear, self-interrupting excessiveness of the prose world. "Tell it consequentially, like an intelligent man," says the bewildered Quixote, but Sancho is already following Tristram Shandy's philosophy of composition, which is to let the world speak, let every singularity have its say, without respect to rules of reason or propositional order. Indeed, one could say that the natural inclination of prose is to organize itself into lists rather than into stories and propositions.

Could a historiographer drive on his history, as a muleteer drives on his mule,——straight forward . . . he might venture to foretell you to an hour when he should get to his journey's end;——but the thing is, morally speaking, impossible: For, if he is a man of the least spirit he will have fifty deviations from a straight line to make with this or that party as he goes along, which he can no ways avoid. He will have views and prospects to himself perpetually soliciting his eye, which he can no more help standing still to look at than he can fly; he will moreover have various

Accounts to reconcile:
Anecdotes to pick up:
Inscriptions to make out:
Stories to weave in:
Traditions to sift:
Personages to call upon:
Panegyricks to paste up at this door;
Pasquinades at that:——All of which both the man and his mule are quite exempt from. (*Tristram Shandy,* 1.14)

The world of prose only comes into its own with the invention of the printing press, which emancipates discourse from the transcendental bondage of narrative and the higher forms of consecutive reasoning. Prose documents its environment from the inside out, not from above, and so it counts things one by one instead of organizing them systematically into accounts that, among other coherent things, begin and end and point a moral. Prose is by its nature realistic in its unpredictable concern with the density of what is singular and refractory to categories. Prose is the unfinished discourse of inhabitants (who themselves never stay in place but, if they have the least spirit, wander maddeningly in every direction, picking up odds and ends, losing bits and pieces: one thinks here of Beckett's Malloy). So the fugitive essay, the decrepit billboard, the meandering joke, entries in an abandoned diary, the muddled quotation, the jotted note, the newspaper page to wrap your cups in, dirty words in the public toilet, menus in French, pointless anecdotes, the crumpled shopping list, the broken-off conversation, police reports, the missent letter, the ad in the window, signs at a rally, gossip or hearsay, a student's answer, the weak radio signal, bureaucratic memos, translations from Japanese, shouting in the street, magazines in the garage, or words to that effect: these are some of the basic genres in the prose of prose.

Shklovsky, of course, is thinking (mostly) of artistic prose, or prose that in some fashion redeems itself from itself, raises itself by its bootstraps into some type of formal coherence. But he recognizes that there is always a historical tension between prose and form, and it is this tension that he seeks to study in the book that follows, which gives us the theory of prose, not as a semiotician or a narratologist might, but through the mediation of historical (one might just as well say random) detail. Russian Formalism is not Structuralism. Its method is historical research rather than the analytical construction of models. Structuralism raises itself on an opposition between system and history, structure and event; Russian Formalism defines itself not against history but against psychology. The difference between Formalism and Structuralism lies in the way the singular is preserved in the one but erased by the other. Structuralism is a method of subsumptive thinking. What matters is the totality of the system. But Shklovsky's formalism is distributed along a diachronic plane. His theory of prose is a *prose* theory of prose, not the systematic construction of a model indifferent to its examples but heterogeneous, internally conflicting descriptions of texts strewn irreducibly throughout the history of writing. Shklovsky's model is not the linguistics of Saussure but historical linguistics and comparative philology. He is closer to Auerbach than to Todorov. He is interested in the historicality of forms rather than in the rules of how formal objects work. So his theory has the richness of practical criticism as well as the lucidity of theoretical reflection, as in his suggestion that an anecdote that is not random (not to say pointless) is not an anecdote.

Not against history but against psychology: the idea here is to foreground the individual text in its formal intelligibility rather than to reconstruct what lies behind the text in the form of an originating expression or rule. The task of Russian Formalism was to emancipate the work of art from the theory of expression, which was Romanticism's way of coping with the world of prose. What's the poet's place in a world of prose? This was essentially Wordsworth's question in his preface to the *Lyrical Ballads.* The idea was to integrate extraordinary events of the mind into the everyday and so to redeem the everyday from its banality. The poet's task is to mediate between the banal and the transcendental—temporality redeemed by its spots. That the poet might come out of this mediation a bit prosy—looking entirely unremarkable, in Geoffrey Hartman's phrase—is fair exchange, since the world comes out looking poetic, even inhabitable and serene, whereas without the poet's intervention it would be a plane of sullen objects impeding movement or escape. Wallace Stevens is perhaps not the last Wordsworthian but he's close: the poet determined to build an inhabitable world from the debris of prose.

But to make the stone stony is to chip away the inscription someone carved on it; it is to turn signs back into things. Formalist poetry (not to say a good deal of modern writing) does this by foregrounding the materiality of language, disrupting the signifying function in order to free words from the symbolic order that rational people say we construct from them. Other sorts of poets just take the world of prose to heart and confound the idea of poetry altogether, as when William Carlos Williams says (pace Stevens) that "A poem can be made out of anything": grocery lists, newspaper clippings, crude love notes, the unrevised doodlings of an exhausted pediatrician. A substantial portion of American writing has tried to work out the consequences of this idea, most recently in the movement called "language poetry," which, among other things, tries to write a poetry that (pace Mallarmé) doesn't seal itself off from whatever is not itself—doesn't, for example, try to seal itself off from the randomness of everyday talk. Here are some lines from Ron Silliman's *What* (1988):

> Woman doctor and male nurse
> are running down the hospital corridor.
> Syntax freezes them forever,
> though I merely made them up.
> Whatness vs. Whichness. 'T's not
> just the large beard on the small guy but
> the way it juts forward. Swivel
> your hips with a knee dip and
> the skateboard serves
> up the curb ramp. Brit flag in window
> serves as curtain. Walker in sweatsuit
> and knit cap—lone figure
> on track at dawn. Pages of xerox
> in a dimestore binder. So let's patent blood
> (knowing the market). So there's Habermas
> in a guest spot on *Miami Vice.* Or the way tabloids
> use quotation marks in place of italics. Like water,
> language runs to the sea, flush with information.
> Not that, aardvark! Prefer poets' yap
> to their lap. Discordance in number
> triggers an audit. Squint
> just to keep glasses
> from sliding down nose. A
> line a day keeps
> the critic away. Re-
> work context for previous vowel.

NO PARK WILL BE TOWED
spray-painted freehand on garage door.
Zen grocer. Eyes ache
after day at CRT.
A teenage girl with a bright smile,
safety pin thru her nose.

As Stephen Fredman says in his book *Poet's Prose,* language poetry like Ron Silliman's is written in prose but is not prose poetry; rather it is poetry that defamiliarizes language by incorporating the overfamiliar, or what belongs to the daily life of a prose environment.

A final point would be that prose is inherently comic precisely because it is the discourse of what is near at hand or everyday. What is remote is always mystified, but what we rub up against every day always inclines us toward laughter, particularly when we see it take the form of language, which is to say language that is not only material but palpable. Prose belongs to the world of flesh and skin. It is in its nature to be corpulent rather than lean. Of course, philosophers try to make prose lean by reducing it to propositional form, because they know that there's no saying anything in prose, no saying something about something and getting it exactly right, not when prose is allowed to go its natural way, growing as much as functioning. There's more to prose than sentences. It overflows thought. One needs paragraphs, chapters, volumes—and still prose will prove uncontainable. Not for nothing Henry James called such novels as he himself did not write "loose and baggy monsters," nor that his prose is distant, distancing, not of this world, impalpable and precise. But even James could hardly stop revising, as if what he had once written had gone to pot and needed to be pounded back into shape, the way of all prose.

# Translator's Introduction

## Shklovsky and the Revolution
### Benjamin Sher

God's voice called for me and said:
"Arise, O prophet, listen and behold,
Fill every sinew with My will,
And as you travel over land and sea,
Set hearts on fire with your Word."
—Pushkin, "The Prophet"

Standing on the brink of the Stalinist nightmare of the 1930s, Viktor Shklovsky declared courageously and forthrightly that the word is autonomous and that the artist who commands its panoply of devices is sovereign and absolute in his domain:

A literary work is pure form. It is neither thing nor material, but a relationship of materials. . . . Humorous works, tragic works, world-encompassing or intimate works, confrontations of worlds or of cats and stones—are all equal in the eyes of literature. It is from this that comes the inoffensive character of art, its sense of being shut up within itself, its freedom from external coercion. . . . An artifact has a soul that is very much like a form, like the geometric relationship of masses. (189, 191)

What exactly does Shklovsky mean?

Is he proclaiming a New Critical manifesto à la Brooks, Warren & Co. centered on the artist as master craftsman? Or is he waging a rearguard battle to preserve a decadent, elitist, art-for-art's-sake individualism against the new dominant Marxist ideology and its mass culture? Or is he perhaps seeking some new synthesis as yet unknown?

One of Shklovsky's most telling distinctions in *Theory of Prose* is between, on the one hand, "recognition," that is, an understanding of an object or thing based on formulas, conventions and preconceptions, and, on the other hand, "seeing," the perception of an object as revealed by an artist wielding the devices of his craft. "Seeing" is an active, dynamic act of perception brought into play by the artist's technique which allows us to see what, until then, had not and could not yet come into view.

Shklovsky has nothing but contempt for any theory of literature that denies or ignores the creative process (in the modern sense of craft). For

*xv*

him the artist is a magician, a supreme master in command of a whole array of "devices" (plot, rhythm, image, wordplay, etc.), without which art does not exist.

If this is so, a Western reader might be tempted to "recognize" affinities between Shklovsky's ideas and certain Western tendencies, when what is called for here is nothing less than a "seeing" that attempts to understand Shklovsky from within, that is, that sees him as a critic who sought to "enstrange," to transform our conventional perceptions of literary history. (See below for a discussion of the key concept of "enstrangement.")

Like Pasternak, Mayakovsky, Tsvetaeva, Mandelshtam, Akhmatova, and other luminaries of the post-Revolutionary era, Shklovsky was undoubtedly an outstanding representative of a *pre*-Revolutionary Russian intelligentsia that called Paris its home no less than St. Petersburg or Moscow. That is, it had strong links with Western values as we have come to know them since the Renaissance. Yet, such values founded on the sensibility of the solitary genius blossomed on Russian soil against the background of a society torn apart by a tug-of-war between the tsar's repressive, myopic regime and a long-suffering people (*narod*) increasingly alienated and radicalized against him.

From this welter of doubt, apprehension and loss of faith emerged a whole array of competing, fanatical ideologies promising salvation to nation and/or individual soul. These isms encompassed the whole spectrum of Russian culture, from politics (Bolshevism, a Russian variant of Marxism), history (Slavophilism), religion (Russian Orthodoxy), literature (symbolism, Acmeism, etc.), nature (primitivism), technology and urbanism (Futurism), etc. These indigenous isms, along with Western imports ranging from cubism and expressionism in art to liberalism in politics, thrived in an apocalyptic age ushered in by the tsar on Bloody Sunday, 9 January 1905, when he unleashed the first revolution by massacring peaceful petitioners on the streets of Saint Petersburg.

Thus, when the Revolution broke out in Russia in 1917 (in February and again in October), it had already been expected for nearly a generation. And for many years thereafter this world-historical cataclysm nurtured the imagination of writers, painters, composers and filmmakers, inspiring them to subordinate their personal sensibilities to the lofty ideals of the Revolution. This was the spirit of the age, embracing one and all, from the aristocratic, delicate Symbolists to the tough, younger breed. As Marc Slonim writes in *Soviet Russian Literature* (1964):

> The Symbolists had had a foreboding of the cataclysm, and they were well qualified to express the belief that the flame kindled in Moscow would set the whole world ablaze. . . . Revolutionary messianism was in the air: in the cities and villages speakers were proclaiming Russia as the savior of humanity and the builder of a new society. . . . Other symbolists and acmeists, such as Anna Akhmatova, also sang of illumination and spoke of the Revolution with messianic fervor. . . . The romantic and heroic poems [of the young] stressed the grandeur, the universal sweep of

events and were frankly utopian and hyperbolic. A group of proletarian poets, calling themselves Cosmists, predicted a conquest of space beyond our planet: "we will first overthrow the earth, then we shall stage the rebellion of the stars. . . ." They expected the World Revolution to come at any moment from just around the corner; they could hear the tread of history. Consciously or unconsciously, the people of Russia welcomed the advent of a new era.

Thrust into this apocalyptic turmoil, Shklovsky must have felt the earth trembling beneath his feet. Yet, he boldly and unequivocally proclaimed the sovereignty of the artist and his vocation in a dying world that was waiting to be reborn.

Looking at a picture of Shklovsky in the company of Mayakovsky and Pasternak—reproduced on the cover—I found myself wondering about the possible relevance of this group photo to the major themes of *Theory of Prose.*

What is the significance of Shklovsky's presence in the company of two revolutionary Futurists? What were the exponents of a spiritual and historical transformation through destruction and regeneration doing side by side with an eccentric devotee of the artist and his devices?

It suddenly struck me that Shklovsky may have considered his role to be far more than a mere defender of the artist and his craft (a role he played, admittedly, with consummate art himself). Is it not conceivable that Shklovsky's preoccupation with craft may have arisen from a heroic, revolutionary conception of the artist as a man-god whose mission is to destroy the old and build the new, that is, the new paradise, on earth? If this is so, then may we not suggest, in turn, that the real thrust of Shklovsky's criticism was directed not merely at establishing the autonomy of the artist through his craft but at the *emancipation* of the artist from his historical bondage to extra-literary forces that have exploited him like a lackey for their own ends? In effect, Shklovsky is striving with might and main, or so it seems, to rehabilitate the artist, whether in the person of the anonymous storyteller of the Middle Ages or the Greek classics or Cervantes, or Dickens or Tolstoi or even Arthur Conan Doyle. He seeks to liberate him from the clutches of the social scientists, psychologists, political scientists, philosophers, theologians, historians, even from the clutches of literary critics themselves.

And it is here that we must ask the cardinal question: Why did Shklovsky strip these masters of their ancient, conventional non-literary layers of interpretation? In other words, why did he enstrange them, why did he, like a magician, remove the superfluous veil from our eyes if not indeed to transform these apparently literary valets into heroic, revolutionary artificers, into demigods with the power given them by their craft to create a new world, or at least a vision of it?

This may also account for Shklovsky's fascination with Sterne's all-encompassing power to create a literary universe that obeyed at will the commands of its one solitary creator, the author. And, incidentally, this hypothesis would help explain Shklovsky's disapproval of Bely's involve-ment with the mystical movement of anthroposophy. For in Shklovsky's opinion, Bely doomed his phenomenological search for his childhood by chaining it to the procrustean bed of anthroposophy.

We may thus consider *Theory of Prose* as Shklovsky's paean to the artists of the past, who had in turn enstranged the materials of their world and art, and who thus succeeded in transforming the formulaic, conven-tional perceptions of *their* age into a true vision of what man is and can be.

In his very style, Shklovsky betrays his kinship to the new revolutionary (though not necessarily Marxist) movement. Like Pasternak, Mayakovsky, and Tsvetaeva, Shklovsky uses a variety of devices to enstrange his material and to provoke in us an irresistible scorn for whatever is hackneyed, trite, and stereotypical in the old world (Lesage, Gogol, Chekhov, Tolstoi) and an equally irresistible desire for a vision of the new age (Rozanov, Bely, Cervantes, even, aesthetically speaking, Sterne). And, like his Futurist comrades, he abandons the smooth, incantatory cadences of the Symbolists (so frequent in their celebrations of death and the world beyond death) in favor of a this-worldly, rough-textured, "laborious" and elliptical style that bristles with extravagant comparisons, witticisms, trenchant puns, liberal use of italics and endless digressions from the main theme. No wonder we find him often contradicting himself or thinking aloud, as it were, as he lunges here or there. His brilliant half analytical, half anecdotal approach to criticism, showing, it seems, little regard for the reader's comfort, "impedes" the reader at every turn, putting him on the defensive, forcing him to question age-old taboos, challenging him to "see" the artifact and not merely to "recognize" it.

Such a revolutionary hypothesis might help us to understand Shklovsky's obsession with the artist's sovereignty. Far from harking back to the Decadence of the 1890s, Shklovsky's whole thrust would then point instead to the future, to a utopian future that apparently was never meant to be. For these same artists and scholars and thinkers who celebrated the messianic age so fervently were later martyred for their faith in an orgy of annihilation that turned the apocalypse of the Revolution upside down.

*

ENSTRANGEMENT: There are, to my knowledge, at least three translations of this key term of Shklovsky. First, let me state the problem: The Russian word *ostraniene* (noun) or *ostranit'* (verb) is a neologism, a fact in itself of supreme importance in a critic as given to serious wit and punning as Shklovsky is. There is no such word in Russian dictionaries. It is clear that the *o* prefix (*o-straniene*), often used to implement an action (though this is only one of its many and even contradictory uses), may be understood to apply to two stems simultaneously, that is, to both *stran* (strange) as well as *storon* (side, which becomes *stran* in such verbs as *otstranit'* [to remove, to shove aside]). It is a pretty fair assumption, then, that Shklovsky speaks of *ostraniene* as a process or act that endows an object or image with "strangeness" by "removing" it from the network of conventional, formulaic, stereotypical perceptions and linguistic expressions (based on such perceptions). This being the case, how should we translate this concept into English?

The translation "estrangement" is good but negative and limited. "Making it strange" is also good but too positive. Furthermore, both "estrangement" and "making it strange" are not new, that is, they require no special effort of the imagination. In fact, they exemplify the very defect they were supposed to discourage.

Finally, there is "defamiliarization," a term used in Lee T. Lemon and Marion J. Reis's *Russian Formalist Criticism* (1965). This semi-neologism is very seductive until you realize that it is quite wrongheaded. Shklovsky's process is in fact the reverse of that implied by this term. It is not a transition from the "familiar" to the "unknown" (implicitly). On the contrary, it proceeds from the cognitively known (the language of science), the rules and formulas that arise from a search for an economy of mental effort, to the familiarly known, that is, to real knowledge that expands and "complicates" our perceptual process in the rich use of metaphors, similes and a host of other figures of speech. "Defamiliarization" is dead wrong!

And so, after some reflection, I decided to coin the word "enstrange," "enstrangement," built on the same cognate root. While positive (see other *en*- prefix words such as "enthrall"), it is also strongly associated with the counterpointing "estrange," "estrangement."

A final word on the subject: The Russians I talked to reacted to *ostranit'* exactly the way an American reader would react to "enstrange," that is, they immediately assumed that it was a misprint for *otstranit'* (that is, the Russian equivalent, for the sake of this discussion, of "estrange").

THE TEXT: *Theory of Prose* was originally published in 1925 in a book of around 190 pages, some of whose chapters had been previously published as journal essays. I have selected the expanded 1929 edition of *Theory of Prose* (250 pages plus index) for the following reasons: (1) University Microforms Inc. (Ann Arbor) chose the 1929 edition for its photocopy edition, available in many libraries. (2) Ardis Press, the famous Russian publisher also in Ann Arbor, chose the 1929 edition for its facsimile reprint in 1971. (3) While mentioning both editions, Victor Erlich, an authority on Formalism, shows an apparent preference for the 1929 edition (*Russian Formalism: History and Doctrine*).

PREVIOUS TRANSLATIONS: I would like to acknowledge the work of others who have helped to shape my approach to Shklovsky. First, I would like to mention the pioneering work of Richard Sheldon and Robert Sherwood. Though problematic in places, their published translations to date demonstrate how maddeningly elusive Shklovsky can be.

On the other hand, Lemon and Reis are professional, lucid and empathic, and I hope I've matched their passionate commitment with my own. Naturally, our terms often differ, but that is inevitable in translating a writer as challenging as Shklovsky.

QUOTATIONS: All translations from Russian texts are mine unless otherwise noted. For other non-English works, standard translations have been used and translators credited. Although Motteux's baroque translation of *Don Quixote* is no longer considered standard, I've used it because it has a magnificence and nobility I find irresistible.

TRANSLITERATION: Russian names have been transliterated according to the system used in Victor Terras's *Handbook of Russian Literature* (Yale University Press, 1985). This excellent reference book also served as the authority for book titles, names of characters, literary terms, and English versions of untranslated Russian works.

ACKNOWLEDGMENTS: I wish to express my deep appreciation to Sophia and Mischa Kukuy, originally from the Soviet Union, for their kind, unselfish help over many years.

My heartfelt gratitude to my two secretaries who believed in me and in my project and who gave of their very best: Celia Brewer, whose passion for literature and scholarly research were absolutely indispensable, and Jeanette Hornot, whose professional expertise and inexhaustible patience made it all possible. My thanks also to Peter Gallim, who did a great job as a typist in the first phase of the project.

My deep thanks to Jean Laves Hellie of Chicago, an expert on early twentieth-century Russian literature, for her extraordinary generosity in sharing with me her erudition and insight.

My thanks to Natasha Ramer of Tulane University, a native of the Soviet Union, for her unselfish assistance, patience and understanding.

My deep appreciation to Ms. Zitzelsberger and her Russian staff at the New York Public Library for their splendid assistance, knowledgeability and immense patience.

My thanks to Ms. Arthur and the Russian staff at Harvard's Widener Library for their invaluable and unselfish help.

My deep thanks to the Baker Street Irregulars, especially Mr. John Bennet Shaw of Santa Fe and Mr. Peter Blau of Washington, D.C., Sherlock Holmes experts, for their enthusiastic, unselfish research into the arcane mysteries of the Sherlock Holmes canon and apocrypha. My gratitude also to Frederick Page and Jayne Stanton of Ann Arbor, Michigan. Thanks to their magnificent work, the Sherlock Holmes references are all complete.

My thanks to Prof. Felix Oinas of Indiana University for his assistance with some of the more obscure aspects of Russian folk tales.

My thanks to Prof. Andy Horton of the University of New Orleans for sharing his Russian materials with me.

My profound personal and professional debt to Robert Olivier (Olive Tree Bookshop) and Carey Beckham (Beckham's Bookshop) of New Orleans goes back many, many years. Always generous with time and money and books, they have consistently shown their encouragement, support and loyalty.

My thanks also to the following:

Emilia Resende, for going out of her way to borrow urgently needed materials from Tulane University.

Justin Winston, for his immense store of knowledge and analytical acumen.

Jeremy Machalek, for his great intelligence and analytical abilities.

Linda Huber, for her devotion and encouragement.

Debbie Kaufman, for her proofreading and enthusiasm.

Tom Hardin, for his untiring encouragement and wise counsel.

Channing and Carolyn Hardin, for their unquestioning love and support.

Samu, Dvora and Ilanit Tof, brother-in-law, sister and niece, respectively, of Melbourne, Australia, for their enthusiastic support and encouragement during many lean years. Special thanks to Samu Tof for providing me with my Panasonic word processor, without which, as we all know, this project would have never gotten off the ground.

Helen Sher, my mother, of New Orleans, who has kept me going year after year in her own special way as long as I can remember.

Finally, my thanks to Mr. John O'Brien and the staff at Dalkey Archive Press for their faith, dedication, meticulousness and exemplary professionalism. Mr. O'Brien guided this project to its happy conclusion with a firm but gentle hand.

# Chapter 1

# Art as Device

"ART IS THINKING IN IMAGES." This phrase may even be heard from the mouth of a lycée student. It serves as the point of departure for the academic philologist who is making his first stab at formulating a theory of literature. This idea, first propounded, among others, by Potebnya, has permeated the consciousness of many. In *Notes on the Theory of Literature* he says: "There is no art without imagery, especially in poetry." "Like prose, poetry is, first and foremost, a mode of thinking and knowing."

Poetry is a special mode of thinking—to be precise, a mode of thinking in images. This mode entails a certain economy of mental effort that makes us "feel the relative ease of the process." The aesthetic sense is a consequence of this economy. This is how academician Ovsyaniko-Kulikovsky understands it, and his recapitulation of this theory, based as it was on his teacher, whose works he had studied with great care, was in all likelihood quite accurate. Potebnya and the numerous members of his movement consider poetry to be a special form of thinking (i.e., of thinking with the aid of images). The raison d'être of the image consists, in their opinion, in helping to organize heterogeneous objects and actions into groups. And the unknown is explained through the known. Or, in Potebnya's words:

> The relationship of the image to that which is explained by means of it may take one of two forms: (a) either the image serves as a constant predicate to a succession of ever-changing subjects—a permanent means of attracting changeable percepts, or else (b) the image is much simpler and clearer than that which is to be explained.

Thus, "since the purpose of imagery is to bring the significance of the image closer to our understanding, and since, without this, an image has no meaning, then, the image ought to be better known to us than that which is explained by it."

It would be interesting to apply this law to Tyutchev's comparison of summer lightning with deaf-and-dumb demons or to Gogol's simile of the sky as the raiments of the Lord.

"There is no art without images." "Art is thinking in images." Enormous energy has been put into interpreting music, architecture, and song along the lines of literature. After a quarter of a century of effort, Ovsyaniko-Kulikovsky has finally recognized the need for a special category of non-imagistic art encompassing song, architecture, and music. Separating them from literature, he defines this category as that of the lyrical arts, whose essence lies in a spontaneous play of the emotions. And so it has turned out that at least one huge chunk of art is not subject to the imagistic mode of thinking. And one of these (i.e., the song) resembles, nonetheless, "imagistic" art: it too deals with words. What is even more important, imagistic art passes imperceptibly into non-imagistic art. And yet our perceptions of them are similar.

Still, the assertion that "Art is thinking in images," and therefore (leaving out the intervening steps known to everyone) the proposition that art is the creator, above all, of symbols, has persisted to this day, having survived the collapse of the theory on which it is based. It is particularly very much alive in the Symbolist movement, especially among its theoreticians.

Consequently, many people still believe that thinking in images (i.e., in "paths and shades," "furrows and boundaries") is the distinguishing feature of poetry. Therefore, these people must have expected the history of this "imagistic" art, to use their own words, to consist of the changes in the history of the image. It turns out, however, that images endure and last. From century to century, from country to country, from poet to poet, these images march on without change. They belong to "no one," except perhaps to "God." The more you try to explain an epoch, the more you are convinced that the images you thought were created by a given poet were, in reality, passed on to him by others with hardly a change. The work of successive schools of poetry has consisted essentially in accumulating and making known new devices of verbal arrangement and organization. In particular, these schools of poetry are far more concerned with the disposition than with the creation of imagery. In poetry, where imagery is a given, the artist does not so much "think" in images as "recollect" them. In any case, it is not imagistic thinking that unites the different arts or even the different forms of verbal art. And it is not the changes in imagery that constitute the essential dynamics of poetry.

We know of cases where we stumble onto a poetic something that was never meant, originally, to serve as an object of aesthetic contemplation. For example, we may point to Annensky's opinion concerning the special poetic character of Church Slavonic or to Andrei Bely's rapture over the practice by eighteenth-century Russian poets of placing the adjective after the noun. Bely raves about this as if there were something intrinsically artistic about it. Or, more precisely, Bely goes beyond this in assuming that this artistic quality is also intentional. In fact, though, this is nothing but a general peculiarity of the given language (the influence of Church Slavonic). In this way a work may be either created as prose and experienced as poetry, or else created as poetry and experienced as prose. This points out the fact that the artistic quality of something, its relationship to poetry, is a result of our mode of perception. In a narrow sense we shall call a work artistic if it has been created by special devices whose purpose is to see to it that these artifacts are interpreted artistically as much as possible.

On the basis of Potebnya's conclusion, which asserts that poetry equals imagery, a whole theory has arisen declaring further that imagery equals symbolism. This presupposes that an image is capable of serving as a constant predicate to a succession of changeable subjects. This conclusion, lying at the heart of the Symbolist movement, has seduced, by virtue of its kinship of ideas, such writers as Andrei Bely and Merezhkovsky with his "eternal companions." This conclusion flows partly from the fact that Potebnya did not distinguish the language of poetry from the language of prose. Thanks to this he has failed to notice that there exist two types of imagery: imagery as a practical way of thinking, that is, as a means of uniting objects in groups, and, secondly, imagery as a way of intensifying the impressions of the senses. Let me illustrate. I'm walking along the street and I see a man walking ahead of me wearing a hat. Suddenly, he drops a package. I call out to him: "Hey, you with the hat, you dropped a package!" This is an example of a purely prosaic use of an image. A second example. Several men are standing at attention. The platoon leader notices that one of the men is standing awkwardly, against army regulations. So he yells at him: "Hey, clean up your act, you crumpled hat!" This image is a poetic trope. (In one case the word *hat* serves as a metonymy, while in the other example we're dealing with a metaphor. And yet I'm really concerned here with something else.)

A poetic image is one of the means by which a poet delivers his greatest impact. Its role is equal to other poetic devices, equal to parallelism, both simple and negative, equal to the simile, to repetition, to symmetry, to hyperbole, equal, generally speaking, to any other figure of speech, equal to all these means of intensifying the sensation of things (this "thing" may well be nothing more than the words or even just the sounds of the literary work itself). Still, the poetic image bears only a superficial resemblance to the fairy-tale image or to the thought image (see Ovsyaniko-Kulikovsky in *Language and Art,* where a young girl calls a round sphere a "watermelon"). The poetic image is an instrument of the poetic language, while the prose image is a tool of abstraction: the watermelon instead of the round lampshade or the watermelon instead of the head is nothing more than an act of abstracting from an object and is in no way to be distinguished from head = sphere or watermelon = sphere. This is indeed a form of thinking, but it has nothing to do with poetry.

The law governing the economy of creative effort also belongs to a group of laws taken for granted by everyone. Here is what Herbert Spencer says:

> On seeking for some clue to the law underlying these current maxims, we may see shadowed forth in many of them, the importance of economizing the reader's or the hearer's attention. To so present ideas that they may be apprehended with the least possible mental effort, is the desideratum towards which most of the rules above quoted point. . . . Hence, carrying out the metaphor that language is the vehicle of thought, there seems reason to think that in all cases the friction and inertia of the

vehicle deduct from its efficiency; and that in composition, the chief, if not the sole thing to be done, is to reduce this friction and inertia to the smallest possible amount. (*The Philosophy of Style*)

And Richard Avenarius writes:

If the soul possessed inexhaustible resources, then it would be of no moment to it, of course, how many of these inexhaustible resources had actually been spent. The only thing that would matter would be, perhaps, the time expended. However, since our resources are limited, we should not be surprised to find that the soul seeks to carry out its perceptual activity as purposefully as possible, i.e., with, relatively speaking, the least expenditure of energy possible or, which is the same, with, relatively speaking, the greatest result possible.

By a mere allusion to the general law governing the economy of mental effort, Petrazhitsky dismisses James's theory, in which the latter presents the case for the corporeal basis of the effect. The principle of the economy of creative effort, so seductive especially in the domain of rhythm, was affirmed by Aleksandr Veselovsky. Taking Spencer's ideas to their conclusion, he said: "The merit of a style consists precisely in this: that it delivers the greatest number of ideas in the fewest number of words." Even Andrei Bely, who, at his best, gave us so many fine examples of his own "laborious," impeding rhythm and who, citing examples from Baratynsky, pointed out the "laboriousness" of poetic epithets, found it, nonetheless, necessary to speak of the law of economy in his book. This work, representing a heroic attempt to create a theory of art, demonstrates Bely's enormous command of the devices of poetry. Unfortunately, it also rests on a body of unverified facts gathered from out-of-date books, including Krayevich's physics textbook, in fashion when he was a student at the lycée.

The idea that an economy of effort lies at the basis of and governs the creative process may well hold true in the "practical" domain of language. However, these ideas, flourishing in the prevailing climate of ignorance concerning the nature of poetic creation, were transplanted from their native soil in prose to poetry.

The discovery that there are sounds in the Japanese poetic language that have no parallels in everyday Japanese was perhaps the first factual indication that these two languages, that is, the poetic and the practical, do not coincide. L. P. Yakubinsky's article concerning the absence of the law of dissimilation of liquid sounds in the language of poetry, and, on the other hand, the admission into the language of poetry, as pointed out by the author, of a confluence of similar sounds that are difficult to pronounce (corroborated by scientific research), clearly point, at least in this case, to the fundamental opposition of the laws governing the practical and poetic uses of language.

For that reason we have to consider the question of energy expenditure and economy in poetry, not by analogy with prose, but on its own terms.

If we examine the general laws of perception, we see that as it becomes habitual, it also becomes automatic. So eventually all of our skills and experiences function unconsciously—automatically. If someone were to compare the sensation of holding a pen in his hand or speaking a foreign tongue for the very first time with the sensation of performing this same operation for the ten thousandth time, then he would no doubt agree with us. It is this process of automatization that explains the laws of our prose speech with its fragmentary phrases and half-articulated words.

The ideal expression of this process may be said to take place in algebra, where objects are replaced by symbols. In the rapid-fire flow of conversational speech, words are not fully articulated. The first sounds of names hardly enter our consciousness. In *Language as Art,* Pogodin tells of a boy who represented the sentence "Les montagnes de la Suisse sont belles" in the following sequence of initial letters: *L, m, d, l, S, s, b.*

This abstractive character of thought suggests not only the method of algebra but also the choice of symbols (letters and, more precisely, initial letters). By means of this algebraic method of thinking, objects are grasped spatially, in the blink of an eye. We do not see them, we merely recognize them by their primary characteristics. The object passes before us, as if it were prepackaged. We know that it exists because of its position in space, but we see only its surface. Gradually, under the influence of this generalizing perception, the object fades away. This is as true of our perception of the object in action as of mere perception itself. It is precisely this perceptual character of the prose word that explains why it often reaches our ears in fragmentary form (see the article by L. P. Yakubinsky). This fact also accounts for much discord in mankind (and for all manner of slips of the tongue). In the process of algebrizing, of automatizing the object, the greatest economy of perceptual effort takes place. Objects are represented either by one single characteristic (for example, by number), or else by a formula that never even rises to the level of consciousness. Consider the following entry in Tolstoi's diary:

As I was walking around dusting things off in my room, I came to the sofa. For the life of me, I couldn't recall whether I had already dusted it off or not. Since these movements are habitual and unconscious, I felt that it was already impossible to remember it. If I had in fact dusted the sofa and forgotten that I had done so, i.e., if I had acted unconsciously, then this is tantamount to not having done it at all. If someone had seen me doing this consciously, then it might have been possible to restore this in my mind. If, on the other hand, no one had been observing me or observing me only unconsciously, if the complex life of many people takes place entirely on the level of the unconscious, then it's as if this life had never been. (29 February [i.e., 1 March] 1897)

And so, held accountable for nothing, life fades into nothingness. Automatization eats away at things, at clothes, at furniture, at our wives, and at our fear of war.

If the complex life of many people takes place entirely on the level of the unconscious, then it's as if this life had never been.

And so, in order to return sensation to our limbs, in order to make us feel objects, to make a stone feel stony, man has been given the tool of art. The purpose of art, then, is to lead us to a knowledge of a thing through the organ of sight instead of recognition. By "enstranging" objects and complicating form, the device of art makes perception long and "laborious." The perceptual process in art has a purpose all its own and ought to be extended to the fullest. *Art is a means of experiencing the process of creativity. The artifact itself is quite unimportant.*

The life of a poem (and of an artifact) proceeds from vision to recognition, from poetry to prose, from the concrete to the general, from Don Quixote, the scholarly and poor aristocrat enduring half-consciously his humiliation at court, to Turgenev's broad and hollow Don Quixote, from Charlemagne to Charles the Fat. As the work of art dies, it becomes broader: the fable is more symbolic than a poem and a proverb is more symbolic than a fable. For that reason, Potebnya's theory is least self-contradictory in its analysis of the fable, which, he believed, he had investigated thoroughly. Alas, his theory never dealt with the "eternal" works of imaginative literature. That accounts for the fact that Potebnya never did complete his book. As is well known, *Notes on the Theory of Literature* was published in 1905, thirteen years after the author's death. Potebnya himself had managed to work out fully only the section on the fable.

After being perceived several times, objects acquire the status of "recognition." An object appears before us. We know it's there but we do not see it, and, for that reason, we can say nothing about it. The removal of this object from the sphere of automatized perception is accomplished in art by a variety of means. I wish to point out in this chapter one of the devices used almost constantly by Tolstoi. It is Merezhkovsky's belief that Tolstoi presents things as he sees them with his eyes without ever changing them.

The devices by which Tolstoi enstranges his material may be boiled down to the following: he does not call a thing by its name, that is, he describes it as if it were perceived for the first time, while an incident is described as if it were happening for the first time. In addition, he foregoes the conventional names of the various parts of a thing, replacing them instead with the names of corresponding parts in other things. Let me demonstrate this with an example. In "Shame" Tolstoi enstranges the idea of flogging by describing people who, as punishment for violating the law, had been stripped, thrown down on the floor, and beaten with switches. A few lines later he refers to the practice of whipping their behinds. In a note on this passage, Tolstoi asks: "Just why this stupid, savage method of inflicting pain and no other: such as pricking the shoulder or some such other part of the body with needles, squeezing somebody's hands or feet in a vise, etc."

I apologize for the harshness of this example but it is typical of the way Tolstoi reaches our conscience. The usual method of flogging is enstranged by a description that changes its form without changing its essence. Tolstoi constantly makes use of this method of enstrangement.

In "Kholstomer," where the story is told from the point of view of a horse, the objects are enstranged not by our perception but by that of the horse. Here is how the horse views the institution of property:

What they were saying about flogging and about Christianity I understood very well. But I was completely mystified by the meaning of the phrase "*my* colt" or "*his* colt." I could see that humans presupposed a special relationship between me and the stable. What the nature of that relationship was I could not fathom at the time. Only much later, when I was separated from the other horses, did I understand what all this meant. At that time, however, I couldn't possibly understand what it meant when I heard myself called by people as the property of a human being. The words "*my* horse" referred to me, a living horse, and this seemed to me just as strange as the words "my land," "my air" or "my water."

And yet, these words had an enormous impact on me. I thought about this night and day, and it was only after many diverse contacts with humans that I learned at last the significance of these strange words. The gist is this: People are guided in their life not by deeds but by words. They love not so much the opportunity of doing (or not doing) something as the chance to talk about a host of things in the possessive language so customary among them: *my* book, *my* house, *my* land, etc. I saw that they applied this "my" to a whole gamut of things, creatures and objects, in fact, even to people, to horses, to the earth itself. They have made a compact among themselves that only one person shall say "my" to any one thing. And, in accordance with the rules of this game, he who could say "my" about the greatest number of things would be considered to be the happiest of men. Why this is so I don't know, but it is so. For a long time I tried to see in this some direct benefit to me, but in the final analysis, it all seemed so unjust.

Many of the people, for example, who call me their horse did not ride on me. Others did. These same people never fed me. Others did. Once again, I was shown many kindnesses, but not by those who called me their horse. No, by coachmen, veterinarians and strangers of all sorts. As my observations grew, though, I became increasingly convinced that this concept of *mine* was invalid not only for us horses but also for human folk, i.e., that it represents nothing more than man's base and beastly instinct to claim property for himself. A landlord, for instance, says "my house" but never lives in it, concerning himself only with the structure and maintenance of the house. A merchant says "my shop," "my clothing shop," yet he himself does not wear any clothes made from the fine material displayed in it.

There are people who call a piece of land theirs but have never laid eyes on it nor walked it. There are people who call other people theirs, but who have never seen them. And their entire contact with these people consists of doing them evil.

There are people who call women "theirs" or "their" wives, yet these women live with other men. And people do not aspire to do good. No, they dream of naming as many objects as possible as *their own.*

Leaving aside other good reasons for our superiority, I am now convinced that what distinguishes us from humans and gives us the right to claim a higher place on the ladder of living creatures is simply this: that the human species is guided, above all, by *words,* while ours is guided by *deeds.*

The horse is killed off long before the end of the story, but the mode of telling the story, its device, does not change:

Much later, they dumped Serpukhovsky's body into the ground. He had walked the earth. He had drunk and eaten of it. Neither his skin nor flesh nor bones were of any use to anybody.

For twenty years, this dead body walking the earth was a great burden to everyone. Now, the dumping of this body seemed like another hardship to others. He was no longer of any use to anyone and could no longer cause anyone any grief. Nevertheless, the dying who buried the dead had found it necessary to dress up this bloated body, which was about to rot, in a dress uniform and to lower him, with his good boots on, into a fine coffin adorned with new tassels at the four corners. They then put this new coffin into another coffin made of lead, took it to Moscow, where they dug up ancient human bones and buried this body infested with worms in its new uniform and polished boots. Then they poured earth all over his coffin.

We see by the end of this story that Tolstoi continues to make use of this device even when no motivation for it exists.

In *War and Peace* Tolstoi describes battles using the same device. They are all presented, above all, in their strangeness. Unfortunately, I cannot offer any full examples, because this would require excerpting a large portion of the monumental novel. However, a description of the salons and the theater will suffice for the moment:

Level boards were spread out in the center of the stage. Along the wings stood painted pictures depicting trees. Behind them, a canvas was stretched on boards. In the middle of the stage sat young girls in red bodices and white skirts. One young girl, very fat, and attired in white silk, was sitting separately on a low bench to which a green cardboard was attached from behind. They were all singing something. When they finished singing, the young girl in white walked over to the prompter's box and a man in tight-fitting silken hose on his fat legs approached her, sporting a plume, spread his arms in despair and began singing. The man in tight-fitting hose sang alone, then she sang. Then they both fell silent, the music roared, and the man began fingering the hand of the young girl dressed in white, evidently waiting again for his turn to join her in song. After their duet, everyone in the theater applauded and shouted. Gesticulating, the lovers then smiled and bowed to the audience.

The second act included scenes depicting monuments. The moon and stars peeped in through holes in the canvas and lampshades were raised in frames. Then, to the sound of bass horns and double basses, hordes of men rushed onto the stage sporting black mantles and brandishing what looked like daggers. Then still others ran up and started pulling on the arm of a young girl. Dressed earlier in white, she was now dressed in a light blue dress. They did not drag her off right away. First, they joined her in a song for what seemed like a very long time. At long last, after whisking her off, they struck three times on some metallic object offstage. Then, everyone fell on his knees and began singing a prayer. Several times the actions of the protagonists were interrupted by the enthusiastic screams of the audience.

So also in the third act:

... But suddenly a storm broke out and in the orchestra you could hear the chromatic scales and diminished seventh chords and they all ran up and dragged another of the characters offstage as the curtain fell.

Or in the fourth act:

> There was a certain devil on the stage who sang, with arms outspread, until someone pulled the board from under him and he fell through.

Tolstoi describes the city and court in *Resurrection* in the same way. Similarly, he asks of the marriage in *The Kreutzer Sonata:* "Why should two people who are soul mates sleep together?"

But the device of enstrangement was not used by Tolstoi to enstrange only those things he scorned:

> Pierre got up and walked away from his new friends and made his way among camp fires to the other side of the road where, as he had been told, the captive soldiers stayed. He wanted to have a little talk with them. On the way, a French sentinel stopped him and ordered him to return. Pierre returned, but not to the camp fire, not to his friends, but to an unharnessed carriage that stood somewhat apart. Cross-legged and with his head lowered, he sat on the cold earth by the wheels of the carriage and thought for a long time without moving. More than an hour passed. No one disturbed him. Suddenly, Pierre broke out with a robust, good-natured laugh that was so loud that people looked back from all directions at this evidently strange laugh.
>
> "Ha, ha, ha," Pierre laughed and he began talking to himself: "So the soldier wouldn't let me through, ha, ha, ha! They seized me, blocked my way. Me. Me. My immortal soul. Ha, ha, ha," he continued laughing as tears rolled down his cheeks. . . .
>
> Pierre looked up at the sky, at the playful stars that were receding into the distance. "And all of this is mine and all of this is within me and all of this is me," Pierre thought to himself. "And they seized all of this and shut it off with boards." He smiled, returned to his comrades and went to sleep.

Everyone who knows Tolstoi well can find several hundred examples of this sort. His way of seeing things out of their usual context is equally evident in his last works, where he applies the device of enstrangement to his description of the dogmas and rituals he had been investigating. He replaces the customary terms used by the Orthodox Church with ordinary, down-to-earth words. What results is something strange, something monstrous which was taken by many—quite sincerely, I might add—as a form of blasphemy, causing them great pain. And yet this is the same device that Tolstoi applied to his perceptions and descriptions of the world around him.

Tolstoi's faith was shattered by his perceptions. He was confronting that which he had been trying to evade for a long time.

The device of enstrangement is not peculiar to Tolstoi. I illustrated it with examples from his work for purely practical considerations, that is, simply because his work is known to everyone.

Having delineated this literary device, let us now determine the limits of its application more precisely. In my opinion, enstrangement can be found almost anywhere (i.e., wherever there is an image).

What distinguishes our point of view from that of Potebnya may be formulated as follows: The image is not a constant subject for changing predicates. The purpose of the image is not to draw our understanding closer to that which this image stands for, but rather to allow us to perceive the object in a special way, in short, to lead us to a "vision" of this object rather than mere "recognition."

The purpose of imagery may be most clearly followed in erotic art. The erotic object is here commonly presented as something seen for the very first time. Consider, for example, Gogol's "Christmas Eve":

> Then he moved closer to her, coughed, let out a laugh, touched her exposed, full arm and said in a voice that expressed both cunning and self-satisfaction:
>
> "And what's that you have there, my splendid Solokha?" Saying this, he took several steps back.
>
> "What do you mean? My arm, Osip Nikiforovich!" Solokha answered.
>
> "Hm! Your arm! Heh, heh, heh!" the secretary, satisfied with his opening gambit, said warmly and paced about the room.
>
> "And what's that you have there, Solokha? Why are you trembling?" he said with that same look in his eyes as he started for her again and touched her neck lightly with his hand. He then pulled back as before.
>
> "As if you didn't see, Osip Nikiforovich!" Solokha answered. "It's my neck and on my neck there is a necklace."
>
> "Hm! So there is a necklace on your neck! Heh, heh, heh!" and the secretary again paced up and down the room, wringing his hands. "And what's that you have there, my peerless Solokha?"
>
> Who knows how far the secretary would dare go with those long fingers of his?

Or in Hamsun's *Hunger:* "Two white miracles showed through her blouse."

Or else erotic objects are depicted allegorically, where the author's intent is clearly something quite other than a conceptual understanding.

Here belongs the description of private parts in the form of a lock and key (e.g., in Savodnikov's *Riddles of the Russian People*), or in the corresponding parts of a loom, or in the form of a bow and arrow, or in the game of rings and marlinespikes. We find the latter in the traditional bylina (folk epic) about Stavyor, where the husband fails to recognize his wife, who has put on the armor of a bogatyr (folk) heroine. She poses the following riddle:

> "Do you remember, Stavyor, remember, dear?
> How we strolled along the street when young,
> How we played rings and 'spikes together:
> Your marlinespike was made of silver,
> While my ring was made of gold.
> *I* would hit the target now and then
> But *you* struck bull's-eye every time . . ."
> Stavyor, son of Godinovich, says in turn:
> "I have never played marlinespikes with you!"
> Vasilisa Mikulichna fires back, quote:
> "Don't you remember, Stavyor, don't you recall

> How we learned our alphabet together:
> Mine was the silver inkwell, and your pen was golden?
> *I* moistened your pen then and there,
> Yes, I moistened it, all right, then and there."

There is another version of this bylina where a riddle is answered:

> At this point the fearsome ambassador Vasilyushka
> Raised her dress all the way up to her navel.
> And behold, young Stavyor, the son of Godinovich
> Recognized the gilt-edged ring . . .

But enstrangement is not a device limited to the erotic riddle—a euphemism of sorts. It is also the foundation of all riddles. Every riddle either defines and illustrates its subject in words which seem inappropriate during the telling of it (for instance: "What has two rings with a nail in the middle of it?") or else it represents a peculiar audio form of enstrangement (i.e., a kind of mimicry: "*slon da kondrik*" instead of "*zaslon i konnik*").

Similarly, erotic images that are not riddles may also be a form of enstrangement. I mean, of course, the whole range of colorful obscenities associated with the burlesque. The device of enstrangement is perfectly clear in the widely disseminated image—a kind of erotic pose—in which bears and other animals (or the devil, prompted by a different motivation for non-recognition) do not recognize man. Very typical is this tale of non-recognition, one of the *Great Russian Tales of the Perm Province* collected by D. S. Zelenin:

A peasant was cultivating a field with a piebald mare. A bear approaches him and asks: "Hey, brother. Who made this mare piebald for you?"

"I myself, of course," the peasant replied.

"Really, and how?" the bear fired back.

"Come on, let me make you piebald too."

The bear agreed.

The peasant tied the bear's legs with a rope, removed the ploughshare from the plough, heated it in the fire, and off he went to apply it to the bear's flanks. This scorched his coat to the very bone, making him piebald. After the peasant untied him, the bear moved away and lay under a tree.

A magpie swooped down on the peasant to peck at his flesh. The peasant seized it and broke one of its legs. The magpie then flew off and sat down on the same tree against which the bear was resting.

Finally, a horsefly came along and sat on the mare and began biting it. The peasant seized the horsefly, shoved a stick up its behind, and let it go. The horsefly flew off and sat in the same tree where the magpie and bear were reposing.

All three were resting together when the peasant's wife arrived on the scene with her husband's dinner. After eating his dinner in the open air, the peasant beat his wife, throwing her repeatedly to the ground.

Seeing this, the bear said to the magpie and the horsefly: "My God! Looks like this peasant is out to make someone piebald again."

"No, no," the magpie answered, "no, he wants to break someone's leg."

"Oh, no, fellows, you got it all wrong," the horsefly announced solemnly: "Not at all. He wants to shove his stick up her behind!"

The similarity of the enstrangement device here with its use by Tolstoi in "Kholstomer" is, I believe, quite obvious.

The enstrangement of the sexual act in literature is quite frequent. For example, in the *Decameron,* Boccaccio refers to "the scraping of the barrel," "the catching of the nightingale," "the merry woolbeating work" (the last image is not deployed in the plot). Just as frequent is the enstrangement of the sexual organs.

A whole series of plots is built on "non-recognition," for example, Afanasiev's *Indecent Tales.* The whole tale of the "Bashful Lady" revolves around the fact that the object is never called by its proper name (i.e., it is based on a game of non-recognition). The same is true of Onchukov's "A Woman's Blemish" (tale no. 525) and "The Bear and the Rabbit," also from *Indecent Tales,* in which a bear and a rabbit give each other a "wound."

To this device of enstrangement belong also constructions such as "the pestle and the mortar" or "the devil and the infernal regions" (*Decameron*).

Concerning enstrangement in the form of psychological parallelism, see my next chapter on plot formation. Here let me say only, what is important in psychological parallelism is for each of the parallel structures to retain its independence in spite of obvious affinities.

The purpose of parallelism is the same as that of imagery in general, that is, the transfer of an object from its customary sphere of perception to a new one; we are dealing here with a distinct semantic change.

In our phonetic and lexical investigations into poetic speech, involving both the arrangement of words and the semantic structures based on them, we discover everywhere the very hallmark of the artistic: that is, an artifact that has been intentionally removed from the domain of automatized perception. It is "artificially" created by an artist in such a way that the perceiver, pausing in his reading, dwells on the text. This is when the literary work attains its greatest and most long-lasting impact. The object is perceived not spatially but, as it were, in its temporal continuity. That is, because of this device, the object is brought into view.

These conditions are also met by "poetic language." According to Aristotle, poetic language ought to have the character of something foreign, something outlandish about it. In practice, such language is often quite literally foreign: just as Sumerian might have been regarded as a "poetic language" by an Assyrian, so Latin was considered poetic by many in medieval Europe. Similarly, Arabic was thought poetic by a Persian and Old Bulgarian was regarded likewise by a Russian. Or else it might indeed be a lofty language, like the language of folk song, which is close to literature. To this category belong also the widespread archaisms of poetic language, the difficulties of the language of the twelfth century called "dolce stil nuovo," the language of Daniel, with its dark style and difficult forms, *presupposing difficulties in pronunciation.* Yakubinsky has demonstrated in his article the law of difficulty for the phonetics of poetic language, particularly in the repetition of identical sounds. In this way, therefore, the language of poetry may be said to be a difficult, "laborious," impeding language.

In certain isolated cases, the language of poetry approaches the language of prose, but this does not violate the principle of "difficulty." Pushkin writes:

> Her sister was called Tatiana.
> Willfully shall we shed light
> On the tender pages of this novel,
> Naming her so for the first time.

For the contemporaries of Pushkin, the elevated style of Derzhavin *was* poetic language, while the style of Pushkin, due to its banality (as was thought then) represented for them something unexpectedly difficult. Let's not forget that Pushkin's contemporaries were horrified at his trite expressions. Pushkin employed folk speech as a special device of arresting the reader's attention precisely in the same way that his contemporaries interspersed *Russian* words in their everyday French speech (see the examples in Tolstoi's *War and Peace*).

At this point, an even more characteristic phenomenon takes place. Though alien to Russia by its nature and origin, the Russian literary language has so deeply penetrated into the heart of our people that it has lifted much of popular speech to unheard-of heights. At the same time, literature has become enamored of dialect (Remizov, Klyuev, Esenin, and others, all of these so uneven in their talent and yet so near to a consciously provincial dialect) and of barbarisms (we might include here Severyanin's school). Maksim Gorky, meanwhile, is making a transition at this very moment from the literary tongue of Pushkin to the conversational idiom of Leskov. And so folk speech and the literary tongue have changed their places (Vyacheslav Ivanov and many others). Finally, a powerful new movement is making its debut with the creation of a new, specialized poetic language. At the head of this school, as is well known, stands Velimir Khlebnikov.

All things considered, we've arrived at a definition of poetry as the language of *impeded, distorted* speech. Poetic speech is *structured* speech. Prose, on the other hand, is ordinary speech: economical, easy, correct speech (Dea Prosae, the queen of correct, easy childbirth, i.e., head first). I shall speak in more detail of the device of impeding, of holding back, when I consider it as a general law of art in my chapter on plot construction.

Still, those who favor the economy of artistic energy as the distinctive feature of poetic language seem to be quite persuasive when it comes to the question of rhythm. Spencer's interpretation of the role of rhythm seems on the face of it quite unshakeable:

Just as the body in receiving a series of varying concussions, must keep the muscles ready to meet the most violent of them, as not knowing when such may come: so, the mind in receiving unarranged articulations, must keep its perspectives active enough to recognize the least easily caught sounds. And as, if the concussions recur in definite order, the body may husband its forces by adjusting the resistance needful for each concussion; so, if the syllables be rhythmically arranged, the mind may economize its energies by anticipating the attention required for each syllable.

This apparently convincing remark suffers from a common defect, that is, the turning upside-down of the laws that govern poetry and prose. In his *Philosophy of Style,* Spencer completely failed to distinguish them. It may well be that there exist two types of rhythm. The rhythm of prose or of a work song like "Dubinushki" replaces the need for an order from a supervisor by its rhythmic chant: "let's groan together." On the other hand, it also eases and automatizes the work. And indeed, it is easier to walk with music than without it. Of course, it is just as easy to walk while talking up a storm, when the act of walking disappears from our consciousness. In this sense, the rhythm of prose is important as a factor leading to *automatization.* But such is not the rhythm of poetry. There is indeed such a thing as "order" in art, but not a single column of a Greek temple fulfills its order perfectly, and artistic rhythm may be said to exist in the rhythm of prose *disrupted.* Attempts have been made by some to systematize these "disruptions." They represent today's task in the theory of rhythm. We have good reasons to suppose that this systemization will not succeed. This is so because we are dealing here not so much with a more complex rhythm as with a disruption of rhythm itself, a violation, we may add, that can never be predicted. If this violation enters the canon, then it loses its power as a complicating device. But enough of rhythm for the time being. I shall devote a separate book to it in the future.

# Chapter 2

# The Relationship between Devices of
# Plot Construction and General Devices of Style

"Why walk on a tightrope? And, as if that were not enough, why squat every four steps?" asked Saltykov-Shchedrin about poetry. Every person who has ever examined art closely, apart from those led astray by a defective theory of rhythm as an organizational tool, understands this question. A crooked, laborious poetic speech, which makes the poet tongue-tied, or a strange, unusual vocabulary, an unusual arrangement of words—what's behind all this?

Why does King Lear fail to recognize Kent? Why do both Kent and Lear fail to recognize Edward? So asked Tolstoi in utter astonishment about the underlying laws of Shakespearean drama. This comes from a man who knew greatly how to see things and how to be surprised by them.

Why does the recognition scene in the plays of Menander, Plautus and Terence take place in the last act, when the spectators have already had a presentiment by then of the blood relationship binding the antagonists, and when the author himself often notifies us of it in advance in the prologue?

Why is it that in dance a partner requests "the pleasure of the next dance" even after the woman had already tacitly accepted it?

What keeps Glahn and Edvarda apart in Hamsun's *Pan,* scattering them all over the world in spite of their love for each other?

Why is it that, in fashioning an *Art of Love* out of love, Ovid counsels us not to rush into the arms of pleasure?

A crooked road, a road in which the foot feels acutely the stones beneath it, a road that turns back on itself—this is the road of art.

One word fits another. One word feels another word, as one cheek feels another cheek. Words are taken apart and, instead of one complex word handed over like a chocolate bar at a candy store, we see before us a word-sound, a word-movement. Dance is movement that can be felt. Or more accurately, it is movement formed in order to be felt. And behold, we dance as we plow. Still, we have no need of a field. We can dance even without it.

There's an old story in some Greek classic . . . a certain royal prince was so impassioned with the dance at his wedding that he threw off his clothes and began dancing naked on his hands. This enraged the bride's father, who shouted, "Prince, you have just danced yourself out of a wedding." To which the young man, addressing the would-be father-in-law, said, "Your Majesty, I couldn't care less!" and went on dancing anyway, his feet up in the air.

# The Ethnographic School

The ethnographic school, represented amongst us most forcefully by A. N. Veselovsky, has come to the following conclusion in its quest for a poetics of plot structure—but before going any further, it would behoove us to let Veselovsky define the concepts of "plot" and "motif":

A) By *motif* I mean the simplest narrative *unit,* corresponding imagistically to the diverse needs of a primitive mind and to the needs of ordinary perception. As a result of the similarity or, rather, unity of *material and psychological* conditions existing at the early stages of human development, such motifs could have arisen independently of each other and nonetheless could still have exhibited similar features at one and the same time. As examples, we may cite the following:

1) The so-called *legendes des origines,* the sun/eye simile, the sun (brother or husband)/moon (sister or wife) comparison, sunrise and sunset myths, myths about spots on the moon, eclipses, etc.

2) Everyday situations: abduction of a young woman (the folk wedding episode), abduction of "Rostan" (in fairy tales), etc.

B) By *plot* I mean a theme, into which a variety of motif-situations have been woven. For example:

1) Tales of the sun and his mother (cf. the Greek and Malaysian legends of the cannibalistic sun).

2) Tales of abduction. The more complex and illogical the combination of motifs (as in a song, where we are dealing with an integration of stylistic motifs), the greater the number of its component motifs, the more difficult it is to suppose, when faced with, e.g., two similar tales originating in two different tribes, that each of them arose by process of psychological self-generation against a background of identical concepts and realities. In such cases one may raise the possibility of *borrowings in historical time* of a plot structure by one nationality from another.

Thus:

If in different national milieus we encounter a formula with an identical, random sequence of x (a-x, x(1), x(2), etc.) then such a resemblance must not be unconditionally replaced by analogous processes of the psyche. If we posit 12 such x's, then, according to Jacobs's calculations (*Folklore*) the probability of its independent formation takes on the ratio of 1:479,001,599. In that case, we have the right to speak of borrowing something from another nationality.

However, this coincidence of plot structures may be encountered even where there is no presumption of borrowing; for example, the American Indian legend of how the birds chose for themselves a king, with the smallest bird managing to win the honor through sheer cunning, is remarkably similar to a European legend on the same subject (Klinger). Similarly, as Veselovsky notes, a certain legend from Zanzibar resembles Grimm's tale no. 15.

Especially remarkable is the Potanian parallel between the story of Bat and his wife Anupa (the Egyptian tale of the two brothers) and the Turkic tale of Idiga (in *Oriental Motifs*).

I would like to point out that an interval of four thousand years separates these records. True, it is a common practice in such cases to resort to the hypothesis that such a story was carried there by colonists. Yet such an explanation reminds us too easily of Voltaire's hypothesis that fossil sea-shells found on the Alps were brought there by pilgrims. Besides it is quite inexplicable as to why the *random* sequence of motifs should be preserved during this borrowing, when eyewitness testimony shows that it is precisely the sequence of events that is usually most deeply distorted under such circumstances. Moreover the (fairy) tale, even when remaining within the same linguistic milieu, is not distinguished for its textual stability. Rybnikov explains:

> Let's listen to the *storyteller*. If he is a good one, his words will weave themselves into place like beads on a string. You can hear the rhythm itself. Whole lines of verse. But all of this is true for stories which the storyteller has *learned by heart*, which he has told and retold. The fortuitous cadence, the lines of verse, come evidently from the traditional locutions of the heroic "bylina." Force him to repeat and he will express much of it differently. Ask him if anyone else knows the story, and he'll point to a *fellow villager*, a certain So-and-So, and he'll tell you that this So-and-So heard this story along with him from a certain old man or minstrel. Then go ask this So-and-So to tell this same story, and you will hear the story told not only in a different language and with different figures of speech, but often in a different key. One storyteller introduces (or preserves) the piteous details, another contributes (or perpetuates) the satirical point of view in certain episodes, while a third story-teller adapts a denouement from another tale (or from the general *fund* that is available to all *storytellers*, of which later). In addition, new characters and new adventures appear on the scene. Then, following up, you ask him how he learned this story and he will answer by saying that he was fishing on the shores of Lake Ladoga or Lake Onega or that he was in a shelter or in some *dwelling* or sitting by a campfire when he first heard it and many others like it told. Some were told by Povenchians, others by Zaolongenans, still others by Kopels and still others by Swedes (Finns). He crammed as many of these stories into his head as he could. Yet, he had no more than two or three of these stories in his repertoire. The well-known, communally shared conceptions had put on a certain costume and were expressed with a certain turn of speech. *Story = Structure.*

The story disintegrates and is rebuilt anew.

To sum up: Fortuitous coincidences are impossible. Coincidences can be explained only by the existence of special laws of plot formation. Even the admission of borrowings does not explain the existence of identical stories separated by thousands of years and tens of thousands of miles. For this reason, Jacobs is wrong: he presupposes an absence of laws governing plot formation, positing instead a fortuitous arrangement of motifs into series or clusters. As a matter of fact, such stories are forever disintegrating and forever being rebuilt in accordance with special laws of plot formation still unknown to us.

# Motifs

Many objections may be raised against the ethnographer's theory of the origin of motifs. Proponents of this theory have explained the resemblance of narrative motifs by the presence of identical socioeconomic forms and religious conceptions. This theory is concerned exclusively with motifs as such and deals with the influence of story schemata upon each other only in passing. As for the laws governing plot construction, the ethnographers couldn't have cared less.

Yet, even apart from this consideration, the ethnographic theory is flawed to its very core. According to this theory, story motif-situations constitute recollections of relationships that have actually existed in reality. So, for example, the presence of incest in certain stories attests to a primitive "hetaerism." Similarly, the presence of helpful beasts attests to traces of totemism, while the abduction of brides alludes to the practice of elopement.

The works of these scholars, especially Veselovsky, are practically chock-full of such explanations. In order to show just how far such an explanation of the origin of motifs may go, I shall analyze one classic study of the origin of a tale, namely of the legend of Dido, who had seized control of land through cunning. This story has been analyzed by V. F. Miller in an essay in *Russian Thought* (1894).

Miller connects the plot dealing with the seizure of land (by covering it with cowhide cut into strips) with the following: (1) the classical Greek legend of Dido, used later by Vergil; (2) three local Indian legends; (3) an Indo-Chinese legend; (4a) a Byzantine legend of the fifteenth century and (4b) a Turkish legend timed to coincide with the building of a fortress on the shore of the Bosporus; (5) a Serbian legend; (6) an Icelandic saga concerning Ragnar Lodbrok's son Ivar; (7) the Danish story of Saxo Grammaticus of the twelfth century; (8) the Gottfried chronicle of the twelfth century; (9) a certain Swedish chronicle; (10) the legend of the founding of Riga, as recorded by Dionysius Fabritz; (11) the legend concerning the founding of the Kirillo-Belozersky monastery (with a tragic denouement); (12) the folk legend from Pskov concerning the erection of the walls of the Pechersky monastery under the reign of Ivan the Terrible; (13) the Chernigovsky Little Russian legend about Peter the Great; (14) the Zyryansky legend of the founding of Moscow; (15) the Cabardinian legend of the founding of the Kydenetov Caucasian village (a Jewish hero); (16) the stories of the North American Indians having to do with the deceitful seizure of land by European colonists.

Having thus exhaustively traced all of the variants of this plot, Miller directs our attention to the peculiar fact that the deceived party in these stories never protests against the violent takeover of land by the other party. This is brought about, of course, by the convention lying at the heart of every work of art, namely, that the situations in question, isolated from their interrelationship in reality, affect each other only in accordance with the laws of the given artistic nexus: "In this story one has the sense of a *conviction* that the act of covering a parcel of land with a strip of cowhide constitutes a juridical act having the force of law."

The meaning of this act is conveyed in some sense in the Vedic legend recorded in the oldest Indian religious work entitled *Kathaka-Brahmana.* According to this legend the Asuri spirits, who are hostile to the gods, measure out land with the hide of a bull and divide it among themselves. Corresponding to this legend, the ancient Indian word *go* stood for "land" or "cow." The word *gocarman* (cowhide) stood for a definite piece of land: "We have a parallel to this ancient Indian measurement (*gocarman*)," says Miller,

in the Anglo-Saxon word *hyd* and in the English "hide," signifying, first, the skin (German *haut*) and, secondly, a specific strip of land, equivalent to forty-six morgens. This leads us to believe with a high degree of probability that the Indian *gocarman* had originally designated a piece of land that could be covered by the strips of a cowhide. Only later it seems, when its ancient meaning was forgotten, did this word come to designate an area occupied in toto by one hundred cows with their calves and bull.

As we have seen above, the attempt to clarify the socioeconomic substructure is carried not only to the bitter end but to absurdity. It turns out that the deceived party—and all variations of the story are based on an act of deception—did not protest against the seizure of land because land was, generally speaking, measured by this means. This results in an absurdity. If, at the moment of the alleged action of the story, the custom of measuring land (i.e., of covering a portion as far as possible with strips of cowhide) actually existed and was known to both sellers and buyers, then not only was there no act of deception, but neither was there a story plot-line, since the seller himself knew what it was all about.

The abduction of brides, which has similarly been taken as a depiction of a real custom, can likewise hardly be regarded as a reflection of a socioeconomic institution. There is every reason to believe that the wedding rituals that allegedly survive as vestiges of this custom are really charms and spells designed to ward off the Evil Spirit, lest it harm the newlyweds. According to N. S. Derzhavin,

We can be quite certain of this in part and by analogy with other particulars of the wedding ceremony, at least, with the wedding rooster, who serves ordinarily as an object of amusement and plays a large role in Little Russian and Bulgarian weddings. . . . And so we shall not be mistaken if, in summarizing our conclusion, we say that in those modern nationalities *where the predatory abduction of women still takes place, this practice has arisen as a corruption of an original ritual abduction.* Although wedding rites have been traditionally regarded as an echo of the abduction ritual, these must be considered only as measures designed to protect the wedding procession from the Evil Spirits. This is so because these rites, like the custom of ritual abduction, are closely bound up with the primitive religious conceptions of the nation.

Much the same can be said for the plot (motif) "husband at the wedding of his wife." Kruk and Veselovsky explain its occurrence by alluding to the custom of *levirat,* the acknowledgment that the husband's relatives have a right to his wife. If this is true, then the wrath of Odysseus, who evidently did not know of this custom, is reduced to nonsense.

Without denying the possible emergence of these motifs on a socioeconomic basis, I would like to point out that it is a common practice in the creation of such motifs to make use of a clash of customs (i.e., of their conflict).

The recollection of a custom no longer in existence may be used in the setting up of this conflict. So we find in Maupassant a whole series of stories (e.g., "The Old Man") based on the depiction of a simple, non-emotional attitude towards death as experienced by a French peasant. It appears that the story is based on a simple description of everyday reality. On the contrary! The whole story achieves its effect by presupposing a reader from a different milieu with a very different attitude towards death.

The same technique is found in "The Return": a husband returns home after a shipwreck. He discovers that his wife has remarried. The two husbands drink wine amicably. Even the tavern keeper isn't surprised. This story is meant for a reader who is familiar with the plot motif of "A Husband at His Wife's Wedding" and who has, therefore, a more sophisticated attitude toward things. We see here the embodiment of the law that underlies the formation of a motif on the basis of an obsolete custom.

I would like to add the following as a general rule: a work of art is perceived against a background of and by association with other works of art. The form of a work of art is determined by its relationship with other preexisting forms. *The content of a work of art is invariably manipulated, it is isolated, "silenced."* All works of art, and not only parodies, are created either as a parallel or an antithesis to some model. *The new form makes its appearance not in order to express a new content, but rather, to replace an old form that has already outlived its artistic usefulness.*

*Note:* I would single out only one group of non-sensuous forms, the most important group by far in my opinion, that is, *differential perceptions or perceptions involving distinctions.*

Whenever we experience anything as a *deviation* from the ordinary, from the normal, from a certain guiding canon, we feel within us an emotion of a special nature, which is not distinguished in its kind from the emotions aroused in us by sensuous forms, with the single difference being that its "referent" may be said to be a perception of a discrepancy. What I mean is that its referent stands for something inaccessible to empirical perception. This is a field of inexhaustible richness because these differential perceptions are qualitatively distinguished from each other by their point of departure, by their forcefulness and by their line of divergence. . . .

Why is the lyrical poetry of a foreign country never revealed to us in its fullness even when we have learned its language?

We hear the play of its harmonics. We apprehend the succession of rhymes and feel the rhythm. We understand the meaning of the words and are in command of the imagery, the figures of speech and the content. We may have a grasp of all the sensuous forms, of all the objects. So what's missing? The answer is: differential perceptions. The slightest aberrations from the norm in the choice of expressions, in the combinations of words, in the subtle shifts of syntax—all of this can be mastered only by someone who lives among the natural elements of his language, by someone who, thanks to his conscious awareness of the norm, is immediately struck, or rather, irritated by any deviation from it.

Yet, the domain of the norm in a language extends far beyond this. Every language possesses its own characteristic degree of abstraction and imagery. The repetition of certain sound combinations and certain forms of comparison belong to the realm of the norm, and any deviation from it is felt fully only by a person who is thoroughly at home in the language. Every change of expression, of imagery, of a verbal combination, strikes him as a sensuous perception. . . .

Moreover, there is the possibility of dual and inverse differentials. A given deviation from the norm may, in its turn, become the point of departure and yardstick for other deviations. In that case every return to the norm is experienced as a deviation. . . .

This idea has been expressed essentially by Nietzsche in his aphorism on "good prose": only in the presence of poetry can one write good prose. Prose, writes Nietzsche, is engaged in a continual war of courtesy with poetry, and all of its charms consist in this, that it constantly seeks to flee from it and contradict it. If poetry by nature holds itself at some remove from everyday prose, then we may say similarly that good prose holds itself at some remove from poetry.

Anything which may serve as a norm may become the starting point for active differential perceptions. In poetry, this may take the form of a geometrically rigid system of rhythm: words submit to this order, but not without certain nuances, not without conflicts that weaken the severity of the meter. Each word insists on its own syllabic stress and length, thereby expanding or contracting the space allotted to it in the verse line. This is why we perceive minute aberrations from the rigid demands of the meter.

Furthermore, there is the opposition of meaning and verse. The verse line demands the emphasis of certain syllables on which the main stress falls, while the sense of the text imperceptibly transfers the accent onto other syllables.

Again, there is also the delimitation of each line of verse from its adjacent lines. The connection demanded by the sense leaps over these intervals, allowing only an occasional pause, if any (which should come at the end of a line), and carries it over, into, perhaps, the middle of the next line. Thanks to the stresses and pauses called for by the meaning, we witness a continual violation of the basic meter. These distinctions bring life to the structure of verse. Meanwhile, the metric scheme fulfills a function other than that of serving as a basis for formal, rhythmic perceptions. It also serves as a standard by which to gauge deviations from the norm, and therefore, it serves as a foundation for the differential perceptions themselves.

This same phenomenon is familiar to us from music: the mathematical conception of the beat is felt as a background against which a living stream of sound flows, and this is attained by the combination of the most subtle nuances and distinctions. (S. V. Khristiansen, *Philosophy of Art,* 1911)

## Stepped Construction and Deceleration

There are those who think that the purpose of art is to facilitate something or to inspire or to generalize. Lacking a sufficient number of steam hammers, these people enlist the help of rhythm to do the job (see, chiefly, Bücher's *Work and Rhythm*). And yet, those who have looked deeply into this matter know better. Indeed, how thoroughly alien is generalization to art. How much closer it is instead to "particularization."

Art is not a march set to music, but rather a walking dance to be experienced or, more accurately, a movement of the body, whose very essence it is to be experienced through the senses.

The practical mind seeks generalizations by creating, insofar as possible, wide-ranging, all-encompassing formulas. Art, on the contrary, with its "longing for the concrete" (Carlyle), is based on a step-by-step structure and on the particularizing of even that which is presented in a generalized and unified form.

Progressive structure includes under its rubric such devices as repetition (with its particular form of rhythm), tautologies, tautological parallelism, psychological parallelism, retardation of the action, epic repetitions, the rituals of fairy tale and legend, peripeteia and many other devices of plot construction.

The convergence of many identical phrases of the type "I command you," "I order you," and so forth, are often encountered in refined English business speech (as pointed out by Dickens in *David Copperfield*). This was common practice in ancient oratory (Zelinsky). This phenomenon represents a kind of general principle in folk poetry. Here are some examples from Dovnar-Zapolsky's *Songs of the Pinchuks:* "They are beating the drums — they are pounding on them; tambourines — drums; the wind blows — the wind wafts; cherry — wild cherry; to order — to command; walks — strolls; weeps — grieves; drank — caroused; knock — rattle," etc.

Here are some examples from Professor Speransky's *Russian Oral Literature:*

Russian poetry is apparently quite enamored of this device and has evolved in this respect a great diversity of forms: this consists either of a simple repetition of one and the same word or of consonants synonymous in meaning, e.g., "*chudnim chudno"; "divnim — divno,"* etc. This device may also take (with especial frequency) the form of a repetition of the preposition, such as "in" glorious "in" old "in" Kiev, etc., or, again, this device may frequently take the form of a repetition of one and the same word or phrase in two adjacent lines of verse, where the final word of one line reappears as the first word of the next line:

> Of this sable, perhaps, from abroad,
> From abroad, a sable with earflaps,
> A sable with earflaps, covered with down . . .

Sometimes this repetition takes the form of a denial of an antithesis: "by a direct route, not a circuitous one"; "from great rather than little vexation"; "a bachelor, an unmarried man." Here belong also such synonymous expressions as "without a fight, without bloodshed"; "from grief, from sorrow"; "an estate — fortune"; etc., etc. Sometimes this expression consists of two words, one native, the other borrowed or dialect in origin, as for example, "luck — fate," etc. Or else of a species concept modifying a genus concept: "pike fish," "feathergrass," "titmouse."

A more advanced form, a simple repetition, may involve entire episodes of a story. These can be especially effective and pleasing. Such, for example, are the bylina episodes concerning the battle between Dobrynya and Dunaya (the description of Duna's tent, Dobrynya's arrival, Dobrynya and Alyosha, Dobrynya's punishment of his wife and its consequences). As an especially clear example of repetition, we may point to Potyck's wrestling with the underground serpent (Gilferding, no. 52). Finally we ought also to include under this rubric combinations of two words, each of which belongs to a different grammatical category yet linked by the root: "to build a building," "to gild with gold," "to cry out with a cry," etc.

The use of synonyms was Gogol's favorite stylistic device.

The distinguishing feature of Gogol's style lies in the unusual frequency, indeed, the constancy with which the author employs two synonymous expressions in succession, even though this does not necessarily contribute to greater clarity or precision of thought. Nearly always one of the expressions turns out to be completely superfluous, being in every sense a full repetition of the other expression and only rarely serving to bring the symbol into greater relief. The reader may satisfy himself as to the truth of this phenomenon by examining its occurrence even within a comparatively narrow scope: ". . . with *firmness* in the cause of life, with *cheerfulness* and with the *encouragement* of all around you." Or, in the same vein, but in the form of a verb: "so that he may *help* his fellow man with good counsel . . . so that he may *cheer* and *invigorate* him with intelligent words of parting." Or else in the form of a participle or adjective: "you will therefore carry it out precisely as one should, and as required by the government, i.e., with *invigorating* and *encouraging* strength . . ."; "You may act with measures that are neither *coercive* nor *violent* . . ."; "Direct passages have *become weaker,* have *lost their strength* due to the introduction of indirect . . ."; "Do not *hurry,* do not *hasten* to add them on," and so on.

In his book *The Nature of Gogol's Style,* Professor Mandelshtam offers numerous such examples. In Pushkin too we find such examples as "the thunderstorm thunders" and "locked in by a lock" (cf. Brik's "Sound Repetitions").

This phenomenon expresses the common principle: *form creates for itself its own content.* For that reason, whenever the corresponding twin of a word is absent, its place is taken by an arbitrary or derivative word. For example: helter-skelter, topsy-turvy, pell-mell, and so on. All of these examples of an impeded, progressive construction do not usually appear together and a separate explanation has been offered by some for each of these cases. So for example, an attempt has been made to sharply delimit psychological and tautological parallel structures. A parallelism of the type

> Our Yelinochka is happy winter and summer
> Our Malashka is wonderful every day

constitutes, in Veselovsky's opinion, an echo of totemism and of a time when individual tribes regarded trees as their ancestors. Veselovsky therefore believes that if a singer compares a man to a tree, then either he is confusing them or else his mother had confused them. This psychological parallelism is, in his opinion, sharply distinguished from a rhythmic parallelism as practiced in Jewish, Finnish, and Chinese poetry. Veselovsky offers the following example:

> The sun did not know where to find his peace,
> The moon did not know where to find his strength.

Psychological parallelism is sharply distinguished from this musical-rhythmic tautology originating, according to Veselovsky, in the method of performance—trochaic or iambic. Yet even formulas of psychological parallelism occasionally turn into or, in Veselovsky's words, "sink" into a type of tautologically musical parallelism. Even Veselovsky acknowledges here, if not an affinity, then at least a predilection on the part of each of these types of structure for each other. They share a common, peculiar poetic cadence. Each of these cases reveals a need for deceleration of the imagistic mass and for its arrangement in the form of distinct steps. In one case, an incongruity of images is used for the formation of these steps, in the other case, a formal-verbal incongruity. For example:

> How shall I curse whom God has not cursed?
> How shall I abhor whom the Lord does not abhor?

Here is an example from Psalms illustrating a variety of steps:

> Give unto the Lord, oh ye sons of the Lord,
> Give unto the Lord glory and strength.

Or a movement forward with a kind of enjambment from line to line:

> For the Lord knows the way of the impious,
> And the way of the impious leads to perdition.

Here we observe a phenomenon common in art: a particular form seeks to complete itself in a manner analogous to the way that words seek completion in certain sound-blurs in lyrical poetry (see Veselovsky's "Three Chapters from Historical Poetics" and Hugo's comments on completing the space between rhymes). For this reason, in the Finnish epic where synonymous parallelism is the norm and where the stanzas take the form of

> If you take back your incantation,
> If you withdraw your evil spell . . .

and where numbers are found in the verse which, as is well known, lack synonyms, then the number that is next in order is selected that does not numerically call attention to a distortion in meaning. For example:

> He finds six seeds on the ground,
> Seven seeds he raises from the ground.

Or consider the Finnish *Kalevala:*

> On the seventh night she passed away,
> On the eighth night she died.

In my opinion, a triolet presents a phenomenon that is very close to a tautological parallelism. As in the case of the rondeau, this device has already been canonized (i.e., it serves as the foundation for the "web" and pervades the entire work). The effect of the triolet lies partly in the fact that one and the same line of verse lands in different contexts, a fact which produces a much needed differential impression. A similar degree of differentiality is represented by psychological parallelism, and the development of a negative parallelism alone shows that there was never a question here of confusing a human being with a tree or a river. Here we encounter two unequal figures that partially overlap: the effect consists in this, that in spite of the incongruity thus created, the first part of the parallel is echoed by the analogous phrase in the second part.

As refutation of a totemistic interpretation, we may also assert that a parallel is often established, not between objects or actions of two objects, but between an analogous relationship between two sets of objects, each set taken as a pair. Here is an example taken from a lovely folk ditty:

> Not along the sky do rain clouds drift,
> Not along the sky's heights,
> Not for virgins do lads pine,
> Not for a virgin's beauty.

The synonymous (tautological) parallelism with a transition and repetition from stanza to stanza turns into what is called in the poetics of the Russian song a "deceleration." As an example, here is an excerpt from a bylina concerning Ilya Muromets, as recorded for P. V. Kireevsky in the province of Simbirska:

> Ilya walked out onto a high hill,
> Onto a high hill that's rolling,
> Spread out the white flaps of his tent.
> After arranging his tent, he started a fire.
> He started a fire, began unpacking.
> Fanning the fire, he began to cook his stew,
> After cooking his stew, he ate it all,
> He gobbled up the stew and lay down.

We find the same device in the song recorded by Kireevsky in Moscow:

> Shall I go then, lovely damsel,
> To stroll in the open field,
> To gather the harmful roots?
> Gathering the harmful roots,
> I shall wash them out white as snow.
> Washing out the roots,
> I shall dry them out as dry as sand.
> After drying the harmful roots,
> I shall crush them to little bits.
> After crushing the harmful roots,
> I shall boil some sweet honey.
> Having boiled some sweet honey,
> I shall invite a friend as a guest.
> After inviting my friend as a guest,
> I shall sit her down on my bed.
> Having sat her down on my bed . . .

There are numerous examples of this type of deceleration. However, thanks to the negligence of those people who have been seeking in these songs a social message, a soul, a philosophy, many examples have been lost. For example, all of the repetitions in Professor A. I. Sobolevsky's collection of Russian songs have been deleted. In all probability, the esteemed professor believed, along with many others, that literature is of interest only insofar as it reflects the history of a culture.

We find peculiar instances of deceleration in the old French poem concerning Renaud de Montauban. In it we come across just such an endlessly drawn-out episode. Charles wants to hang the captive Richard and proposes to Beranger the knight to carry out the sentence. Beranger answers: "May he be cursed who has shamefully thought of seizing the captive's estate for himself." Charles then turns to Ozier and to the six other knights and, with minor changes, repeats his declaration. He receives from them the exact same answer. And each time Charles exclaims: "Scoundrel, God will punish you, but I swear by the beard of Charles, the captive shall be hanged." Finally one of the knights takes upon himself this commission. . . .

What is true of deceleration is equally true of parallelism: a particular form seeks fulfillment and, if numerals happen to occur in the creation of the steps, then the author deals with it in a very original way, in accordance with the laws of a given "web":

> My young nightingale,
> Do not sing early in the spring!
> Do not sing sweetly, do not sing loudly!
> The young man won't feel so wretched,
> Not so wretched or so bitter.
> I myself do not know why, I only know
> That I long for her, for my beloved,
> My beloved who has left me behind,
> Left me behind—left behind four hundred,
> Four hundred, five hundred, twelve cities,
> Twelve cities, thirteen cities,
> And came to the glorious city of Moscow.

In "Epic Repetitions as a Chronological Factor," Veselovsky tried to explain these peculiar repetitions with their enjambment from stanza to stanza by alluding to their mechanism of execution (his usual explanation): he assumed that these works (or prototypes of these works—a crucial factor insufficiently explained in his article) were executed iambically, and that these repetitions accompanied each singer as he joined in the song. Here are some of Veselovsky's examples of repetitions:

The Saracens surrounded Charlemagne's rear guard; Olivier tells his companion Roland that there are many enemies about; Olivier tells him to blow his horn so that Charlemagne will hear it and come to their rescue. But Roland refuses, and this circumstance is developed three times in the following manner:

1) Comrade Roland, blow your horn! Charlemagne will hear it and his army will return. Roland answers: I would be acting senselessly in that case; I would lose my glorious fame in sweet France. I shall strike mighty blows with my sword Durendal, so that the blade of my sword shall become crimson to its very hilt. The vile pagans have come to the mountain gorges at a bad hour; I guarantee you that they are all doomed to a certain death.

2) Comrade Roland, blow your horn. Charlemagne will hear it and order his army to return. Roland answers: God will not permit my kith and kin to be shamed on my account and for sweet France to be denigrated, were I to blow my horn on account of these pagans. On the contrary, I shall begin to hack away mightily with my sword Durendal. . . . You will all see the bloody blade of my sword. These vile pagans have gathered here at a bad hour. I guarantee you that they are all condemned to a certain death.

3) Comrade Roland, blow your horn! Charlemagne shall hear it and come rushing across the gorges. I guarantee you that the French troops shall return. And Roland answers: But the Lord shall not permit that someone among the living should say that I had blown my horn on account of pagans; I shall not go against the traditions of my family. In the heat of battle I shall rain down a thousand and seven hundred blows. You shall see the blade of Durendal made crimson with blood. . . .

Finally, Roland, who has been wounded, decides to blow his horn.

1) Roland places his horn in his mouth, grasps it firmly with his hand and begins to blow forcefully. The mountains are tall. You could hear the echoes far away. On the thirty major peaks you could barely hear its echo. Charlemagne and his troops hear it. The emperor says: It's our boys! They are fighting the good fight. But Ganelon answers him: Had anyone said that, it would have been considered a great lie.

2) Count Roland blows his horn with much effort, difficulty and great pain. Scarlet blood streams out of his mouth and the veins on his temples burst. Far away the sound of his horn is heard. Charlemagne hears it as he advances through the gorges. Duke Nemon hears it. The French troops hear it. The emperor says: I hear Roland's horn. Ganelon answers: No, there is no battle. He twits the aged emperor for his childish gullibility, as if he didn't know how haughty Roland was. Why, he was just showing off before his peers. Let's go forward, France is still so far away.

3) Blood streams out of Count Roland's mouth. The veins on his temples are bursting. He blows his horn with pain and difficulty. Charlemagne hears him. The French troops hear him. The emperor says: This horn is mighty and powerful. Duke Nemon answers: Barons, a loyal vassal is fighting the good fight. In my opinion, a battle is raging. He suspects Ganelon. We must help our own men. . . .

Meanwhile, Roland, dying, (a) tries to smash his sword Durendal so that it won't fall into the hands of infidels; and (b) confesses his sins. Each of these motifs is developed in three consecutive "laisses."

1) Roland feels that death is at hand. Before him is a dark stone. In anger and anguish he strikes it ten times with his sword. The steel scrapes but does not break nor is it notched. An address to the sword with which the hero had been victorious in so many battles follows.

2) Roland strikes his sword against the hard stone. The steel scrapes but does not break and is not notched. Plaints follow along with epically developed reminiscences. . . .

3) Roland strikes the grey stone and chips off more than I could ever tell you. The sword scrapes but does not break and is not shattered. . . .

Innumerable similar examples analogous to the three strikes by Roland can be found elsewhere, although in other epics such a device is not the norm.

For example, the three strikes by Ilya against Svyatogor's coffin or the three strikes inflicted by Tor against the giant. I would like to call your attention to the fact that in all such comparisons it is my purpose to stress not so much the similarity of motifs, which I consider of little significance, as the similarity of the plot schemata.

In spite of this repetition, the action does not come to a stop. It advances, but more slowly. The factory song about Marusa is constructed along the same lines. Marusa, who has been poisoned, is visited first by her girl-friends, then by her mother, and finally by her close friend. These visitors are given an answer first by the nurse, then by the doctor, and finally by the watchman: "Marusa is in delirium"; "She is unconscious"; "She is in the mortuary." This device of the three arrivals is also utilized in the Little Russian duma (Ukranian folk ballad):

> Shaded by the Beskid's snowball trees,
> Stands a new tavern proud and strong.
> Within, a Turk sits drinking away,
> As a girl kneels before him and cries:
> "Oh, Turk, oh, Turk, oh, Turk!
> Don't kill me, for I am so young!"

The young woman says that her father has already paid for her ransom. But her father does not show up and the young woman weeps. The following stanza repeats the same scene: Beskid, the inn, and the young woman's entreaty. This time it appears that her mother has paid her ransom. The third time the same thing happens and finally a kind man appears with the ransom.

Similarly, a young wife's call home in the vernal songs of the Malmariée type is also broken down into three stages. Many Russian songs are based on the same technique (Veselovsky).

Similarly, in Perrault's tale, the deceived wife of Bluebeard waits for help:

"My sister Anna! Please go up the tower to see if our brothers are coming: they promised to come see me today. And if you see them, give them a sign so that they may hurry."

The sister climbed up to the tower and the poor woman screamed out to her: "Anna, my sister Anna! Do you see anything?"

"I see only the dust gleaming in the sun and the green grass."

Meanwhile Bluebeard, holding in his hand a large kitchen knife, screamed at the top of his voice: "Come down quickly or else I'll come up myself!"

"One more minute I beg of you," replied his wife. Again she called softly to her sister: "Anna, my sister Anna, do you see anything?"

And her sister answered: "I see only the dust gleaming in the sun and the green grass."

"Come down quickly," Bluebeard cried, "or I'll come up myself."

"I am coming," his wife answered again. And again she shouted to her sister: "Anna, my sister Anna, do you see anything?"

"I see," answered the sister, "a cloud of dust approaching."

"Are those my brothers?"

"Alas, no, my sister. I see a herd of rams."

"Will you come down, for goodness sake!" Bluebeard shouted.

"Just one more minute," answered his wife and then shouted to her sister: "Anna, my sister Anna, do you see anything?"

"I see," she answered, "two horsemen traveling in our direction, but they are still far away."

"Thank God!" she exclaimed. "Those are our brothers. I'll try my very best to give them a sign to hurry."

This schema, among other things, has been widely used in England, where it is found in parodies.

I shall refrain from offering further examples, so as not to turn this essay into a chrestomathy.

Constructions of the type a + (a+a) + ([a + (a+a)]) + . . . follow an arithmetic progression.

There are tales constructed on a peculiar plot tautology of the type a + (a+a) + ([a + (a+a)] + a2), etc. For example, these tales from E. R. Romanov's *Belorussian Anthology:*

## The Slave Hen

Grandpa and Grandma had a slave hen. She lay a basketful of eggs. Grandpa beat on them, beat on them but didn't break them; Grandma beat on them, beat on them but didn't break them. A mouse passed by, wagged its tail and broke them. . . . Grandpa wept, Grandma wept, the hen cackled, the gate creaked, the fire crackled, the dogs barked, the geese honked, people yelled.

A wolf came along and said: "Grandpa, why are you crying?"

Grandpa answered: "Why should I not be crying? Grandma and I were living peacefully. We had a slave hen. She lay a basketful of eggs. I beat on them, beat on them but didn't break them. Grandma beat on them, beat on them but didn't break them. A mouse passed by, wagged its tail and broke them. . . . Grandpa cried, the hen cackled, the gate creaked, the fire crackled, the dogs barked, the geese honked, people yelled. . . ."

The wolf howled. Along came a bear who said: "Why are you howling, oh wolf?"

"Why should I not be howling," said the wolf. "Once there was a Grandpa and a Grandma. They had a slave hen. She lay a basketful of eggs for them. Grandpa beat on them, beat on them but didn't break them. Grandma beat on them, beat on them but didn't break them. A mouse passed by, wagged its tail and broke them. . . . Grandpa cried, the hen cackled, the gate creaked, the fire crackled, the dogs barked, the geese honked, people yelled, and I, a wolf, am howling. . . ."

And the bear growled. Along came an elk who said: "Why are you growling, oh bear?"

"And why should I not be growling? Once there was a Grandpa and a Grandma. They had a slave hen. She laid a basketful of eggs for them. Grandpa beat on them, beat on them but didn't break them. Grandma beat on them, beat on them but didn't break them. A mouse passed by, wagged its tail and broke them. . . . Grandpa cried, Grandma cried, the hen cackled, the gate creaked, the fire crackled, the dogs barked, the geese honked, people yelled, the wolf howled, and I, a bear, am growling."

And the elk lowered its horns. . . .

This round of questioning eventually leads to the priest's servants, who crush a bucket from grief. And then to a deacon who rends his books out of sympathy. And, finally, to the priest himself, who, from sheer woe, sets the church aflame.

## The Rooster and the Hen

Grandpa and Grandma had a rooster and a hen. Once they were digging a hole in the dump. The hen dug up a pin and the rooster dug up a pea. The hen then said to the rooster: "Give me your pea, and I'll give you my pin!" The rooster gave the hen the pea, and the hen gave him the pin. The hen ate the pea, while the rooster swallowed the pin and started choking on it.

The hen ran to the sea for water and said: "Oh my sea, my sea, give me water. The rooster is choking to death."

"No, no, I shall not give you water. Go down to the badger. Go down and ask the badger to give me his tusks."

The hen ran up to the badger and said, "Oh badger, my badger, give the sea your tusks. Then the sea will give me water, for the rooster is choking to death."

"No, no, I shall not give you my tusks, go down to the oak and ask him to give me his acorns!"

The hen ran to the oak and said: "My oak, my oak, give the badger your acorns."

"No, no, I shall not give him acorns. Go down to the cow, and ask her to give me some of her milk."

The hen ran up to the cow and said: "Oh cow, my cow, give the oak some of your milk!"

"No, no, I shall not give any milk. Go down to the reaper and tell him to give me his hay!"

The hen ran up to the reaper and said: "Oh reaper, my reaper, give the cow some of your hay!"

"No, no, I shall not give him hay. Go down to the linden tree and ask him to give me bast for my shoes."

The hen ran up to the linden tree and said: "Oh linden tree, my linden tree, give the reaper bast for his shoes!"

"No, I shall not give him the bast. Go down to the blacksmith and ask him to give me a knife!"

The hen ran down to the smith and said: "Oh smith, my smith, give the linden tree a knife, so that he may give the reaper bast for his shoes."

"No, I shall not give the linden tree a knife. Go down and get me some peas and bring them to me. Then I will give you a knife."

The hen scoured the yard till it found a pea, then brought the pea to the smith and the smith gave her a knife. She then brought the knife to the linden tree. The linden tree gave the hen the bast for the reaper's shoes. The reaper then gave the hen hay. She carried the hay to the cow. The cow ate the hay and gave the hen milk. The hen carried the milk to the oak. The oak gave acorns to the badger. The badger gave the hen the tusks. The hen took the tusks from the badger and ran off to meet the sea. And the sea gave the hen water. The hen then carried the water to the rooster and poured it into his mouth and the rooster screamed: Kuka-reku!

It is absolutely impossible, if I may observe, to fathom from this tale why the sea needs the badger's tusks as a form of ransom. The motivation here is obviously an artistic one. That is, the author feels a need to create a step-by-step structure.

Some versions involve a peculiar, everyday interpretation of this motif. In these variants, when the rooster returns, he finds that the hen has already been eaten up by the worms. (In some versions, it is the rooster who runs for help, in others, it is the hen.)

Along these lines (Fedorovsky), a little boy, born miraculously from the saliva of a blade of grass, demands that the latter rock it like a cradle. The blade of grass refuses. He sends for the goat, then for the wolves, then for people, and finally for fire, etc. They all refuse. Finally, the hens are on their way to peck the worms. The worms are on their way to sharpen the pin, and so on. The goat is foraging for a blade of grass.

Similarly, that which is designated in prose by an "A" is expressed in art by means of an "A(1) A" (for example, a tautology) or by means of an A A(1) (for example, psychological parallelism). This is the foundation of all technical devices. In accordance with this, if the realization of a certain task demands a degree of effort equal to $A(n)$, then it would take the form of $A(n—2)$, $A(n—1)$, $A(n)$. Thus, in the bylina it is Alyosha Popovich who takes the field of battle first, then Dobrynya Nikitich, and finally Ilya Muromets. This is the order of battle for the heroes of these tales. This device was preserved and utilized by Tennyson in his *Idylls of the King.* Similarly, the "koshchei," the hobgoblin of Russian folklore, was beaten three times in order to get him to confess where Death is. In the Bible, too, Samson confesses the secret of his strength three times.

In the Belorussian tales of E. R. Romanov, Ivan is bound "as a test of his strength" first with canvas, then with silk (or with a strand of hair), and finally with a piece of rough rope. The delivery of the ring or the kiss of the princess through the twelve panes of glass is similarly constructed. The first time he jumps, but he doesn't reach it, three crowns. The second time he jumps, almost reaching it, two crowns. The third time he jumps and reaches it and attains the goal.

Seeking refuge from king/maiden, the prince finds at each way station a valiant horse waiting for him at the hut of Baba Yaga, the witch. With each station the race brings him closer and closer to the goal. At first, fifteen verst, then ten verst, and finally five. And the prince saves himself by hiding in the grass and leaving behind him a deceptive inscription.

Osip Brik observed ingeniously that the dead and living waters represent nothing more than the concept of "healing waters" broken down into two separate concepts (as is well known, the "dead water" of legend joins together the hacked-off limbs of a body), that is, A is depicted as: $A(1)$, $A(2)$. In the same way, a certain "type" is reduplicated in Gogol's *Inspector General.* Undoubtedly, Bobchinsky and Dobchinsky form a double, a fact which is evident from their surnames. Here too, A is presented as $A(1)$, $A(2)$.

The answer usually given in this case is that we are dealing here with the "rituals of legends." However, in saying this, a critic may fail to realize that this ritual characterizes more than just legend. It is also the ritual and sacrament of all art. So, for example, *The Song of Roland* is not a legend, and neither is a film a legend. Even now we can see a chase in a film: with the enemy breathing down his neck, our hero suddenly makes his getaway in a car. Let me suggest a comparison with the description of a chase after Jean Valjean in Hugo's *Misérables.* The concluding effect consists of climbing over a wall and finding refuge in a monastery.

# Deceleration as an Artistic Device

In general, the device of a belated rescue, as a fitting theme for a step-by-step structure, is widely used in legends and in adventure novels. The prince is near death. Animal helpers, rushing to his rescue, eat their way through twelve iron doors. The prince asks for permission to bathe.*

Ivan Tsarevich walks up to the bathhouse and starts lighting the fire. Suddenly, a crow flies up to him, crying out:

"Caw! Caw! Ivan Tsarevich. Light the fire. Light the fire! It's going out! Your greyhounds are rushing to your rescue! They have already broken through four doors."

Behold Ivan Tsarevich as he lights the fire. Still, it keeps going out.

No sooner does the crow vanish than Koshchei, the evil spirit who knows not death, appears to the boy:

"Ivan Tsarevich, is the bathhouse ready?"

"No, not yet, the stones are not yet in place."

"Well then, try harder!"

At that very moment a second crow flies up to the boy, crying out: "Caw! Caw! Ivan Tsarevich, light the fire, light the fire! It's gone out again. Your greyhounds have broken through another four doors."

No sooner does the second crow vanish than Koshchei, the goblin who knows not death, appears again:

"Ivan Tsarevich, Ivan Tsarevich, is the bathhouse ready yet?"

"Not yet, but I've just set the stones in place," the lad replies.

"Well then, hurry up and light the fire!"

Behold again how Ivan lights the fire.

A third crow flies up and cries out: "Caw! Caw! Ivan Tsarevich, light the fire, light the fire! It's gone out again. Your greyhounds have broken through the last four doors."

At that moment Ivan finally lights the fire. When the fire is hot and ready, Koshchei, the spirit who knows not death, appears and says:

"Well go on, take your bath. I can wait a little longer."

As soon as Ivan walks into the bathhouse, his greyhounds rush in ... (E. R. Romanov, *Belorussian Anthology*)

In another version, Ivan Zlatovus received permission before his death to play the zhuleika, a wooden flute:

He climbed up the birch tree. When he played the flute, a bird flew up to him. When he played it the second time, more birds flew up. When he played it for the third time, all of the beasts of the field ran up to him. (Ibid.)

---

*This brief introduction is in single space, without quotes, in the Russian text, as is, of course, the tale that follows it. Shklovsky's (his editor's?) punctuation, paragraph division, etc. are, like so much else in *Theory of Prose,* so erratic and arbitrary that one cannot always be sure what his real meaning in a given context is. In this case, it seems that Shklovsky himself is speaking. [Trans. note]

So also does Solomon play under the gallows tree as he climbs up step by step calling for help (see A. N. Veselovsky, "Solomon and Kitovras").

The existence of rituals in legend has been, generally speaking, acknowledged by everyone to be canonical for this genre. I would like to offer several examples out of the thousands available: the three underground kingdoms of honey, silver and gold; the hero's three battles with the characteristic graduated nature of the tasks—for example: the capture of the Fire Bird, the capture of the steed, the capture of the Beautiful Vasilisa. This series of tasks is preceded by an exposition which explains the necessity for the tasks. This type ("threading" of the tasks) passed on into the adventure and chivalrous novel.

The tasks themselves are extremely interesting. They serve as a motivation for the creation of an apparently unresolvable situation. Here the posing of riddles serves as the simplest means of creating such a hopeless situation. Characteristic of this type are the tales of the "seven years" (Afanasiev).

A task is imposed: do not come by foot, do not come on horseback, do not come naked, do not come dressed, and so on. A young woman is wrapped in a net, and rides on the back of a rabbit, etc. Here the story is constructed backwards, as a motivation is sought to justify a successful resolution of the story. The recognition of one of twelve look-alikes with the help of a bee is similarly constructed, etc. The "wisdom" here is more complex, that is, it calls, for example, for distinguishing young maidens from adolescent girls. Similarly, it calls for identifying the illegitimate son by the latter's "inappropriate thoughts," as, for instance, in the case of the smith's son, who has been fraudulently replaced by Solomon. Upon seeing the beautiful place, he says: "Here should we put the blacksmith's forge" (Onchukov, *Legends of the North*).

Consider also the thief in *A Thousand and One Nights,* who, among his other tasks, recognizes the cook as the sultan's son because the latter confers upon him an award in the form of food. We meet with an echo of this in the nobility of "mistaken children" in adventure novels—for example, Le Destin in Scarron's *Le roman comique* and the numerous heroes of children's tales.

(An interesting story about a falsely exchanged "counterfeit white boy" is to be found in Mark Twain's *Pudd'nhead Wilson*.)

The part preceding the tasks constitutes what in the poetics of cinematography is called a "segue" (i.e., a scene that has no independent significance, serving only as preparation for what follows).

As I have already said, the fulfillment of the tasks often occupies the tale in its entirety. We may distinguish (looking at it from the standpoint of technique rather than essentials) two types of such fulfillments, or resolutions: resolution by the guessing of riddles or resolution by means of some magical or non-magical creature such as animal helpers. The classical type of resolution in the latter case has each wild animal carry out a task that it alone can do. The ant gathers seeds (tale from Apuleius). Sometimes, the ant is called upon to accomplish a specific task, such as gathering and bringing (or taking out) seeds into (or out of) a closed barn. A fish or crab is called upon to bring a ring from the depths of the sea. A mouse purloins the ring from the teeth of the abducted princess. The eagle or falcon captures a duck. In cases where the tasks are of a similar nature, each animal is called upon to perform its task with a progressively greater degree of strength (tale of Prince Larokoney). The animal helpers may be replaced by helpful people and helpful magical objects or of the type "Oak-Slayer" ("felling the oak") or "Mountain-Tamer" ("overturn the mountain") and so on, or by strong men of progressively greater strength (compare the names of dogs of the type of tale represented by "Beast-milk," "Crushmountain," "Breakwall," "Breakiron"). Or else people wielding magical powers possess specific attributes. This mirrors the specific tasks of the wild beasts. We encounter here the "glutton" or "guzzler," the man who trembles with cold in the fire and "a marksman shooting a pestle from a mortar." We encounter echoes of these helper figures in novels, for example, in the form of helpful strong men, such as Ursus in Sienkiewicz's *Quo Vadis?,* Maciste in d'Annunzio's film *Cabiria,* Porthos in *The Three Musketeers* by Dumas, and others. Similarly, Rabelais employed in his *Pantagruel* the well-known legendary character of the helper acrobat. In the contemporary "scientific" adventure novel a special role is assigned to the helpful scientist. Under this rubric falls also the type of tale represented by "The Seven Semions," the seven brothers who each possess a unique skill (e.g., how to steal, or how to build a ship [Afanasiev]).

This entire collection of devices associated with the genre of the legend makes possible the construction of a tale in which the fate of the hero, caught, it seems, in a hopeless predicament, is unexpectedly resolved. A situation that is capable of creating such plot complications is selected as a motif—for example, the motif of the "two keys to the same door" (Spanish drama), or of the "secret door" (*A Thousand and One Nights*), the Egyptian tale of the cunning thief (reported by Herodotus). Thanks to this, certain motifs have become special favorites—for example, the motif of the shipwreck or of the abduction of the hero in adventure novels. The hero is not killed immediately, since he is still needed for the recognition scene. If they want to remove him from the picture, then they drag him off somewhere. Quite frequently, these episodes involving stealing and restealing, escapes and other vain attempts are complicated by the fact that their victims, in love with each other, strive towards their goal by the most circuitous path. The episodes, following one upon the other, are hard to distinguish from each other and play in adventure novels the same role of deceleration that the task or rituals of legend play in tales, or that parallelism and the slowing of the narrative do in song. The motifs of the shipwreck, of abduction by pirates, etc., are introduced into the plot not out of realistic but rather out of technical-artistic considerations. No more of the real world impinges upon a work of art than the reality of India impinges upon the game of chess. The adventure novel is to this day interrupted, according to Veselovsky, by schemata and methods inherited from the genre of the legendary tale. Veselovsky himself considers "adventures" to be a stylistic device ("Belle Lettres in Ancient Greece").

This type, the type of the circuitous path, very closely resembles the game called "Move Up" ("Staraysya Vverkh") or the game of "Goose" ("Gusyek"), which is played in the following way: Dice are cast; in accordance with the number of points allotted, you receive a place on a chart. Depending upon the number shown by the dice, the player's position either moves up or down on the chart. This is precisely the kind of labyrinth represented by the adventure novel. This similarity has been pointed out by the creators of adventure novels themselves. In Jules Verne's *Testament of an Eccentric,* the different coincidences and adventures of the heroes are motivated by the fact that the heroes must go where the dice point. In this case, the map of the United States is divided into quadrants and represents a playing field, while the heroes represent nothing more than figures—that is, "geese."

The motivation for the difficulties undergone by the hero of the adventure tale is very much worth noting. Let me offer two examples, again from Jules Verne, who is presently under consideration. The first novel bears the title *The Return Home,* which tells of the return of certain acrobats from North America to France by way of Canada, the Straits of Dezhnev and Siberia, due to their having lost their money. In the other novel, a stubborn Turk by the name of Keriban travels from one shore of the Bosporus to the other by a roundabout path which takes him all over the Black Sea. The reason for this is that he refuses to pay a few kopecks required by customs. Naturally, these crooked paths are called into being by specific conditions—by the demands of the plot. As an example of the difference between resolutions of a problem in prose and poetry, I recommend the reader look at Mark Twain's *Adventures of Huckleberry Finn.* The matter at hand concerns the freeing of a fugitive Negro. Huck Finn represents the method of prose, when he suggests:

"My plan is this," I says. "We can easy find out if it's Jim in there. Then get up my canoe to-morrow night, and fetch my raft over from the island. Then the first dark night that comes, steal the key out of the old man's britches, after he goes to bed, and shove off down the river on the raft, with Jim, hiding day-times and running nights, the way me and Jim used to do before. Wouldn't that plan work?"

"*Work?* Why cert'nly, it would work, like rats a-fighting. But it's too blame' simple; there ain't nothing *to* it. What's the good of a plan that ain't no more trouble than that? It's as mild as goose-milk. Why, Huck, it wouldn't make no more talk than breaking into a soap factory." (chap. 34)

And there you have it! A poetically laborious plan is concocted. A leg from a bed is sawn off. It is wrapped in a chain. Although it could have been lifted with little effort, an underground passage is dug up, a rope ladder is constructed and handed over to the prisoner in a pirogue, the neighbors are warned of the abduction—in a word, everything is played according to the rules of art. At the conclusion of the novel, it turns out that Jim is not a fugitive at all. He had been emancipated long before. We may see a parallel here with a "recognition" and with the attendant collapse of all obstacles standing in the way of a marriage. It is precisely this marriage, after all, that the parents of the concerned parties desire. So how do we answer Tolstoi's question "Why didn't Lear recognize Kent, and why didn't Kent recognize Edward?" Simply by saying that this is necessary for the creation of a drama, that Shakespeare was as undisturbed by the unreality of the literary work as a chessplayer is undisturbed by the fact that a knight can only move obliquely on the board.

I would like to now return to the abduction and recognition plot. Zelinsky supposes that it has a foundation in reality. Concerning a certain play by Apollo Karistsky, he writes:

> No doubt about it! You couldn't find a better planned story line. There's nothing superfluous in it, all the scenes hold together beautifully. Similarly, there is no viola-tion of the principle of verisimilitude, except perhaps for the capricious play of Fate. But people saw things quite differently in those troubled times before the advent of passports and telegrams. Unexpectancy ruled their lives. For that reason, it was permissible for an author, in constructing his work, to select from a multitude of meaningless, fortuitous events by which he was surrounded, to select those events in which an intelligent plan and good will made themselves manifest.

First and foremost, Zelinsky's explanation fails to explain precisely how the plot could have survived beyond the times of Alexandria to the times of Molière and almost to our own day. Besides, this explanation is factually incorrect. By the time of Menander, the plot having to do with the recogni-tion of abducted babies had already passed from an actual phenomenon to pure literary tradition. So, for example, the slave in the play *Epitrepontes,* having found the baby with items indicating its origin, speaks of the possi-bility that this child might be recognized by his parents, alluding thereby not to reality as such, but to the play seen by him in the theater (cf. G. Tseretely's *The Newly Discovered Comedies of Menander*). In precisely the same way, Merezhkovsky is too soft-hearted when he laments the breakdown of mores in the city of Alexandria:

> We must point out a similar characteristic in the mores [of the times] in the frank and naive admission made by Daphnis' father: he had abandoned his little son to the vicissitudes of fortune only because it seemed to him that he had already had enough children. Daphnis was born a superfluous child, of little account. His father threw him out of the house like a puppy. The father deals with Chloë similarly. However, he apologizes for his poverty and for the predicament that made it impossible for him to bring up (and marry off) his daughter in proper style. These features attest to the degenerate state of the family and to the barbarism of late Byzantine culture. This barbarism is capriciously intertwined with a pathological refinement of mores, as in

all periods of decadence. This is not a pagan patriarchal severity, which we encounter in Homer and in the works of the Greek tragedians—rather, it represents a case of savagery, of a coarsening of mores in a degenerating culture. Of course, it would be absurd to condemn the author: he took from life only what he found in it, and a deep artistic objectivity prevented him from embellishing it. (*Eternal Companions*)

As I have already said, the abduction plot had already become a purely bookish affair by that time. To set Merezhkovsky's mind at rest, let me relate the following:

In the age of *Sturm und Drang* in Germany, the overwhelming majority of plays during a space of five years were based on the subject of fratricide. So, for example, all three plays presented at a competition in a theater in Hamburg in 1776 depict just such a crime (*Julius von Tarent* by Leisewitz, *The Twins* by Klinger, and *The Ill-Starred Brothers* by an anonymous author). Schiller's *The Robbers* also bears some relationship to the theme. Nevertheless, this does not prove that cases of fratricide were occurring in massive numbers in Germany at the time. It is worth repeating that Veselovsky considers the adventures of the Greek novel to represent a purely stylistic device.

The abduction device took a long time in dying. Its fate is a curious one. As it degenerated, it began to appear in subsidiary plot lines. Now, however, it has descended to the level of children's literature. It flared up feebly when it was renewed in the so-called war stories of 1914 to 1916. However, even before that, this device suffered a most unusual and curious fate. We should mention in passing that a device in a state of deterioration can still be used to parody the device itself. So Pushkin made use of the banal rhyme "rose/close" even as he pointed out its banality in his verse.

The abduction plot was already parodied by Boccaccio in the seventh story of the second day, the one having to do with the Babylonian sultan who sends one of his daughters to be married to the king of El Gharb. As a consequence of every possible kind of fortuitous incident, she goes through ten husbands in as many localities during the course of four years. Returning at last to her father, she leaves home once again, as a virgin, for her meeting with the king, in order to enter into marriage with him according to the original plan. The point here is that the effect achieved in the classic adventure tale involving a young woman as a heroine lies precisely in her preservation of her innocence even in the hands of her abductors. This virginity, left inviolate (by writers) for the next eighty years, was mocked by Cervantes.

The ending of the story, with its assurances of the maiden's chastity and with the light-headed prank of the mouths that would not shrink from kissing, has the same effect on Veselovsky that a dissonant chord has when it unexpectedly demolishes a fatalistic melody.

However, the correctness of our interpretation of this story as a parody is confirmed by the fact that Boccaccio has several other literary parodies in his book. Let me mention two of them.

The eighth story of the fifth day: In Ravenna a certain Nastagio degli Onesti loves a young woman of the Traversari family. Even after lavishing his fortune on her, his love remains unrequited. At the insistence of relatives, he travels to Chiazza. There he watches as a knight persecutes a young woman, kills her and throws her body to the dogs. Seeing this, he invites his kinfolk and the woman he loves to Chiazza for dinner. During dinner, she sees the dogs ripping the young woman apart. Fearing a similar fate, she decides to marry Nastagio. "Nor was it in her instance alone that this terror was productive of good: on the contrary, it so wrought among the ladies of Ravenna that they all became, and have ever since been, much more compliant with men's desires than they had been wont to be" (Rigg translation).

Boccaccio's women, it turns out, are thus severely punished for their intractability. In the legend which serves as the prototype for this story, however, such a punishment was reserved for adultery only. Veselovsky cautiously suggests that Boccaccio did not draw on this legend for his prototype but on a different, less orthodox one. This is Veselovsky's usual point of view. He has never fully recognized the independent, deliberate changes and transformations effected by the writer himself, and which are the very source of his creativity. We may suppose that Boccaccio had in mind here a work based on the conflict between new and old interpretations of morality and punishment. This assumption is all the more right in that Boccaccio offers us another story with calming assurances concerning retribution beyond the grave. This is the tenth story of the seventh day.

Recognition, however, represents only an isolated case of a peripeteia. The fundamental principle on which peripeteia is based also calls for impeding and retarding it. That which ought to have been revealed immediately and that which is already clear to the spectator is slowly made known to the hero. Example: Oedipus finds out about his misfortune. Here the drama slows down, caught in the torture of deferred pleasure (see Zelinsky's analysis of peripeteia in Sophocles' *Oedipus*). But this question is easier to study in the everyday rituals of life than in a play that is a work of art. Let me recommend, as an example, the best man's story at a Russian wedding, reported by Veselovsky.

The best man declares that he has come neither under duress nor under coercion. Rather he was sent by the bridegroom, and so on:

Our young bridegroom was coming out of the tower chamber onto the wide street just as I, his best man, walked past. I harnessed my brave horse, saddled and reined it and whipped it with a silken lash. My valiant horse became angry and kicked against the ground. Wagging his tail, my brave horse leaped from mountain to mountain and from hill to hill. Across valleys and rivers he leaped till he reached the edge of the blue sea. In the blue sea swam grey geese and white swans and brilliant falcons. I asked the geese, the swans: "Where is that tower chamber of our young bride?" And the geese answered me:

"Go to the blue sea, to the eastern side of the blue sea. There you'll see an oak of twelve roots standing." So I rode to the eastern shore of the sea, I rode up to that oak and a marten jumped out. Not the one who roams the forest, but the one that is a young woman sitting on the lattice chair in the tower chamber, weaving a towel for her bridegroom. I, the groom's best man, followed the marten's track and rode up to the tower chamber, to the tower chamber on the broad street, to the newly wed bride. The marten's tracks led to the gates and there they came to an end. "Show us the marten's tracks or open the door!"

Riddles by the gate:

"Who are you, a mosquito or a fly?"

"I am neither a mosquito nor a fly. I am a man of the Holy Spirit. Show us the marten's tracks or open the gate."

There follows an extremely important passage which I would like very much to insist on. A debate follows. From within they propose to the best man:

a) Stand under a corner window.
b) Climb over the gate.
c) The gates are locked. The keys have been thrown into the sea.
d) He went to the wrong porch.
e) The gates are overgrown with forest and thicket.

To all these proposals the best man responds with: "Show us the marten's tracks or open the gate." Finally, they allow him into the peasant hut.

He answers (c) as follows:

Our bridegroom rode to the blue sea, where he hired some brave fishermen, men of good will. They cast a silken net into the waters and captured a white fish. In that white fish they found the golden keys to the tower chamber.

To (e) he answered:

Our bridegroom rode to the blacksmiths, to the young blacksmiths. They forged heroic axes and hired bold workers, who chopped down the forest and the thicket and battered down the gates.

We see the device of deceleration even more clearly in the extraordinarily curious custom recorded by Roman Jakobson in the village of Kostyushino, of the Rogachesky Volost, Demidovsky District, Moscow Province:

The parents of a young girl have gone into town for the night. The girl invites several of her girlfriends (usually two or three) to her home. She then informs a number of previously designated lads about this in advance or else she spreads a rumor (e.g., through a soldier's wife) that "there will be a house party at such and such a place and time." When everyone in the village goes to sleep, the boys (in the first case—invited, in the second case—on their own volition) approach the hut where the young girl lives. As the other boys move over to the side, one boy knocks on the window. At first no one responds. At the second knock, the hostess responds.

"Who is it?"

"Me" (so and so).

"What do you want?"

"Let me in."

"Of course."

She lets him in and says: "I am alone but there are *many* of you."

"I am alone too."

She exposes him as a liar. He tries to justify himself and says: "But you are not alone either. Nyushka Manyushka and others are with you."

This she denies, saying: "Well now, if I let you in, I won't be able to let you out. Papa is coming back in an hour."

The young fellows say that they came by for just half an hour. Finally she lets them in through the window. They all find a seat. They then demand that she light the lamp.

"I'm out of kerosene. The wick is ruined and Mama hid the glass lid."

All of these arguments are refuted, one by one, by the boys. The lamp is lit.

"Put on the samovar!" the boys cry out.

"We're out of coal and we're out of water," the girl says. "The samovar has been taken apart and Mama has hidden the tea."

All of these arguments are refuted by the boys. The samovar is heated. They drink tea and the boys propose: "Now why don't we all go to sleep."

The girls say no, under all sorts of pretexts. The fellows refute their arguments and, finally, they all go to bed, two at a time. Every attempt at disrobing or immodest advance provokes a motivated reply, but the boys do not give up. By morning, they all disperse. Returning home, the parents pretend they didn't notice a thing.

An analogous custom existed in Germany under the name of "trial nights."

Sumtsov had already commented on the affinity between these "young people's gatherings" and "trial nights."

Apart from elements which consist of borrowings, a work of art also contains an element of creativity, a force of will driving an artist to create his artifact piece by piece as an integral whole.

The laws underlying this creative will must be brought to light. Here is a letter by Tolstoi on the subject:

Dear Princess V:

I am very happy, my dear princess, at the occasion which has caused you to remember me. And, as proof of that, I am hastening to do for you the impossible, that is to answer your question. Andrei Bolkonsky is no more than a character created by a novelist. He does not represent the writer's personality or his memoirs. I would have been ashamed to be published if all of my work consisted of nothing more than copying a portrait from life, or discovering and remembering details about people. I shall endeavor to say who my Andrei is. In the battle of Austerlitz (which was described later) it was necessary for me to kill off a brilliant young man. Later in the same novel I found that I needed old man Bolkonsky and his daughter. Since it is rather awkward to describe a character who is in no way connected with the novel, I decided to make another brilliant young man the son of old Bolkonsky. I then became interested in him and gave him a role in the unfolding plot of the novel. And, feeling charitable, I had him severely wounded instead of killed. And so, my dear princess, here is my totally honest though somewhat vague explanation as to who Bolkonsky is. (3 May 1865)

'I would like to call the reader's attention to Tolstoi's motivation for the blood kinship between his protagonists. If we compared his motivation to the motivation underlying Hugo's novels (e.g., *Les Misérables*), then it would be clear how conventional indeed is the kinship and locality motivation that links the separate parts of Tolstoi's composition. We see a lot more daring in this respect, before Tolstoi.

If, for compositional reasons, an author decides to connect two fragments, then this need not necessarily imply a causal relationship. Such are, for example, the motivations for the connections between stories in Oriental tales. In one of these Oriental tales, a story is told by a hero carrying a spinning wheel on his head (Østrup). This thoroughly untrue-to-life situation did not in any way embarrass or confuse the compiler of the story because the parts of this work are not necessarily linked to each other, nor are they dependent upon each other in accordance with any non-compositional laws.

## Framing as a Device of Deceleration

*Note:* The type of storytelling where the principal characters tell their stories in succession ad infinitum until the first story is completely forgotten may be considered to be specifically Indian in origin.

This method of framing the action is encountered everywhere in the *Panchatantra, Hitopadesa, Vetalapanchavimśati* and in all similar works. As far as the improbability of the situations in which the characters find themselves is concerned, the Hindus couldn't care less. Thus, amidst the most terrifying torments, at death's door, the characters relate or, in turn, hear out with utter calmness all sorts of fables (e.g., a man who tells of his past while a wheel is spinning on his head).

As in the story concerning *The Seven Viziers*—a work of undoubtedly Hindu origin, where we were dealing with a method of transmitting stories that is well known to us—so also in *A Thousand and One Nights* we encounter that same characteristic way of slowing down and prolonging the telling of the stories in order thereby to defer the carrying out of the death sentence.

Similarly, we encounter an absolutely analogous situation in the literature of India, where a whole series of fables is told with the purpose of dragging out the time and forestalling a hasty decision. *Śuka-saptati* (i.e., seventy stories by a parrot) is a story about a certain lady who wants to visit her lover in the absence of her husband. Before leaving on his voyage, however, the husband left his wife a parrot. Every day this parrot recites a different story to its mistress, and each night it ends its story by saying: "You'll find out the rest tomorrow, if you stay home tonight."

I would suggest comparing this story with the song about Alvass (from the *Edda*), in which Tor, seeking to hold back the sunrise, when he would supposedly be turned into stone, keeps asking for the names of various objects among the gods of the elves, turs and carls.

It is worth noting that in this particular case the device is consciously perceived as a delaying tactic.

Let me offer another example:

A vizier disobeys the king's order to kill the queen. Instead, he hides her. The king, not knowing this, laments her death. The vizier, answering the king's query, plays with his impatience in a way analogous to a "framing device." For instance:

The king says: "You have upset my state of mind and increased my sorrow." So he executes the "upaxn."

The "upagh" responds: "There are two kinds of people who deserve sorrow: the one who commits sins every day of his life and the one who never does any good deeds. Why? Because their joy in the world and their bliss are insignificant, while their repentance, i.e., after a long period of punishment, is beyond measure."

The king says: "You are right. If the upaxn were alive, I wouldn't grieve for anything in the world."

The upagh answers: "There are two kinds of people who should not grieve. One of them is the man who exercises himself by doing good deeds," etc.

In one version of this story (*Kalilah and Dimnah*) the vizier's answers (along with the parables) occupy nine pages of the text.

This device of Hindu poetics plays a role similar to that of the rituals found in legends and the "impeding elements" in adventure novels.

Let us return, however, to the question of the artist's intention. Here is an excerpt from chapter 17 of Aristotle's *Poetics*. The reader may wish to compare it with Tolstoi's letter above.

And the argument of the play, whether previously made or in process of composition by oneself, should first be sketched out in abstract form and only then expanded and other scenes ("episodes") added. I mean, as a method for gaining a general view of the play, the following, for example, with the *Iphigenia:* A certain young woman is sacrificed but spirited away without the sacrificers perceiving it. She is established in another country, where the custom is to sacrifice all foreigners to their goddess, and wins this priesthood. A considerable while later the priestess's brother happens to come to the country (the fact that the god ordered him to do so, and for what purpose, is outside of the plot), and having come and been captured he is about to be sacrificed when he recognizes his sister . . . and thence comes his deliverance. At this stage, but not before, one may assign names to the characters and add other scenes; but be sure that these are appropriate, as for example the fit of madness through which he is captured and their escape by means of the purification ceremony are appropriate to Orestes. (Else translation)

From this it follows that the battle between father and son is a result of the artist's conscious choice and not because of matriarchal recollections (Ilya and Sokolnik, Rustem and Sokhrab and so on).

I would like to call the reader's attention to the fact that all of the versions of the story speak of the son's "recognition" by his father. That means that the writer who formed the plot is convinced that the father ought to know his own son.

Of interest to us are the different expositions constructed by the author to enable him to kill off the father and create a state of incest. For example, Yulian Milostivy slays his father and mother, whom he finds sleeping in the guest room, mistaking them for his wife and her lover.

Compare the analogous legend called "On the Poor and Needy": "After a period of absence, a merchant sees two young men lying in his wife's bed. He wants to kill them. They are his sons."

What is evident here is the will of the artist striving to motivate the crime that he needs for his work. Consider the following excerpt from chapter 14 of Aristotle's *Poetics:*

> Since it is the pleasure derived from pity and fear by means of imitation that the poet should seek to produce, it is clear that these qualities must be built into the constituent events. Let us determine, then, which kinds of happening are felt by the spectator to be fearful and which pitiable. Now such acts are necessarily the work of persons who are near and dear (close blood kin) to one another, or enemies, or neither. But when an enemy attacks an enemy there is nothing pathetic about either the intention or the deed, except in the actual pain suffered by the victim; nor when the act is done by "neutrals"; but when the tragic acts come within the limits of close blood relationship, as when brother kills or intends to kill brother or do something else of that kind to him, or son to father or mother to son or son to mother—those are the situations one should look for.

Myths passed on by means of legend ought not to be mutilated. (It is very characteristic, indeed, how certain myths have been altered). In Aeschylus' *Choephori* Orestes alone informs Clytemnestra of her son's death. Sophocles, on the other hand, divides this role between Orestes and Talthybius. While the latter delivers the actual message, Orestes delivers the fictitious remains of the dead son. That is, we are dealing here with the usual device of expressing A through A(1), A(2).

The change, as I understand it, has Clytemnestra killed by Orestes and Eriphyle by Alcmaeon. The poet, however, must be his own inventor and make use of the legend as he sees fit.

Let us be even clearer and say what precisely we mean by "as he sees fit."

The action may be performed as in classical drama, where the characters carry out their deeds consciously. This is how Euripides depicts Medea murdering her children. Yet, one can perform such an action without being fully aware of its horror and discover only afterwards the underlying relationship of blood or friendship that binds one to one's victim, as in the case of Sophocles' Oedipus. In the case of the latter, moreover, the horrible deed is accomplished within the play by Alcmaeon Astydamanta or by Telegonus in *Wounded Odysseus.*

There is a third possibility: A character who intends to commit a certain unforgivable crime comes to recognize his mistake before actually committing his deed. Other than this, there is no other possible alternative. One must either commit the crime or not commit it, whether consciously or unconsciously. Of these alternatives the worst is that where someone has consciously planned to commit the crime but does not go through with it, for this failure to commit the crime is repugnant but not tragic to us. This is so because suffering is absent from the situation. For that reason, no one has composed in that vein except perhaps for a few cases, as for example in *Antigone.* In this play, Haemon intends to kill Creon but does not kill him.

There is also the case where the crime (under similar circumstances) *is* performed. Best of all is a situation where someone commits a crime in ignorance and afterwards recognizes his deed, because such a situation inspires in us not disgust, but astonishment.

The most effective alternative is represented by the case above. As an example, consider the *Kresfont.* Meropa plans to kill his son but does not kill him. Instead, he recognizes his crime before committing it. Similarly in *Iphigenia* a sister intends to kill her brother and does not do so, while in *Helle* a son, who has planned to betray his mother, recognizes her. This is why, as it has been said, tragedies move within the circle of a few families. This method of working out their story line was discovered by poets through chance rather than art. For this reason, they reluctantly seize upon any families who had experienced these types of misfortunes.

Compare this with the descriptions of incest in Maupassant's "The Hermit": (a) father and daughter, in which a recognition takes place by means of a photograph; and (b) brother and sister ("Francoise"), where recognition takes place by means of a conversation.

Let me make a comparison.

The action of a literary work takes place on a field of battle. The masks and types of modern drama correspond to the figures of chess. The plots correspond to the moves and gambits, that is, to the techniques of the game, as these are used and interpreted by the players. The tasks and the peripeties correspond to the moves made by the opponent.

The methods and devices of plot construction are similar to and in principle identical with the devices of, for instance, musical orchestration. Works of literature represent a *web of sounds, movements and ideas.*

In a literary work an idea may take a form analogous to the pronunciatory and sonar aspect of a morpheme or else the form of a heterogeneous element. Here is an excerpt from a letter from Tolstoi to N. N. Strakhov:

> If I wanted to express in words all that which I sought to express in a novel, I'd have no choice but to write the very same novel I had written in the first place. And if the critics now understand me and are able to declare in their feuilletons what it was that I had really meant to say, then I congratulate them and assure them, if I may

be so bold, that they know a lot more about it than I do. And if these myopic critics think that I intended to describe only that which I found to my liking, for example, Oblonsky at dinner or Karenina's shoulders, then they are mistaken.

In everything, in almost everything that I have ever written, I have been guided by the need to collect my thoughts, to connect them in such a way that I may express myself. However, every thought that is expressed in words loses its meaning and degenerates horribly whenever it is taken by itself, that is, whenever it is ripped out of the integral structure of which it is a part. The structure of words consists not of ideas as such (I believe), but of something else, and it is impossible to express the basis of this structure directly through words. This basis can be expressed only through the mediation of words, that is through images, actions, situations. . . .

Now, however, when nine-tenths of what is published consists of criticism, we need people who would show us the absurdity of searching for [individual] thoughts in a work of art and who could guide the reader permanently in that endless labyrinth of interconnections which is the essence of art. And in accordance with those laws which inform these interconnections.

The tale or legend, the short story, the novel—are a combination of motifs. The song is a combination of stylistic motifs. For that reason the plot and the nature of plot constitute a form no less than rhyme. From the standpoint of plot, there is no need for the concept of "content" in our analysis of a work of art. We may consider form in this context to be the principle underlying the construction of an object.

## APPENDIX A

[Trans. note: *Shklovsky begins with abbreviated bibliographic citations to further examples of the kind of story referred to on p. 30 above. The terse citations demonstrate Shklovsky's wide acquaintance with folklore literature, but would mean little to the contemporary reader, and hence are omitted. The text resumes:*]

These tales have close relatives in barter stories. For example, Afanasiev, first tale, variant: The she-fox exchanges a stick for a goose, the goose for a turkey, the turkey for a bride. Same device in the West European tale worked out by Andersen under the title of "Whatever the Little Man Does Is Fine." The barter is made vivid by a humorous interpretation of the ever *diminishing* value of the objects exchanged.

For purposes of comparison I would like to offer an excerpt from the work of S. K. Beilin, *Nomadic or Universal Tales and Legends in Ancient Rabbinical Literature* (1907). Here we encounter the type $a < b < c < d$, i.e., a kind of geometric progression.

In the twelfth tale of the third book of *Panchatantra,* "On the Mouse That Was Turned into a Maiden and Chose Its Betrothed"; also in chapter eight, tale no. seven, from the book of *Kalilah and Dimnah* on the hermit and the mouse, we read the following:

A certain pious and compassionate hermit kept a mouse. Through prayer, he had secretly transformed it into a beautiful woman so that it wouldn't be shunned by his family. When the girl reached adulthood, the good hermit began searching for a worthy suitor for her.

Since she asked for the strongest man alive, the solicitous guardian turned to the sun, who was the most powerful being in the universe, and pleaded with him to marry his daughter. In doing this, he explained why he was turning to the sun and to no one else. But then the sun answered:

"I will show you someone who is stronger. It is the cloud, which covers and detains all of my rays and eclipses my rays."

Then the hermit went to see the cloud and said to him what he had earlier said to the sun. But the cloud answered:

"I too will show you someone who is stronger. Go see the wind, who moves me back and forth and drives me to the east and west."

So the hermit went to see the wind and said to him what he had already said to the cloud. The wind answered:

"I too will show you someone stronger. It's the mountain, which I cannot move."

So the hermit came to see the mountain and repeated his speech. And the mountain said to him:

"I will show you someone stronger. It's the rat, from which I am powerless to protect myself when he bores a hole within me and selects me for his dwelling."

So the hermit went to see the rat and asked it: "Won't you please marry my daughter?" And he answered:

"How can I marry her when my burrow is so narrow. On the contrary, a rat would rather marry a mouse."

So the hermit, with the consent of the young woman, began to pray to his Lord, imploring Him to turn his daughter back into the mouse she had once been. So God turned her back into a mouse and she and the rat lived happily ever after.

This tale was culled by me from the book of *Kalilah and Dimnah,* a collection of fairy tales under the name of Bindnaya, translated from the Arabic by M. O. Attaya and M. V. Ryabinina (Moscow, 1899).

The moral: Human nature does not change.

According to Rumanian legend—"a baby mouse always returns to its burrow"—the wind assures him that the oak is stronger than he, since the latter stands in the way of the mighty whirlwinds. But he informs him what the latter knows already, namely, that the oak will nevertheless soon fall to the ground, since mice have infiltrated its roots. For that reason, the wind advises the baby mouse to return to its own burrow, thinking that thereby the mouse will find there the strongest creature on earth.

We read the following story in the Midrash, Bereshit (Genesis), book 1, chapter 38 (edited between the third and fifth centuries A.D.):

When Terah found out about the heretical ideas and reckless actions of his son Abraham (i.e., that Abraham had intentionally and provocatively smashed the idols of the people, that he had spitefully and pointedly mocked the ancient faith, that he was preaching some new teaching of "the one God"), he handed him over to Nimrod.

"Bow down in worship before the fire!" Nimrod orders Abraham.

"Wouldn't it be more correct to bow down before the water that extinguishes the fire?" objects Abraham.

"Fine, then bow down before the water!" orders Nimrod.

"But wouldn't it be more correct, in that case, for me to bow down before rain clouds, who hold within them water?"

"Well, all right, then bow down before the rain clouds!"

"Of course, but wouldn't it be more correct for me to bow down before the wind, which scatters the rain clouds?" Abraham objects again.

"Fine, then go ahead and bow down before the wind!"

"If so, then wouldn't it make more sense to bow down before the being who contains the wind within himself?"

And the king, incensed, cries out:

"These are foolish ideas that you are uttering. Look here, I shall bow down before the fire, and it is into the fire that I shall cast you. Let your god, the god you believe in, come save you."

We read the following edifying passage in the Babylonian Talmud concerning the mighty and beneficial power of virtue (justice, peace of mind, etc.)*—in which a similar but more detailed parallelism (a kind of order) plays a role, a parallelism in which the physical and spiritual forces of nature dominate each other in turn.

Rabbi Yehuda says: "Justice (the administration of justice, mercy) is infinitely great, because it hastens the day of salvation (secures human happiness on earth), as it is said in the opening verse of Isaiah 56: 'Thus saith the Lord, Keep ye judgment, and do justice: for my salvation is near to come, and my righteousness to be revealed.' " He also said: "Ten powerful objects—one stronger than another—have been created in the world: a hard (stone) mountain—which is pulverized by iron; hard iron—which is melted down by fire; a mighty fire—which is extinguished by water; mighty waters—which are carried to the earth by rain clouds; formidable clouds—which are scattered by the wind; violent winds—which are stopped by a body; (a powerful) body—which is undermined by sorrow; a great sorrow—which is conquered (assuaged) by wine; a strong wine—which loses its effect in sleep. And death overpowers them all. But virtue saves us even from death."

We find a similar step-by-step parallelism in the Midrash Kohelet (chap. 7, no. 46), but with a different interpretation or conclusion. There it is carried out as a satire on "shrewish women."

The idea of this satire lies in the following: one power overcomes another power. One is more mighty (or more fierce) than another. Yet, there is nothing worse than a spiteful shrew. She is more terrifying than anything on earth, even death itself.

This passage from the Midrash says the following:

Rabbi Yehuda said: "There are fourteen things, each of which is mightier than the other (overpowers the other). The abyss is mighty, but the land rises above it, since it encompasses it. The land is mighty, but the mountains are even mightier, since they rise above the plain. The mountain is mighty, but iron can cut into it. The iron, hard though it may be, can be melted by fire. Fire devours all, but it in turn is over-powered by water, which extinguishes it. Waters are mighty, but they are carried to the earth by clouds. The clouds are mighty, but they are scattered by the wind. The winds are mighty, but the wall can stop them. The wall is strong, but a man can destroy it. A man is powerful, but sorrow can lay him low. Sorrow is mighty, but wine can dull its pain and it is forgotten. The power of wine (intoxication) is great, but it is chased away by sleep. Sleep is mighty (salutary), but illness can chase it away. The power of illness is great, but the angel of death prevails and carries the soul into the upper regions. But a shrewish wife is worse than all of these."

---

*These parenthetical variants are Shklovsky's, not mine—Trans.

Similarly, there is a certain Ethiopian parable that runs: "Iron is strong, but fire is stronger than iron; water is stronger than fire, the sun is stronger than water, the cloud is stronger than the sun, the earth is stronger than the cloud, man is stronger than the earth, sorrow is stronger than man, wine is stronger than sorrow, sleep is stronger than wine, but stronger than all of them by far is a woman."

The same caustic or humorous opinion of the shrew, and in the same form (i.e., as in the Midrash), appears in the monuments of ancient Russian texts, and this opinion passed on into the oral folk literature in the form of folk riddles and jokes (see Khudyakov, "Russian Riddles," *Ethnographic Collections* [Russian Imperial Geographical Society, 1864]) and is expressed in the following form:

"The fire has hardly been lit, when it is extinguished by the water. What's stronger than water? Wind. What's stronger than wind? A mountain (because it withstands the wind). What's stronger than the mountain? Man (he cuts into the mountain). What's stronger than man? Wine (it deprives us of the use of legs and arms). What's more fierce than wine? Sleep. What's more fierce than sleep? A shrew." (See also Pypin's *History of Early Russian Literature.*)

Among Lithuanian Jews the song-tale "The Pears Refuse to Fall" is a favorite with the children.

The well-known tale "Khad Gadya" (i.e., An Only Kid) is even more popular—and remains so to this very day—among the Central and Eastern European Jews, the so-called Ashkenazim (or Jews of Germanic extraction). This animal tale has even made its way into the Passover Hagada (Passover legends read on the first two days of the Passover in commemoration of the Exodus of the Jews from Egypt).

In these folk tales we are dealing with animate and inanimate objects that wage war against each other and overpower each other.

The content of the first of them—save for certain insignificant alterations—identical to that which we find in the Germanic folk tale—is the following:

God created the pear tree so that it may bear fruit, but the tree refuses to bear fruit, and the pears refuse to fall from the tree.

It is then that the Lord sends the young boy Yankele to gather (to pick) the ripe pears from the tree, but Yankele, in his turn, refuses to go pick them just as they, in their turn, refuse to fall (refuse to let themselves be picked). The Lord then sends a dog to bite Yankele for his disobedience. The dog refuses to obey. In order to spur on the dog, the Lord sends a cudgel (*shtekele*), but the cudgel also refuses. Finally, the Lord sends fire after the club, and water after the fire, and a steer (*eksele*) to drink up the water, and a ritual slaughterer after him, and an angel of death after the ritual slaughterer (*shokhet*). But all of this is in vain. They all refuse to obey. But when the Lord raises His arm against the angel of death and acts in His own person, then the matter takes a different turn: Everyone suddenly obeys. The angel of death declares his willingness to cut down the ritual slaughterer for his disobedience, the ritual slaughterer cuts down the steer, the steer drinks the water, etc., etc. And in the end the young boy picks the pears from the tree and the pears fall willingly into his hands.

A similar song is found among the Slovenes, relatives of the Russian people, and consists of the following:

They send a dog after Yurik, in order to bring the young boy home, but the dog refuses to go bite him. They then send a cudgel after the dog, but the cudgel would not beat the dog. They then send fire after the cudgel, and water after the fire, and after the water bulls, and after the bulls the butchers, after the butchers the witch, but all in vain. Finally, when they send the Devil himself after the witch to take her away, the witch goes off to put her spell on the butchers, the butchers slaughter the bulls, the bulls drink the water, water puts out the fire, the fire sets the cudgel afire, the cudgel beats the dog, the dog bites Yurik, and Yurik returns home. (Buslaev, "Nomadic Tales and Stories," *Russian Herald,* May 1874.)

A similar song-tale has been a source of amusement among kids all over Russia. Its content is as follows: A goat went looking for nuts, but did not return home. First, they sent the wolves after her, but the wolves refused to eat the goat. They then sent people after the wolves, etc., but all was in vain. No one obeyed. No one would do as he was told. Finally, geese are sent after the worms:

> The geese peck at the worms,
> The worms gnaw at the butt of the ax.
> The butt of the ax strikes down the bulls,
> The bulls drink the water,
> The water puts out the fire,
> The fire consumes the stone,
> The stone sharpens the ax,
> The ax chops down the oak,
> The oak knocks down the bear,
> The bear rips people apart,
> People chase after the wolves,
> The wolves eat the goat—
> There's the goat with the nuts,
> There is the goat with the shelled nuts. (Buslaev, ibid.)

In the above-mentioned Jewish Passover song, "Khad Gadya," as in the other folk tales (Jewish, Russian, German, etc.), we find a whole procession of beings (characters) and objects, who overpower each other in battle.

Victory is always to the last one, i.e., to God.

The difference between this liturgical song and other tales for children similar to it lies only in the relationship inhering between the characters and their actions: in the Passover song they act on their own accord, voluntarily—some of them are motivated by an evil will, others, on the contrary, by a sense of duty and justice, rather than by command, as in the others.

The content of the song "An Only Kid" (Khad Gadya) is as follows: The beloved kid, the one and only kid, purchased by the father for two zuzes (zuz = a monetary unit), is torn to pieces by a wild, ferocious cat. In punishment, the dog bites the cat, the cudgel beats the dog, the fire consumes the cudgel, the water puts out the fire, the bullock drinks up the water, the bullock is cut down by the ritual slaughterer, the ritual slaughterer is struck down by the angel of death.

In the work just cited, the relationship between the author and the object of his investigation is incorrect, since he calls our particular attention to the inessential, namely, to the way a distinct semantic content is applied to the given device. It may well be the case that this moral, attached to the end of the work, bears the same relationship to it that the tears of music lovers have to the music. As is well known, composers at times adapted their chorales for burlesque to the delight of the public that applauded it for its wit and gaiety. Yet, on Sunday morning, the music seemed to them to be religious to its core (Hanslick).

*The chief thing here is that the device is constructed on the basis of deceleration.*

*The purpose of this device is to construct a sensuously experienced work.* If we look at this device from the standpoint of prose, then we, the audience, become impatient and wish to cut it short. Such an attitude is often shared by the gentlemen who, in collecting these tales, delete the retardations and repetitions on their own initiative. The creators of these tales were aware of such a possible perception and even played with it. This is the basis for the so-called "Tedious Tales." An analogous tale of the "ferrying of the goats" is told by Sancho Panza to his knight in *Don Quixote,* part 1, chapter 20.

APPENDIX B (p. 44)

"I have not scorned other influences or themes, which are customarily advanced in these cases, such as the influences of race or environment. However, I believe that of all the influences at work in the history of literature, *the chief influence is exercised by one literary work on another literary work, and it is this influence that I have chiefly sought to trace. I would like to follow a line of investigation that is different from that pursued by my predecessors. It is this influence of artifact upon artifact that is the origin and acting principle responsible for changes of taste and for revolutions in art, including those in literature. There is no question whatsoever here of metaphysics.* * The Pléiade of the sixteenth century wanted to create something different from the work produced by the school of Clément Marot. Racine, in his *Andromaque,* wanted to create something different from Corneille's *Pertharite,* while Diderot in his *Father of the Family* wanted to create something quite different from Molière's *Tartuffe.* Finally, Romantics of our time want to create something different from the works of classical writers. . . . † There is no point in multiplying the causes needlessly or under the pretext that literature is an expression of society. There is no point in confusing the history of literature with the history of mores. These are two completely different things." —F. Brunetière, preface to *Manuel de l'histoire de la littérature française* (1898).

*My reading of "metaphysics" is strictly conjectural. Shklovsky's enigmatic *m'e't'a'z'ki* (*sic!*) is both tantalizing and characteristically frustrating. It looks and sounds like a teasing slant rhyme on the Russian word *ya-zyk* (language) with an obvious play on the word *metafizika.* Or then again, it could all be a weird case of a typo (but how to explain the five apostrophes in the original?). [Trans. note]

† There were also those who wanted "to create something quite similar" to their predecessors. I know them very well, indeed! But it is precisely these who can be excluded from the history of literature and art. [Shklovsky's note]

# Chapter 3

# The Structure of Fiction

## 1

Before I set out to examine the structure of fiction, I feel duty-bound to confess to the reader that I do not have a definition for "story" as such. That is, I do not claim to know what characteristics define a motif or how motifs are actually formed and shaped into a plot. Images alone or parallel structures alone or even mere descriptions of the events do not produce the feeling of a work of fiction in and of themselves.

In chapter 2 I attempted to show the relationship between the devices of plot formation and the general devices of style. In particular, I pointed out the progressive accumulation of motifs. Such accumulations are by their very nature limitless, as are also the adventure novels built on them. This is the source for all those innumerable volumes of Rocambole and also for Alexandre Dumas's *Ten Years Later* and *Twenty Years After*. This explains the need for an epilogue in these novels, where an ending is possible only by changing the time dimension, that is, by "crumpling it."

Yet, it is common practice to enclose this accumulation of stories and tales within the structure of a "framing story." For example, in addition to the devices of abduction and recognition, the writer of an adventure novel may quite frequently adopt a climactic wedding ceremony as a framing story for this work. This is why Mark Twain declares at the end of *The Adventures of Tom Sawyer* that he is at a loss as to how to end his story, since, after all, the boy is obviously too young for the obligatory wedding that ends adult novels. For that reason, Twain ends his book at an opportune point in the narrative. As is well known, the story of Tom Sawyer had a kind of sequel in the story of Huck Finn (who, having played a minor role in his friend's novel, now takes center stage). This theme was later continued in the form of a detective novel. Finally, another "sequel" was produced by Jules Verne in his novel *Five Weeks in a Balloon.*

But what precisely does a story need in order to be understood as something truly complete?

It is easy to see that, in addition to a progressive development, there exists in a story also a structure analogous to a ring or, rather, a loop. The description of happy lovers does not in and of itself create a story. What a story needs is love hindered by obstacles (i.e., it needs happy lovers perceived against the traditional background of love hindered by obstacles). For example, A loves B, but B doesn't love A. By the time B falls in love with A, A has ceased to love B. This is the schema that underlies the relationship between Eugene Onegin and Tatiana. The causes of their ill-timed passion are presented in terms of a complex, psychological motivation. This same device in Boiardo is motivated by a witch's spell. In his *Orlando Innamorato,* Rinaldo is in love with Angelica, but after accidentally drinking water from an enchanted spring, he suddenly forgets his love for her. Meanwhile, after drinking water from another spring, Angelica conceives an ardent love for Rinaldo, whom she had previously hated. As a result, Rinaldo runs away from Angelica's advances, while she, in turn, pursues him from country to country. After wandering all over the globe, Rinaldo, still pursued by Angelica, lands again in the enchanted forest. As they both drink of the water, their roles are reversed once more: Angelica conceives a hatred for Rinaldo, while he falls in love with her again. Here the motivation is nearly laid bare.

Thus, to be a true "story," it must have not only action but counteraction as well (i.e., some kind of incongruity). This reveals a certain affinity between a "motif" and a trope (e.g., a pun). As I have already said in the chapter on erotic enstrangement, the plot lines of erotic tales represent extended metaphors (e.g., the male and female sexual organs are compared in Boccaccio with the pestle and mortar). This comparison is motivated by the entire story, giving rise thereby to a "motif." We see a similar situation in the story about "The Devil and the Nether Regions." Only here the development is more clearly shown, since the author points out frankly at the story's end that such an expression does in fact exist in the vernacular. Obviously, the story is a development of this expression.

Countless stories are, at bottom, really extended puns. As an example, we may cite stories dealing with the origin of names. I myself had occasion to hear from the lips of a certain old resident of Okhtyaska that the name *Okhta* has its source allegedly in Peter the Great's exclamation: "Okh! Ta!" When a name does not admit of such a paronomastic interpretation, then it is broken up into nonexistent proper names. For instance, *Moskva* becomes *Mos* and *Kva,* and *Yausa* becomes *Ya* and *Usa* (as found in the legend of the founding of Moscow).

A motif is not always an extension of linguistic material. For example, the inconsistencies of mores and customs may serve as a basis for the development of a motif. It is worth noting the following detail from the folklore of soldiers (though the influence of linguistic elements is also evident here): the opening of a bayonet is called a "little mule" and it is said about young soldiers that they complain of having lost their little mule.

A similar motif, based on its association with a smokeless fire (electricity), may be found in the story about a warrant officer who was convinced by his compatriots that the electric bulb hanging in the smoke-filled barracks was really a lamp covered in soot.

A conflict also serves as a basis for the motif of a "false impossibility." The device of "prophecy" brings about a clash of purposes on the part of the protagonists, who seek to avoid the fate "predicted" for them by asserting that this prediction has already been fulfilled (the Oedipus motif). Though seemingly unrealizable, this prophecy is, in fact, fulfilled in the form of an apparent pun.

As another example, I may point to the Witch's promise to Macbeth that he shall not be defeated till Birnam wood "remove" to Macbeth and that he cannot be conquered by any man "of woman born." During their assault on Macbeth's castle, the soldiers pick up branches in order to conceal the size of their army. Macbeth's killer, we find out later, was not born of a woman but ripped from the womb.

The same is true of the Alexander legend: Alexander is told that he will die in an iron land under a sky made of bone. In fact, he dies on a shield under a ceiling made of ivory. The same holds for Shakespeare. The king who is told in a prophecy that he will die in Jerusalem dies instead in a monastery cell bearing the name "Jerusalem."

The sense of contrast is the basis for the following motifs: "father vs. son," "brother vs. brother-in-law" (in Pushkin's adaptation of a folk song, this motif is quite complicated), and the motif of "the husband at his wife's wedding" ("husband vs. wife's new husband"). This device serves as the basis also for the motif of the "elusive criminal" introduced into history by Herodotus. We meet this character first in a state of despair and then in his clever resolution. Under this rubric fall also tales based on riddles and riddle solving or, in more advanced forms, tales based on the solving of tasks and on heroic exploits.

In literature of a later time, the motif of the "innocent criminal" came to the fore. In this type of motif we see first the establishment of the very possibility of such an indictment, then the indictment itself, and, finally, the innocent man's acquittal. This acquittal is often attained by juxtaposing the perjured testimony of witnesses (as a Susanna type, this is found also in the Kamoanksky tales of Minaev), or by the intervention of a conscience-stricken witness.

This case may lack a denouement, but then we do not feel the presence of a plot either.

Consider, if you will, Le Sage's *Asmodeus or the Devil on Two Sticks,* where there are scenes that exhibit no plot structure at all. For example:

You observe that new building, which is divided into two wings. One is occupied by the proprietor, the old gentleman whom you see, now pacing the apartment, now throwing himself into an easy chair. He is evidently immersed in some grand project, said Zambullo: who is he: If one may judge by the splendour which is displayed in his mansion, he is a grandee of the first order. Nevertheless, said Asmodeus, he is but an ancient clerk of the treasury, who has grown old in such lucrative employment as to enable him to amass four millions of reals. As he has some compunctions of conscience for the means by which all this wealth has been acquired, and as he expects shortly to be called upon to render his account in another world, where bribery is impracticable, he is about to compound for his sins in this, by building a monastery; which done, he flatters himself that peace will revisit his heart. He has already obtained the necessary permission; but, as he has resolved that the establishment shall consist of monks who are extremely chaste, sober, and of the most Christian humility, he is much embarrassed in the selection. He need not build a very extensive convent.

The other wing is inhabited by a fair lady, who has just retired to rest after the luxury of a milk bath. This voluptuary is widow of a knight of the order of Saint James, who left her at his death her title only; but fortunately her charms have secured for her valuable friends in the persons of two members of the council of Castile, who generously divide her favours and the expenses of her household.

Hark! cried the Student; surely I hear the cries of distress. What dreadful misfortune has occurred? A very common one, said the Demon: two young cavaliers have been gambling in a hell (the name is a scandal on the infernal regions), which you perceive so brilliantly illuminated. They quarrelled upon an interesting point of the game, and naturally drew their swords to settle it: unluckily they were equally skillful with their weapons, and are both mortally wounded. The elder is married, which is unfortunate; and the younger an only son. The wife and father have come just in time to receive their last sighs; and it is their lamentations that you hear. Unhappy boy, cries the fond parent over the still breathing body of his son, how often have I conjured thee to renounce this dreadful vice!—how often have I warned thee it would one day cost thee thy life. Heaven is my witness, that the fault is none of mine! Men, added the Demon, are always selfish, even in their griefs. Meanwhile the wife is in despair. Although her husband has dissipated the fortune she brought him on their marriage; although he has sold, to maintain his shameful excesses, her jewels, and even her clothes, not a word of reproach escapes her lips. She is inconsolable for her loss. Her grief is vented in frantic exclamations, mixed with curses on the cards, and the devil who invented them; on the place in which her husband fell, and on the people who surround her, and to whom she fondly attributes his ruin. (Thomas translation)

Obviously, such a passage (or a fragment of it) doesn't qualify as a story, and this is not because of its brevity. On the other hand, the sense of completion is conveyed by the short scene that interrupts the story told by Asmodeus:

Asmodeus was at this moment interrupted in his recital by the Student, who thus addressed him: — My dear Devil, interesting as is the history you are relating to me, my eyes have wandered to an object which prevents my listening to you as attentively as I could wish. I see a lady, who is rather good-looking, seated between a young man and a gentleman old enough to be his grandfather. They seem to enjoy the liqueurs which are on the table near them, but what amuses me, is, that as from time to time the amorous old dotard embraces his mistress, the deceiver conveys her hand to the lips of the other, who covers it with silent kisses. He is doubtless her gallant. On the contrary, replied the cripple, he is her husband, and the old fool is her lover. He is a man of consequence,—no less than a commandant of the military order of Calatrava; and is ruining himself for the lady, whose complaisant husband holds some inferior place at court. She bestows her caresses on the sighing knight, for the sake of his gold; and is unfaithful to him in favour of her husband, from inclination.

The sense of completeness, of a finished state, derives from the fact that the narrative moves from a false recognition to a revelation of the true state of affairs (i.e., the formula is realized).

On the other hand, even in more substantial short stories and tales, we often sense a certain incompleteness, as if they were never quite truly finished. Such a story is to be found at the end of the tenth chapter. It begins with a description of a serenade, interspersed here and there with lines of verse.

... but enough of these couplets, continued he, you will hear music of another kind.

Follow with your eyes those four men who have suddenly appeared in the street. See! they pounce upon the serenaders: the latter raise their instruments to defend their heads, but their frail bucklers yield to the blows which fall on them, and are shattered into a thousand pieces. And now see, coming to their assistance, two cavaliers; one of whom is the gallant donor of the serenade. With what fury they charge on the four aggressors! Again, with what skill and valour do these latter receive them. What fire sparkles from their swords! See! one of the defenders of the serenade has fallen,—it is he who gave it,—he is mortally wounded. His companion, perceiving his fall, flies to preserve his own life; the aggressors, having effected their object, fly also; the musicians have disappeared during the combat; and there remains upon the spot the unfortunate cavalier alone, who has paid for his gallantry with his life. In the meanwhile, observe the alcade's daughter: she is at her window, whence she has observed all that has passed. This lady is so vain of her beauty,—although that is nothing extraordinary either,—that instead of deploring its fatal effect, she rejoices in the force of her attractions, of which she now thinks more than ever.

This will not be the end of it. You see another cavalier, who has this moment stopped in the street to assist, were it possible, the unfortunate being who is swimming in his blood. While occupied in this charitable office, see! he is surprised by the watch. They are taking him to prison, where he will remain many months; and he will almost pay as dearly for this transaction as though he were the murderer himself.

This is, indeed, a night of misfortunes! said Zambullo.

The story is felt to be incomplete. At times, such "story pictures" are supplemented by what I shall call a "false ending." This false ending is usually fashioned from a description of nature or the weather, like the ending of a certain Christmas story ("the frost turned fierce and violent") that became so famous thanks to the *Satyricon.* You might wish, dear reader, to try your hand at composing something along similar lines. I'd suggest a description of Seville at night or a description of an "indifferent sky" and append it to the excerpt from Le Sage.

Very typical of a false ending is a description of autumn accompanied by the exclamation: "How boring is life, gentleman!" found in Gogol's "Tale of How Ivan Ivanovich Quarreled with Ivan Nikiforovich."

This new motif corresponds to the preceding material and the story then appears to be complete.

There is an entirely special type of story that involves what may be called a "negative ending." Let me first explain the term by analogy. In words like *chairs, skies,* or *oxen,* the letters *s, -ies,* and *-en* represent inflectional endings that are attached to their respective stems (*chair, sky, ox*). Normally, these words, when used in the singular, are perceived as "positive form." However, against the background of plural inflectional endings, a word in the singular (i.e., a word without an ending) may be perceived in this instance as "negative form." (Fortunatov's term. This has also been termed a "0 ending" by Baudouin de Courtenay.) Such negative forms are frequently encountered in short stories, particularly in the stories of Maupassaunt.

For example, a mother travels to see her illegitimate son, who has been sent to the country for his education. It turns out that he has become a coarse peasant. In grief, his mother runs away and ends up plunging into the river. The son, knowing nothing about her, scours the bottom of the river with a pole and finally drags her out by her dress. This is where the story ends. This story is perceived against the background of traditional stories with an "ending." Incidentally (insofar as I can tell), the French novel of everyday life of the epoch of Flaubert made wide use of this device of the unconsummated story (*Sentimental Education*).

The story usually represents a combination of circular and step-by-step construction, complicated by development.

In Chekhov's complete works it is the volume containing his short stories that shows the most wear and tear. The public at large favors, above all, his youthful stories, those which Chekhov himself considered to be most uneven. When we examine the plots of these stories, we come to the realization that Chekhov's themes are of the most ordinary type. Chekhov tells stories mostly about petty bureaucrats and merchants, a sphere of life already conquered for literature a long time before (see the works of Leikin and Gorbunov). In fact, contemporary audiences find this theme rather old hat by now.

The explanation for Chekhov's success in these stories is in their plot structures. Russian literature had paid scant attention to the short story genre. For years Gogol waited for an anecdote that could be developed into a story or tale.

Goncharov's structure, from the point of view of the plot, was quite hopeless. In *Oblomov* the nineteenth-century writer Goncharov has people of the most diverse types troop in and out in the course of one day. From this incompetent exposition, the reader is forced to conclude that Oblomov lives a life of turmoil and disorder.

Turgenev's *Rudin* consists of one story, one episode, and Rudin's confession.

In the world of the short story proper, Pushkin's stories exhibit special energy when it comes to plot structure. Other short story writers include Kalashnikov, Vonlyarlyarsky, Sologub, Lermontov and Marlinsky, author of monotonous society tales.

Chekhov's stories constitute a sharp break with that tradition. Mundane in content, they're distinguished nevertheless from the innumerable "physiological" sketches—which in their time competed with the society tale—by distinct plot lines with unexpected resolutions.

The fundamental structural device used by Chekhov is the "error." The first story, "In the Bathhouse," is based on the historical fact that in pre-Revolutionary Russia long hair was worn by both nihilists and the clergy. In order to make this "error" work, it was necessary for Chekhov to eliminate all secondary elements from his story. That is why the action takes place in a bathhouse. In order to heighten the impact of this conflict, Chekhov selects the season of Lent for the time of the action (i.e., when issues concerning the clergy are most in vogue). The replies by the priest, who is mistaken for a nihilist, are structured in such a way that, when we discover that the priest is indeed a deacon and not a nihilist, we feel an unexpected sense of recognition. Yet this recognition is legitimate, since it reveals the meaning of the priest's obscure muttering. To make the denouement work, Chekhov had to involve the protagonist in the denouement. He had to bring out the recognition scene in bold relief: The barber is distressed to discover that he has insulted a member of the clergy during Lent, before confession, by thinking that he was harboring some strange ideas in his head.

We have before us here a correctly formed equation, both parts of which function in mutual harmony.

The short story entitled "Fat and Thin" occupies only a few pages. It is built on a social inequality between two former schoolmates. This is a thoroughly elementary situation, but it is developed with an unexpected and precise inventiveness. At first, the old comrades greet each other with a big bear hug as they look joyously into each other's tear-soaked eyes. The thin man hastens to tell his comrade about his family. His words pour out uncontrollably, as one might expect of an old friend. In the middle of the story, that is, in the middle of the first page, the thin man realizes that the fat one is a State Councillor, and, suddenly, a chasm of inequality opens up between them. This is quite clear, because, prior to this recognition, the friends were represented as if in their former state of poverty. The thin man, stammering, repeats to the fat man almost word for word everything he had said earlier about his family, but now he speaks without emotion, perfunctorily, as if he were reciting an official report. In spite of this symmetry, the repetition carries a different nuance the second time around, thereby revealing the full meaning of the story's structure.

The parallel structure is continued to the very end of the story. It has a double denouement based on a difference in the feeling of the two comrades who have met. The State Councillor is almost nauseated by the courtesies bestowed upon him by his former friend. Finally, he turns away from the thin one and shakes his hand in farewell. The thin one shakes three of his fingers, bows with his whole body, and begins to giggle like a Chinese, hee-hee-hee! His wife smiles. Nafanail shuffles his feet and drops his peak-cap. All three are pleasantly dumbfounded.

Quite frequently, Chekhov bases his work on a violation of some traditional plot convention.

There's a story by him entitled "A Terrifying Night" concerning a man who finds coffins at night in every apartment that he visits, including his own. The story begins in a primitive-mystical manner. The storyteller's surname is Requiem. He lives at the corner of Death and Grave Streets in the home of a government clerk by the name of Corpse. To soften the impact of a device laid bare, Chekhov adds the phrase: "And so it happened in one of the most obscure localities of Arbat."

By this accumulation of inert horrors, Chekhov achieves a thoroughly unexpected ending. The ending is based on a clash between the coffin as a mystical object in a terrifying story and the coffin as the property of a coffin-maker. To elude his creditors, the coffin-maker hides his coffins clandestinely with his friends, who discover their surprise with horror when they get home.

"An Enigmatic Nature" is filled with an irony played on the epigones of the high society tale. By telling her story directly to the writer, the heroine lays bare the device. The action takes place in a first-class coupé against a background that has become traditional for the high society heroine: "Next to her in the coupé sits a provincial official, a young writer, who has been publishing short stories ('novellas,' he calls them) about high society life in the provincial press."

The beginning of this story, told by a woman, is completely traditional: She was a poor woman, who "endured the ugly upbringing of a boarding-school girl, read lots of stupid novels, committed the usual indiscretions of youth, and experienced her first timid love."

She has fallen in love with a certain young man and wants to be happy. This is followed by another parody on the epigones of the psychological novel: " 'How splendid,' the writer prattles, as he kisses her bracelet. 'I am not kissing you, my divine creature. Rather, I am kissing suffering humanity.' "

The woman marries an old man. This is followed by a parodic description of her life in a few lines. The old man dies and leaves her a fortune. Happiness knocks on her door, but on the way she encounters another obstacle: " 'What stood in your way?' 'Another rich old man.' "

The doubling of this same motif completely deprives it of its original motivation and incorporates the high society story within the framework of an ordinary business transaction.

Parody also serves as a foundation for the story called "It Was She," a work of lesser quality. This story, once again, is built on the inertia of a Christmas story, on an encounter with an unknown woman, whose mystery is not asserted but implied. When she turns out to be the wife of the story-teller, the listeners protest and the storyteller is forced to adopt a traditional ending.

An ambiguous stance towards one and the same thing, carried out without the static quality of another genre, informs Chekhov's remarkable story "A Familiar Face." A prostitute is released from a hospital without her former professional costume (i.e., without her fashionable short blouse, tall hat and bronze-colored shoes). Looking at her internal passport, she discovers that she is now Natasha Kanavkina and not Wanda, the professional hooker, and this makes her feel naked. Since she is in need of money on this day, Wanda/Natasha, the dual woman, pawns her last ring for a ruble and goes to see her friend Finkel, the dentist. She had originally intended to surprise him, and to ask him, face beaming with laughter, for twenty-five rubles. She knocks on his door. Dressed in ordinary clothes, she walks in and timidly asks, "Is the doctor home?" The staircase seems to her luxurious, and above the staircase is a mirror. Wanda again sees herself without a hat, without the fashionable blouse, without the bronze-colored shoes. She enters the doctor's office and from sheer bashfulness says she has a tooth-ache. Finkel soils her lips and gums with his tobacco-stained fingers and pulls out her tooth, whereupon Wanda gives him her last ruble.

The structure of this short story is based on the ambiguous nature of a person's station in life. Here we are dealing with two people of very different professions—a prostitute and a dentist. Besides, she approaches him now as an amateur vis-à-vis a professional. Wanda's changed state of affairs is constantly counterpointed by the author's reminder of her change of attire. At bottom, we are dealing here with shame. The shame of saying who you are; the shame that leads to pain. This is the crux of the entire story:

> Going outside, she felt an even greater shame than before. But now she was no longer ashamed of her poverty. She no longer noticed that she was lacking a tall hat and a fashionable blouse. She was walking along the street spitting blood and every red spittle told her of her life, of her bad and hard life, of those insults which she had borne and which she shall continue to bear tomorrow, a week later and a year after that till her death.

Chekhov rarely makes use of purely legendary material. Yet he has an unsurpassed story called "Polyenka" where legendary material is utilized for a compositional purpose.

A salesman, talking to a dressmaker about his love for her, suggests that the student she is in love with will someday deceive her. This conversation is taking place even as the protagonists are negotiating over trimmings for sale. The intonations of their voices seem to contrast sharply with the drama in progress. The sale is intentionally drawn out, because the man is in love while the woman feels guilty.

> "The most fashionable trimmings nowadays are from bird feathers, the most fashionable color, if you will, is heliotrope or else the color of *kanak,* that is, bordeaux

with a tinge of yellow. We have a huge selection. And where is this story heading? I really don't know . . ."

The woman is pale and tears roll down her cheeks as she selects the buttons.

"We'll be making it for the merchant's wife," she says, "so give me something outstanding, out of the ordinary."

"Indeed! If it's for the merchant's wife," he says, "then, by all means, we must have a little more color. Here are some buttons. A combination of blue, red and fashionable gold. They're as big as eyes. More refined people prefer the dull black buttons with a brilliant fringe. It's just that I don't understand! Can't you see all this for yourself?! Well, what's the point of all these . . . 'strolls' of yours?"

"I really don't know . . ." Polyenka whispers as she bends down to look at the buttons. "I really don't know what's happening to me, Nikolai Timofeich."

The story ends with an almost meaningless series of deliberately gallant words and tears.

Nikolai Timofeich shields Polyenka with his arm, as he tries desperately to conceal her agitation from the other customers in the shop. He forces a smile and says with a loud voice:

"There are two kinds of lace, madam. Cotton and silk. Oriental, British, Valenciennes, crochet, torchon—these are cotton. On the other hand, rococo, soutache and cambric are silk. . . . For God's sake, wipe away your tears. People are coming."

Seeing that she is still sobbing, the salesman continues, louder than ever: " 'Spanish lace, rococo, soutache, cambric . . . Fildecosovian stockings, cotton, silk stockings.' "

Chekhov's short stories made their appearance originally in the humor magazines favored by the young. Chekhov's literary reputation was first made in the theater and in the genre of the tale. It is high time for Chekhov not only to be republished but reexamined as well. Everyone who does so will surely admit that his most popular stories are also the most formally perfect.

## 2

Let us now look closely at parallelism as a device of special importance in the formation of a short story. We'll do so with a particular emphasis on Tolstoi.

In order to transform an object into a fact of art, it is necessary first to withdraw it from the domain of life. To do this, we must first and foremost "shake up the object," as Ivan the Terrible sorted out his henchmen. We must extricate a thing from the cluster of associations in which it is bound. It is necessary to turn over the object as one would turn a log over the fire.

The following example appears in Chekhov's *Notebooks.* Someone walks along a certain alley for fifteen or maybe thirty years. Each day he reads the sign that hangs above a certain shop: LARGE SELECTION OF BEARS, and each day he asks himself: "So who needs a large selection of 'bears'?" Well, one fine day, for reasons unknown, the sign is taken down and laid against the wall. It is then that he reads for the first time: LARGE SELECTION OF PEARS.

A poet removes all signs from their places. An artist always incites insurrections among things.

Things are always in a state of revolt with poets, casting off their old names and adopting new names and new faces. A poet employs images as figures of speech by comparing them with each other. For instance, he may call fire a red flower or he may attach a new epithet to an old word, or else, like Baudelaire, he may say that a carcass lifts its legs like a woman with lascivious intent. In this way he brings about a semantic shift. He wrests the concept from the semantic cluster in which it is embedded and reassigns it with the help of the word (figure of speech) to another semantic cluster. We, the readers, sense the presence of something new, the presence of an object in a new cluster. The new word envelops the object, as new clothes envelop a man. The sign has been taken down. This is one of the ways in which an object can be transformed into something sensuous, into something capable of becoming an artifact. Another way is represented by a progressive, stepped structure. The object divides into two or three segments that reflect or confront each other.

> Oh my apple, who are you courting?
> Oh Mama, do you want to marry?

sings a vagabond from Rostov, perpetuating, in all probability, the tradition represented by:

> An apple rolled down from the bridge.
> Katichka asked to be excused from the table.

We see here two thoroughly incongruous concepts. Yet, each displaces the other from its respective cluster of conventional associations.

At times the object is reduplicated or dismembered. In Aleksandr Blok, for example, the adjective *railroad* is broken up in "rail road melancholy." Or again Leo Tolstoi, in his most formally musical pieces, creates structures informed by the principles of enstrangement and step-by-step development.

I have already spoken of Tolstoi's enstrangement elsewhere. One of the variety of ways in which this device is used involves focusing on a certain detail in the "picture" and emphasizing it in such a way that its conventional proportions are altered. For example, in his depiction of a battle scene, Tolstoi develops the detail of the moist, masticating mouth. Singling out such a detail creates a peculiar displacement. (Konstanin Leontiev showed little understanding of this device in his book on Leo Tolstoi.)

The most common device in Tolstoi, however, may be characterized as the author's refusal to recognize things by their names (i.e., he insists on describing things as if they were seen for the first time [enstrangement]). For example, he calls theatrical scenery in *War and Peace* pieces of painted cardboard, or he calls the communion bread a bun and assures us that Christians eat their God. I believe that this Tolstoian device has its source in French literature, perhaps in Voltaire's Huron, nicknamed "L'ingénu," or perhaps in the description of the French court made by Chateaubriand's "Savage." In any case, Tolstoi enstranges Wagnerian things, describing them precisely from the point of view of an intelligent peasant (i.e., from the point of view of someone unencumbered with the customary associations of things, in the manner of the French primitives). Besides, the technique of describing a city from the standpoint of a peasant had already been used in the ancient Greek novel (Veselovsky).

The second device, that of step-by-step construction, was carried out by Tolstoi in a most original way.

I shall not attempt even a cursory essay on the process by which Tolstoi created his original poetics. Instead I shall confine myself here to several examples.

The young Tolstoi was rather naive in the way he constructed his parallel structures. In order to work out the theme of "dying," that is, in order to illustrate it, Tolstoi felt it necessary in "The Three Deaths" to carry out three subthemes: the death of the mistress of the house, the death of the peasant, and the death of the tree. The three parts of the story are connected by a specific motivation: the peasant is the lady's coachman, and the tree is chopped down to serve as a cross on the peasant's grave.

In later folk lyrics, parallelism is also occasionally motivated. For example, the conventional parallel "to love is to trample upon the grass" is motivated by the fact that the lovers trample upon the grass as they go for a stroll.

In "Kholstomer" Tolstoi supports the parallelism horse/man with the following phrase: "Much later, they dumped into the ground the body of Serpykhovsky that had eaten and drunk of the earth and had walked on it. They found no use for either his skin or bones."

These parts of the parallelism are linked together motivationally by the fact that Serpykhovsky had once been Kholstomer's master.

In "The Two Hussars," the parallel structure, quite evident from the title itself, is carried out also in the details of love, cards, and friends. The relationship among the parts is motivated by the kinship ties that bind the protagonists.

If we compare Tolstoi's devices with the devices of Maupassant, then we may wish to make the following observation:

In making use of parallelism, Maupassant omits, as it were, the second part of the parallel structure. Instead he seems to imply it. Such an implicit, tacitly understood second part is usually represented by the traditional framework of the short story, which he violates (i.e., his stories seem to lack an ending), or else it is represented by the ordinary, conventional French bourgeois attitude towards life. So, for example, in many of his stories, Maupassant depicts the death of a peasant. He describes it simply but with astonishing enstrangement by "comparing" it with the literary description of the death of a townsman. However, this literary description is never introduced into the story proper. Rather, it is implied. Sometimes, this second part of the parallelism is brought into the story in the form of the narrator's personal assessment.

In this respect, Tolstoi is more primitive than Maupassant, since he feels the need to expose the parallel structure, as, for example, in his "Fruits of Enlightenment," where he juxtaposes the kitchen and the living room. I believe that this phenomenon is to be explained by the greater clarity found in the French literary tradition vis-à-vis ours. The French reader feels the violation of norms with greater force or else he finds it easier to search for the appropriate parallel implied in the text. Our Russian reader, on the other hand, operates with a much more nebulous conception of literary norms.

I would like to mention in passing that, when I speak of a literary tradition, I do not have in mind a literal borrowing by one writer from another. I conceive of it as a common fund of literary norms from which each writer draws and on which he is dependent. If I were to use the analogy of an inventor and his tradition, I would say that such a literary tradition consists of the sum total of the technical possibilities of his age.

More complex cases of parallelism in Tolstoi may be found in his novels, where one group of protagonists is pitted against another group. For example, the following antithetical relationships are clearly discernible in *War and Peace:*

1) Napoleon – Kutuzov.

2) Pierre Bezukhov – Andrei Bolkonsky. We may also include here Nikolai Rostov, who serves as a coordinate (standard of measurement) for both Bezukhov and Bolkonsky.

In *Anna Karenina* we observe the following composition:

Anna – Vronsky group vs. Levin – Kitty group.

The relationships among these characters are motivated by bonds of kinship. This is a common motivation in Tolstoi and in novelists in general, perhaps. Tolstoi himself writes that he "has made the elder Bolkonsky the father of the brilliant young Andrei because it is awkward to describe a character who bears no relationship whatsoever to the rest of the novel."

Tolstoi made little use of the device of involving a protagonist in several different groupings (a favorite device of English novelists). The one exception perhaps is the Petrushka–Napoleon episode, where he employed it for purposes of enstrangement. In any case, the two parallel lines in *Anna Karenina* are so loosely connected from the standpoint of motivation that one may consider this motivation to serve a strictly artistic need.

Tolstoi exploits the kinship motif in an intriguing way when he resorts to it not for the purpose of motivating a relationship but as part of a progressive construction. We see the two Rostov brothers and their only sister. They are presented as a development of a single type. At times Tolstoi compares them, as for example before Peti's death. Nikolai Rostov is a "radical over-simplification," a "cruder version" of Natasha.

Stiva Oblonsky expresses one side of Anna Karenina's soul. This relationship is presented by means of the phrase "a little bit" uttered by Anna in Stiva's voice. Stiva serves as a stepping stone to his sister. Here the relationship among the characters is not explained by kinship bonds as such. Tolstoi is not too timid here to establish an affinity in his novel between two separately conceived protagonists. Here a kinship bond was necessary for a step-by-step construction.

The depiction of family members is in no way linked in literary tradition with the author's obligation to show the distortions undergone by one and the same character. That this is so is demonstrated by the traditional device of pitting a noble brother against a criminal brother, both offspring of the same parents. Still on occasion, a motivation is introduced such as illegitimacy (Fielding).

Here as always in art, we are dealing with the motivation of a master.

# 3

The modern novel was preceded by the short story collection. I am stating this as a chronological fact, without necessarily implying a causal relationship between these genres.

Collections of short stories were ordinarily put together in such a way that the individual stories bore some relationship, however formal, to each other. This was achieved by enclosing the individual stories within one framing story that held them together as its parts. This explains the composition of *Panchatantra, Kalilah and Dimnah, Hitopadesa, Tales of a Parrot, The Seven Viziers, A Thousand and One Nights,* and *The Book of Wisdom and Lies* (the eighteenth-century Georgian collection of short stories), and many others.

We may distinguish several types of framing stories, that is, techniques of enclosing one story within another. The technique most popular with writers introduces the *telling* of legends and tales into the body of the main story in order to retard its action. So, for example, in *The Seven Viziers,* the viziers restrain the king from executing his own son, while in *A Thousand and One Nights* Scheherazade succeeds in postponing her own execution by telling her tales. In the Mongol short story collection of Buddhist origin entitled *Ardzhi Barzhi,* the wooden statues that serve as steps keep the king from ascending the throne by telling stories. As a matter of fact, much as the first story encloses the second story, so does the second story enclose the third and fourth stories. Similarly, the parrot of *Tales of a Parrot* restrains the wife from betraying her husband by telling its stories until her husband comes home. This principle of *deceleration* also underlies the cycles of stories making up *A Thousand and One Nights.* Their very objective is to ward off the executioner.

A second mode of enclosure may be called a "debate of stories," where tales are introduced to demonstrate some idea. In this case, one story is called upon to refute another story. This technique is of interest to us because it extends also to other materials susceptible of development such as poems or maxims.

It is very important to point out that these devices are confined to the domain of written literature. The cumbersome nature of this material does not permit such an interrelationship of parts in the oral tradition. The relationship among the parts is so formal that it can be discerned, perhaps, only by a reader but certainly not by a listener. The working out of a unifying technique for short stories in the so-called *folk* or anonymous (as opposed to consciously personal) literature was possible only in embryonic form.

From the day of its birth and even before, the novel gravitated towards a literary rather than an oral form.

Quite early in European literature emerged collections of short stories whose unity was achieved by having one story serve as a framing device.

Anthologies of Oriental origin, transmitted into Europe by Jews and Arabs, introduced into the lives of Europeans many tales from abroad, many of which had analogues in the indigenous literature of Europe.

At the same time, a European type of framing device was born, motivated by the desire to *tell the story for the sake of the storytelling itself.*

I am speaking of the *Decameron.*

The *Decameron,* along with its descendants, differs very strongly from the European novel of the eighteenth and nineteenth centuries in that the individual episodes comprising it are not linked to each other by the unity of their characters.

I would go a step further and assert that we are not dealing here with a protagonist at all. The focus is entirely on the unfolding action, while the bearer of the action serves merely as a pretext for the realization of the plot.

Though I have no way of proving it, I would venture to say that this state of affairs lasted a rather long period of time. Even as late as Le Sage's *Gil Blas,* the hero is depicted as a thoroughly spineless character. This has provoked critics to claim that the author's objective in this novel was to depict the man on the street. This is not true. Gil Blas is not a human being at all. He is a *thread,* a tedious thread, by means of which all of the episodes of the novel are woven together.

A much stronger relationship between the action and its bearer exists in *The Canterbury Tales.*

A framing device was widely used in picaresque novels.

Of great interest to us is the fate of this device in the works of Cervantes, Le Sage, and Fielding and, through Sterne, its refraction in the European novel.

Very curious indeed is the composition of the "The Tale of Kamar al-Zamán and the Princess Budur." This story extends from the 170th to the 249th night of *A Thousand and One Nights.* It immediately breaks up into a number of separate tales:

1) The story of the son (Kamar al-Zamán, son of Shahriman) with his demon assistants. The structure of the story is very complex, culminating in the lovers' wedding and in Princess Budur's desertion of her father.

2) The story of the king's two sons (Amjad and As'ad). This story is connected with the first story only by the fact that these sons are the off-spring of King Kamar's wives. The king wants to punish them, but they run off and undergo all sorts of adventures.

The king's daughter, Marjanah, falls in love with As'ad, who met her first as a mameluke slave. Landing in one adventure after another, he falls repeatedly into the clutches of Bahram the wizard. At long last As'ad and Marjanah are reunited. On this occasion, the wizard, after repenting and converting to Islam, tells them the story of "Ni'amah and Naomi." This story is very complex and is nowhere interrupted by the story of the two brothers. "Listening to the story intently, the king's sons are filled with astonishment."

It is around this time that Marjanah, the king's daughter, arrives on the scene at the head of her army. She demands the return of the beardless mameluke, who had been abducted from her earlier. This is followed by the arrival of the army of King Ghayúr, the father of Queen Budur, who is, in turn, the mother of Amjad. A third army headed by Kamar arrives soon thereafter. Kamar has been busy searching for his children, after learning of their innocence. Finally, the army of King Shahriman makes its entrance. This king, whom we have almost completely forgotten, has also arrived at this place looking for his son.

By means of this artificial device, several stories have been welded together.

It is worth noting how the plot of the folk drama *King Maximilian* has evolved over the years. The basic plot structure is very simple. The son of King Maximilian, who had married Venus, refuses to worship idols and suffers death at the hands of his father for it. The father, along with the entire court, is struck down by death. This text is later adopted as a kind of scenario.

Supported by the most diverse motivations, highly developed motifs are interpolated at different points into the narrative of the story. For example, consider the folk drama *The Boat* or *The Gang.* Sometimes they are attached to King Maximilian without any motivation, just as pastoral scenes are incorporated into *Don Quixote* or as poems are introduced into *A Thousand and One Nights.*

At other times, however, and I take this to be a later historical development, these motifs are interpolated with the following motivation: Adolf, refusing to submit to his father, runs away to join a gang. Just previous to this we heard the story of "Anika and Death." Perhaps this had already taken place in the version of the text that was found first in the country (and which we may, for the sake of simplicity, consider, though wrongly, the original text).

The episode concerning the mock requiem mass, familiar to us from outside this comedy, was inserted into the text at a much later date.

In many places, new episodes and wordplay, particularly in the form of an accumulation of homonyms motivated by deafness, grew with such luxuriance that Maximilian himself was nearly smothered by them. In fact, he served as a pretext for many a new comedy. The road from the original *King Maximilian,* which has close affinities with the South Russian school of drama, to the later *Maximilian* disintegrating in a text rife with puns and opposed to it in principle, was no shorter than the path that leads from Derzhavin to Andrei Bely.

Incidentally, Derzhavin's poetry occasionally finds its way into these aforementioned plays. We have here, more or less, a history tracing the changes in the technique of plot development in the *King Maximilian* text. With the addition of local material, the text changed and developed.

## 4

If we consider any typical story-anecdote, we shall see that it represents something complete and finished. If, for example, we look at the successful answer by which a person extricates himself from a certain predicament, then we will discover a motivation for the predicament, the hero's answer, and a definite resolution. Such is the structure of stories based on "cunning" in general. For example, if, after the commission of a crime, a man finds himself marked by the clipping of a tuft of hair, he may impose the same tonsorial style on his comrades and thereby save himself. The same holds true for the analogous tale of the house marked by chalk (*A Thousand and One Nights* and Andersen's tales). We witness here a definite completed circle of plot structure, which at times deploys descriptions or characterizations, but which, in itself, represents something completely resolved. As I have said above, several such stories may form a more complex structure by being incorporated within one framework, that is, by being integrated into one plot structure.

Yet another device of plot composition, namely, the "threading" device, is even more widely disseminated. In this mode of composition one finished story motif succeeds another motif and is linked to it by the unity of the protagonist. The complicated tale of the conventional type with its tasks set before the hero already represents a composition of the threading type.

It is precisely this device of threading that makes it possible for the motifs of one story to be assimilated by the motifs of another. Some tales comprise two or even four such motifs.

Let us establish at the outset two types of threading:

1) In one type the hero is neutral. The adventures spring upon him, so to speak. He is not responsible for their appearance. Such a phenomenon is quite common in the adventure novel, where a young man or woman is abducted back and forth by different groups of pirates and where the ships of these pirates are incapable of reaching their appointed rendezvous. This situation gives rise to an endless series of adventures.

2) In other works, on the other hand, we see some attempts at linking the action and the bearer of the action (i.e., an attempt at motivating the adventure). The adventures of Odysseus are motivated, though only externally, by the anger of the gods, who do not give our hero any peace. Odysseus' Arabic cousin, Sinbad the Sailor, keeps the explanation for his numerous adventures (if, indeed, he has an explanation) to himself. Because Sinbad has such a passion for travel, the author succeeds in weaving into his hero's seven voyages the entire travel folklore of his age.

In Apuleius' *Golden Ass,* the threading motivation is woven around the curiosity of Lucius, who is always eavesdropping or spying. Incidentally, *The Golden Ass* represents a combination of the two devices of the framing story and threading. By means of the threading device, Apuleius has managed to interpolate into his text the episodes covering the battle with the wineskins, the stories concerning metamorphoses, the adventures of the robbers, the anecdote about the donkey in the attic, etc.

On the other hand, the device of the framing story has made possible the interpolation of stories about a sorceress, the famous story of "Cupid and Psyche" and many little stories to boot.

In the concluding parts of works composed along the threading principle, we very frequently have the feeling that these constituent parts once had an independent existence all their own. For example, in *The Golden Ass,* after the episode with the donkey, which had taken refuge in the attic and which was finally recognized by its shadow, we encounter the suggestion that this very situation had spawned a proverb (i.e., it is presupposed that the story is known to its audience either in its entirety or in its basic structure).

Still, the most popular motivation by far for the threading device has been (and from very early time, I might add) the journey, and in particular a journey in search of a certain place. Such a construction characterizes *Lazarillo of Tormes,* one of the oldest of the Spanish picaresque novels.

This novel depicts the variety of adventures experienced by a little boy in search of a certain place. It is customary to suggest that certain episodes and certain expressions from *Lazarillo* had entered into the (humorous) idiom of the Spanish bazaar. I, for one, am of the opinion that they were there even before their inclusion in the novel. The novel ends strangely with fantastic adventures that involve metamorphoses, again, a rather common phenomenon, since the organizing idea that informs the first part of such a novel nearly always exhausts itself by the second part. These second parts therefore are usually constructed on a whole new base. Such was the case with

*Don Quixote* and with Swift's *Gulliver's Travels.*

On occasion we find that the threading device is used with material that is not part of the plot. In Cervantes' "Man of Glass," a short story about a scholar who had broken away from his people and who had afterwards gone mad after drinking a love potion, we encounter his interpolated, or rather, threaded sayings for whole pages at a time:

He also had no end of fault to find with the puppet masters, saying that they were a lot of vagabonds who were guilty of indecency in the portrayal of sacred things: the puppets they employed in their shows made a mockery of devotion, and they some-times stuffed into a bag all or nearly all the personages of the Old and New Testament, and then would sit down upon them to eat and drink in the alehouses and taverns. In short, it was a wonder that perpetual silence was not imposed upon them, or that they were not banished from the realm.

When an actor dressed like a prince went by, Glasscase looked at him and said, "I remember having seen that fellow in the theater: his face was smeared with flour and he was wearing a shepherd's coat turned inside out: but at every step he takes off the stage, you would swear upon your word of honor that he was a gentleman."

"That may very well be," someone reminded him, "for there are many actors who are well born and sons of somebody."

"That is true enough," replied Glasscase, "but what the stage stands least in need of is individuals of gentle birth. Leading men, yes, who are well mannered and know how to talk, that is another matter. For it might be said of actors that they earn their bread by the sweat of their brows, with an unbearable amount of labor, having con-stantly to memorize long passages, and having to wander from town to town and from one inn to another like gypsies, losing sleep in order to amuse others, since their own well-being lies in pleasing their public. Moreover, in their business, they deceive no one, inasmuch as their merchandise is displayed in the public square, where all may see and judge of it.

"Authors, too, have an incredible amount of work to perform and a heavy burden of care: they have to earn much in order that by the end of the year they may not be so far in debt that they will have to go into bankruptcy; yet for all of that, they are as necessary to the state as are shady groves, public walks and parks, and other things that provide decent recreation."

He went on to cite the opinion of a friend of his to the effect that a servant to an actress was a servant to many ladies at one and the same time: to a queen, a nymph, a goddess, a kitchen wench, a shepherd lass, and many times a page or a lackey as well, since the actress was used to impersonating all these and many other char-acters. (Putnam translation)

These sayings supplant the action in the story. When, at the end of the story, the scholar recovers, a phenomenon quite common in art intervenes: the motivation may have ceased to exist, but the device continues to func-tion unaltered (i.e., the scholar continues to spout his mad sayings even after making a full recovery). His speech on the court is quite similar to his previous pronouncements.

So also in Tolstoi's "Kholstomer," where the peculiar description of life from the standpoint of a horse continues even after the horse's death. Only now it issues directly from the lips of the author.

In Andrei Bely's *Kotik Letaev,* the paronamastic constructions, motivated by an infant's perception of the world, exploit material that the baby itself could never have known.

To return to my theme: we may say in general that both the framing device and the threading device, historically speaking, led in the course of the novel's history to a closer bond between the interpolated material and the main body of the novel. We can follow this process very clearly in a work known to everyone, that is, in *Don Quixote.*

# Chapter 4

# The Making of *Don Quixote*

## 1. The Speeches of Don Quixote

In classical drama, monologues often end with a pithy saying, a "gnome." A gnome was a forceful figure of speech that was etched into the memory. The pithy sayings of Sophocles and Euripides had already achieved distinction among the ancients themselves. Sophocles' sayings always bear the mark of a moral maxim independent of the character of the person speaking, while in Euripides the conclusion of a monologue may be either moral or immoral, depending upon the person who pronounces it.

The ancients explained this difference rather naively by asserting that Sophocles did not want anyone to associate a blasphemous saying with him. There is, however, another possible interpretation. The speeches of the principal characters constitute one of the means by which the writer develops his plot. The author, for instance, introduces new material through them. That is, the protagonists' speeches originally served only to motivate the introduction of such new material. The relationship between the speech and the person making the speech, as between the action and the initiator of the action, has never been a constant one in the history of literary form. In Sophocles, the "speech" is nevertheless the speech of the author, who does not as yet wish to individualize the speeches of his masks.

Don Quixote was conceived by Cervantes to be a person of rather limited intelligence: "The sun would have melted the brains of this hidalgo, if only he had had any" (Motteux translation, rev. John Ozell [1719]). And yet already in the first pages of the novel, in fact, in the very preface, Cervantes laments—ironically, to be sure—the fact that

Now I want all these Embellishments and Graces: I have neither marginal Notes nor critical Remarks; I do not so much as know what Authors I follow, and consequently can have no formal Index, as 'tis the Fashion now, methodically strung on the Letters of the Alphabet, beginning with Aristotle, and ending with Xenophon, or Zoilus, or Zeuxis; which last two are commonly cramm'd into the same Piece, tho' one of them was a famous Painter, and t'other a saucy Critick.

Elsewhere in the preface Cervantes says that

you have no need to go begging Sentences of Philosophers, Passages out of Holy Writ, Poetical Fables, Rhetorical Orations, or Miracles of Saints. Do but take care to express your self in a plain, easy Manner, in well-chosen, significant, and decent Terms, and to give an harmonious and pleasing Turn to your Periods: Study to explain your Thoughts, and set them in the truest Light, labouring, as much as possible, not to leave 'em dark nor intricate, but clear and intelligible.

Notwithstanding this disclaimer, Cervantes went on to write a novel with the breadth and scope of an iconostasis or an encyclopedia.

We should, however, also take into consideration the fact that the dimensions of this novel, which was laid out like a dining table, evidently far surpass Cervantes' original intentions.

Let us now return to Don Quixote.

So Don Quixote was originally conceived as a "brainless" knight. But as the novel progressed, Cervantes found that he needed Don Quixote as a unifying thread of wise sayings. Cervantes valued the poor knight and ennobled him, much as he had earlier ennobled the madness of the "Man of Glass."

The first of numerous discourses which reflect this changed perception in the course of the novel is delivered by Don Quixote in part 1, chapter 11. This is the speech on the Golden Age. Here is its opening:

O happy Age, cry'd he, which our first Parents call'd the Age of Gold! not because Gold, so much ador'd in this Iron-Age, was then easily purchas'd, but because those two fatal Words, Mine and Thine, were Distinctions unknown to the People of those fortunate Times; for all Things were in common in that holy Age: Men, for their Sustenance, needed only to lift their Hands, and take it from the sturdy Oak, whose spreading Arms liberally invited them to gather the wholesome savoury Fruit; while the clear Springs, and silver Rivulets, with luxuriant Plenty, offer'd them their pure refreshing Water. In hollow Trees, and in the Clefts of Rocks, the labouring and industrious Bees erected their little Commonwealths, that Men might reap with pleasure and with Ease the sweet and fertile Harvest of their Toils.

As you can see, this is an almost verbatim translation from Ovid's Golden Age. The motivation for this speech is a curious one. This entire speech (which we could have most excellently done without) was delivered by our knight on the occasion of the presentation to him of acorns, which reminded him of the Golden Age. Cervantes himself comments on this speech:

All this long Oration, which might very well have been spar'd, was owing to the Acorns that recall'd the Golden Age to our Knight's Remembrance, and made him thus hold forth to the Goat-herds, who devoutly listen'd, but edify'd little, the Discourse not being suited to their capacities. Sancho, as well as they, were silent all the while, eating Acorns, and frequently visiting the second Skin of Wine, which for Coolness-sake was hung upon a neighbouring Cork-Tree. As for Don Quixote, he was longer, and more intent upon his speech than upon his Supper.

That is, the author himself considers this speech to be out of place. I recall in passing Chichikov's monologue on Plyushkin's list of fugitive peasants. This speech by its material and form is undoubtedly not Chichikov's but

Gogol's. Similarly, it is no less interesting to note Tolstoi's vacillation when adapting a specific set of ideas to his hero. For example, the ideas on war in *War and Peace* are first put in the mouth of Andrei Bolkonsky and only later does Tolstoi strip him of these thoughts and express them as his own.

I shall skip over Don Quixote's speech on procuring as well as over several of his discourses on knighthood and shall pass directly to the fourth book of part 1. Here Don Quixote, after a series of recognitions in the tavern, delivers his speech on the military and scholarly professions. It is interesting to observe that in the opening section Cervantes reminds us of his hero's speech to the shepherds: "Don Quixote, to raise the Diversion, never minded his Meat, but inspir'd with the same Spirit that mov'd him to preach so much to the Goat-herds, he began to hold forth in this Manner" (chap. 37).

This allusion by Cervantes to an earlier speech along similar lines is most curious. Likewise, in the critical passages incorporated into *Don Quixote* (the examination of Don Quixote's library, the conversation with the inn-keeper, and so on) we hear mention of the housekeeper who had burned the knight's books—the first act of criticism.

In the complex novelistic schemata of our new age, the relationship between kindred episodes is achieved by the repetition of certain words, very much in the manner of Wagnerian leitmotivs (for example, in Andrei Bely's *The Silver Dove;* see also the work of Aleksandra Beksler).

Again, Don Quixote's speech is essentially out of place. He was supposed to speak about the vagaries of fate. Instead, he praises the military profession. It is interesting to observe how Cervantes shifts to this new theme:

"Certainly, Gentlemen, if we rightly consider it, those who make Knight-Errantry their Profession, often meet with most surprising and stupendous Adventures. For what Mortal in the World, at this Time entering within this Castle, and seeing us sit together as we do, will imagine and believe us to be the same Persons which in reality we are? Who is there that can judge, that this Lady by my side is the great Queen we all know her to be, and that I am that Knight of the woeful Figure, so universally made known by Fame? It is then no longer to be doubted, but that this Exercise and Profession surpasses all others that have been invented by Man, and is so much the more honourable, as it is more expos'd to Dangers. Let none presume to tell me that the Pen is preferable to the Sword; for be they who they will, I shall tell them they know not what they say: For the Reason they give, and on which chiefly they rely, is that the Labour of the Mind exceeds that of the Body, and that the Exercise of Arms depends only upon the Body, as if the use of them were the Business of Porters, which requires nothing but much Strength. Or, as if This, which we who profess it call Chivalry, did not include the Acts of Fortitude, which depend very much upon the Understanding. Or else, as if that Warriour, who commands an Army or defends a City besieg'd, did not labour as much with the Mind as with the Body. If this be not so, let Experience teach us whether it be possible by bodily Strength to discover or guess the Intentions of an Enemy. The forming [of] Designs, laying of Stratagems, overcoming of Difficulties, and shunning of Dangers, are all

Works of the Understanding, wherein the Body has no Share. It being therefore evident, that the Exercise of Arms requires the Help of the Mind as well as Learning, let us see in the next place, whether the Scholar or the Soldier's Mind undergoes the greatest Labour."

This is followed by a lengthy and, in its own way, brilliant speech comparing the fate of the scholar and the soldier. This speech, of course, is incorporated into the text in much the same way that verse is incorporated into *A Thousand and One Nights* or, for that matter, as one tale is incorporated into another tale in the same work. At its conclusion, Cervantes remembers Don Quixote:

All this long Preamble Don Quixote made, whilst the Company supp'd, never minding to eat a Mouthful, though Sancho Panza had several times advis'd him to mind his Meat, telling him there would be time enough afterwards to talk as he thought fit. Those who heard him were afresh mov'd with Compassion, to see a Man, who seem'd in all other Respects, to have a sound Judgment and clear Understanding, so absolutely mad and distracted, when any mention was made of his curs'd Knight-Errantry.

By this point the wisdom of the "brainless knight" has been definitively established. In a similar way, the image and significance of Pickwick are decisively changed in the structure of Dickens's *Pickwick Papers.*

By now Cervantes has begun to exploit the contrast between the madness and wisdom of Don Quixote. So, for instance, during his conversation with his niece, Don Quixote's speech begins with the madness of the knight, then moves on to moral maxims, which move his niece to exclaim:

"Bless me! dear Uncle," cry'd the Niece, "that you should know so much, as to be able, if there was Occasion, to get up into a Pulpit, or preach in the Streets, and yet be so strangely mistaken, so grosly blind of Understanding, as to fancy a Man of your Years and Infirmity can be strong and valiant; that you can set every thing right, and force stubborn Malice to bend, when you yourself stoop beneath the Burden of Age; and what's yet more odd, that you are a Knight, when 'tis well known you are none? For tho' some Gentlemen may be Knights, a poor Gentleman can hardly be so, because he can't buy it." "You say well, Niece," answered Don Quixote; "and as to this last Observation, I could tell you things that you would admire at, concerning Families; but because I will not mix Sacred Things with Profane, I wave the Discourse. However, listen both of you, and for your Farther Instruction know, that all the Lineages and Descents of Mankind, are reduceable to these four Heads: First, Of those, who from a very small and obscure Beginning, have rais'd themselves to a spreading and prodigious Magnitude. Secondly, Of those, who deriving their Greatness from a noble Spring, still preserve the Dignity and Character of their original Splendor. Third, Are those who, though they had large Foundations, have ended in a Point like a Pyramid, which by little and little dwindle as it were into nothing, or next to nothing, in comparison of its Basis. Others there are (and those are the Bulk of Mankind) who have neither had a good Beginning, nor a rational Continuance, and whose ending shall therefore be obscure; such are the common People, the Plebean Race." (part 2, chap. 6)

Don Quixote concludes his speech with some lines of verse:

> Thro' steep Ascents, thro' strait and rugged Ways,
> Our selves to Glory's lofty Seats we raise:
> In vain he hopes to reach the bless'd Abode,
> Who leaves the narrow Path, for the more easy Road.

"Alack a-day!" cry'd the Niece, "my Uncle is a Poet too! He knows every thing. I'll lay my Life he might turn Mason in case of Necessity. If he would but undertake it, he could build a House as easy as a Bird-cage."

This cage returns us to Alonzo the Brave, that is, to Don Quixote before his madness. It is worth noting here that Cervantes himself did not realize that Don Quixote, with all his cages and toothpicks, could not have been half so wise before his madness as afterwards, when he was dubbed the Knight of the Woeful Figure. Don Quixote's wisdom is not anticipated by the author either at the beginning or even in the middle of the novel. All we can say about Alonzo is that he is "brave" (good). Don Quixote's speech on glory constitutes a kind of collection of quotations and recollections, a kind of chrestomathy. This entire speech has evidently been interpolated into the text in much the same way that passages from a dictionary of synonyms have been incorporated into the text of Fonvizin's *The Minor* (Starodum's conversation with Mitrofanushka). Here is the excerpt:

"What thou say'st, Sancho," answer'd Don Quixote, "puts me in mind of a Story. A celebrated Poet of our Time wrote a very scurrilous and abusive Lampoon upon all the intriguing Ladies of the Court, forbearing to name one, as not being sure whether she deserv'd to be put into the Catalogue or not; but the Lady not finding herself there, was not a little affronted at the Omission, and made a great Complaint to the Poet, asking him what he had seen in her, that he shou'd leave her out of his List; desiring him at the same time to enlarge his Satire, and put her in, or expect to hear farther from her. The Author obeyed her Commands, and gave her a Character with a Vengeance, and, to her great Satisfaction, made her as famous for Infamy as any Woman about the Town. Such another Story is that of Diana's Temple, one of the Seven Wonders of the World, burnt by an obscure Fellow merely to eternize his Name; which, in spite of an Edict that enjoin'd all People never to mention it, either by Word of Mouth, or in Writing, yet is still known to have been Erostratus. The Story of the great Emperor Charles the Fifth, and a Roman Knight, upon a certain Occasion, is much the same. The Emperor had a great Desire to see the famous Temple once called the Pantheon, but now more happily, the Church of All Saints. 'Tis the only entire Edifice remaining of Heathen Rome, and that which best gives an Idea of the Glory and Magnificence of its great Founders. 'Tis built in the Shape of a half Orange, of a vast Extent and very lightsome, tho' it admits no Light, but at one Window, or to speak more properly, at a round Aperture on the Top of the Roof. The Emperor being got up thither, and looking down from the Brink upon the Fabrick, with a Roman Knight by him, who shew'd all the Beauties of that vast Edifice: after they were gone from the Place, says the Knight, addressing the Emperor, 'It came into my Head a thousand Times, Sacred Sir, to embrace your Majesty, and cast myself with you, from the Top of the Church to the Bottom, that I might thus purchase an immortal Name.' 'I thank you,' said the Emperor, 'for not doing it; and for the future, I will give you no Opportunity to put your Loyalty to such a Test. Therefore I banish you [from] my Presence for ever'; which done, he bestow'd some considerable Favour on him. I tell thee, Sancho, this Desire of Honour is a strange bewitching Thing. What dost thou think made Horatius, arm'd at all Points, plunge headlong from the Bridge into the rapid Tyber? What prompted Curtius to leap into the profound flaming Gulph? What made Mutius burn his Hand? What forc'd Caesar over the Rubicon, spite of all the Omens that dissuaded his Passage? And to instance a more modern Example, what made the undaunted Spaniards sink their Ships, when under the most courteous Cortez, but that scorning the stale Honour of this so often conquer'd World, they sought a Maiden Glory in a new Scene of Victory? These and a Multiplicity of other great Actions, are owing to the immediate Thirst and Desire of Fame, which Mortals expect as the proper Price and immortal Recompence of their great Actions. But we that are Christian Catholick Knights-Errant must fix our Hopes upon a higher Reward, plac'd in the Eternal and Celestial Regions, where we may expect a permanent Honour and compleat Happiness; not like the Vanity of Fame, which at best is but the Shadow of great Actions, and must necessarily vanish, when destructive Time has eat away the Substance which it follow'd." (part 2, chap. 8)

It is worth noting that as Don Quixote becomes wiser and wiser, an analogous development takes place with Sancho Panza: " 'Truly, Sancho,' said Don Quixote, 'thy Simplicity lessens, and thy Sense improves every Day' " (part 2, chap. 12).

The point is that Cervantes leaves the wisdom of folklore to Sancho while reserving the worldly-bookish wisdom for Don Quixote. Sancho's wisdom comes into its own in his judgments, which, as is well known, represent an appropriation by the novel of the legends of wise lawgivers.

Here is a sample of one of Sancho's strings of proverbs. These strings are especially characteristic of part 2 of *Don Quixote:*

"Heav'n forbid; Marry and Amen," cry'd Sancho! "Who can tell what may happen? He that gives a broken Head can give a Plaister. This is one Day, but to Morrow is another, and strange things may fall out in the roasting of an Egg. After a Storm comes a Calm. Many a Man that went to Bed well, has found himself dead in the Morning when he awak'd. Who can put a Spoke in Fortune's Wheel? No body here I am sure. Between a Woman's Yea and Nay, I would not engage to put a Pin's-point, so close they be one to another. If Mrs. Quiteria love Master Basil, she'll give Camacho the Bag to hold; for this same Love, they say, looks through Spectacles, that makes Copper look like Gold, a Cart like a Coach, and a Shrimp like a Lobster."

At the end of chapter 3 of part 2, Sancho takes center stage, overshadowing Don Quixote himself. This phenomenon is quite common in the history of the novel. So, for example, in Rabelais, Panurge moves to center stage at the end of the novel. This means, in essence, that the old novel has come to an end, and a new novel based often on new devices has taken its place.

It would be very instructive to follow the device, already used by Cervantes before, of alternating wisdom and madness by eavesdropping, as it were, on the knight's meeting with Don Diego. This conversation, which begins with Don Quixote's "chivalrous" speech and quickly moves on to literary themes, is astonishing for its professional knowledge of literary history. This speech is motivated by the fact that Don Diego has a son who is a poet. At first, the mad knight speaks of the duty of parents before their children. He then moves on to criticism. Unfortunately, shortage of space prevents me from quoting this speech (occupying about half of chapter 16 of part 2). Delivering his wise speeches, Don Quixote remains nonetheless faithful to his own madness, as he dons the barber's basin on his head. The mad knight mistakes this basin for a helmet at precisely the moment when Sanchez has mislain a piece of unfinished cottage cheese in it.

However, Don Quixote's subsequent adventure with the lions, whom he challenges to battle, stands out from the usual, tedious gory finales which crown the conventional adventure novel. There is little parody in Don Quixote's speech, which serves, as always, as a yardstick by which to gauge the discrepancy between the knight's real action and its imagined form:

"But a much nobler Figure is the Knight-Errant, who fir'd with the Thirst of a glorious Fame, wanders through Desarts, through solitary Wildernesses, through Woods, through Cross-ways, over Mountains and Valleys, in Quest of perilous Adventures, resolv'd to bring them to a happy Conclusion. Yes, I say, a nobler Figure is a Knight-Errant succouring a Widow in some depopulated Place, than the Court-Knight making his Addresses to the City Dames. Every Knight has his particular Employment. Let the Courtier wait on the Ladies; let him with splendid Equipage adorn his Prince's Court, and with a magnificent Table support poor Gentlemen. Let him give birth to Feasts and Tournaments, and shew his Grandeur, Liberality, and Munificence, and especially his Piety; in all these things he fulfils the Duties of his Station. But as for the Knight-Errant, let him search into all the Corners of the World, enter into the most intricate Labyrinths, and every Hour be ready to attempt Impossibility itself. Let him in desolate Wilds baffle the Rigor of the Weather, the scorching Heat of the Sun's fiercest Beams, and the Inclemency of Winds and Snow: Let Lions never fright him, Dragons daunt him, nor evil Spirits deter him. To go in Quest of these, to meet, to dare, to conflict, and to overcome 'em all, is his principal and proper Office. Since then my Stars have decreed me to be one of those Adventurous Knights, I think my self obliged to attempt every thing that seems to come within the Verge of my Profession. This, Sir, engag'd me to encounter those Lions just now, judging it to be my immediate business, tho' I was sensible of the extreme Rashness of the Undertaking. For well I know, that Valour is a Virtue situate between the two vicious Extremes of Cowardice and Temerity." (part 2, chap. 17)

In the following chapter we see the literary learning of one Don Quixote, a poor provincial nobleman, Alonzo the Brave, known as a master in the art of coop-making, grow ever more professional. Here are several examples from his speeches:

"If the Composition be design'd for a Poetical Prize, I would advise you only to put in for the second; for the first always goes by Favour, and is rather granted to the great Quality of the Author than to his Merit, but as to the next, 'tis adjudged to the most deserving; so that the third may in a manner be esteem'd the second, and the first no more than the third, according to the Methods us'd in our Universities of giving Degrees. And yet, after all, 'tis no small matter to gain the Honour of being call'd the first." Hitherto all's well, thought Don Lorenzo to himself, I can't think thee mad yet; let's go on —

Or take, for instance, this passage:

"I remember," said Don Quixote, "a Friend of mine, a Man of Sense, once told me, he wou'd not advise any one to break his brains about that sort of Composition; and he gave me this Reason for't, That the Gloss or Comment cou'd never come up to the Theme; so far from it, that most commonly it left it altogether, and run contrary to the Thought of the Author. Besides he said, that the Rules to which Custom ties up the Composers of those elaborate Amusements are too strict, allowing no Inter-rogations, no such Interjections as 'said he' or 'shall I say'; no changing of Nouns into Verbs; nor any altering of the Sense: Besides several other Confinements that cramp up those who puzzle their Brains with such a crabbed way of Glossing, as you yourself, Sir, without doubt must know."

Don Quixote's speeches later demonstrate even more specialized learning. Cervantes equips him with knowledge in linguistics and the theory of transla-tion, such as in this disquisition on Spanish words beginning with *A-*, *Al-*, etc.

"What are the *Albogues?*" quoth Sancho: "For I don't remember I've ever seen or heard of 'em in my Life." "They are," said Don Quixote, "a Sort of Instruments made of Brass-Plates, rounded like Candlesticks: The one shutting into the other, there arises through the Holes or Stops, and the Trunk or Hollow, an odd Sound, which if not very graceful, or harmonious, is however not altogether disagreeable, but does well enough with the rusticity of the Bag-Pipe and Tabor. You must know the Word is Moorish, as indeed are all those in our Spanish, which begin with an *Al-*, as *Almoaza, Almorsar, Alhombra, Alguasil, Alucema, Almacen, Alcanzia,* and the like, which are not very many. And we have also but three Moorish Words in our Tongue that end in *-i;* and they are *Borcequi, Zaquicami* and *Maravedi;* for as to *Alheli* and *Alfaqui,* they are as well known to be Arabick by their beginning with *Al-*, as their ending in *-i.* I cou'd not forbear telling thee so much by the Bye, thy *Quere* about *Albogue* having brought it into my Head." (part 2, chap. 67)

And here is an even more specialized report:

"What is the Name of it pray?" said Don Quixote. "Sir," answer'd the Author, "the Title of it in Italian is *Le Bagatele.*" "And pray, Sir," ask'd Don Quixote, "what's the Meaning of that Word in Spanish?" "Sir," answer'd the Gentleman, "*Le Bagatele* is as much to say 'Trifles'; but though the Title promises so little, yet the Contents are Matters of Importance." "I am a little conversant in the Italian," said the Knight, "and value my self upon singing some Stanzas of Ariosto; therefore, Sir, without any Offence, and not doubting of your Skill, but meerly to satisfy my Curiosity, pray tell me, have you ever met with such a Word as *Pignata* in Italian?" "Yes, very often, Sir," answer'd the Author. "And how do you render it pray?" said Don Quixote. "How should I render it, Sir," reply'd the Translator, "but by the Word 'Porridge-Pot'?" "Body of me," cried Don Quixote, "you are Master of the Italian Idiom? I dare hold a good Wager, that where the Italian says *Piace,* you translate it 'Please'; where it says *Piu* you render it 'More'; *Su,* 'Above,' and *Giu,* 'Beneath.'" "Most certainly, Sir," answer'd t'other, "for such are their proper Significations." (part 2, chap. 62)

We may assert in general that the speeches of part 2 are more fragmentary and episodic than those of part 1. The second part, as I have already observed, exhibits more of a mosaic structure than the first, and if there are no great inset tales or stories in it, such as those that on occasion push Don Quixote from the stage in part 1, yet, nonetheless, we meet with many small episodic anecdotes, delivered extemporaneously by our hero.

Let me, with the reader's indulgence, draw the following conclusions (although it is really for the reader to draw conclusions for himself):

1. The Don Quixote type made famous by Heine and gushed over by Turgenev was not the author's original plan. This type appeared as a result of the novel's structure, just as a change in the mode of execution often created new forms in poetry.

2. Towards the middle of the novel Cervantes realized that in loading Don Quixote with his own wisdom, he was creating a duality in him. At that point he began to take advantage of this duality for his own artistic ends.

## 2. Inset Stories in *Don Quixote*

Most fortunate and happy was the Age that usher'd into the World that most daring Knight Don Quixote de la Mancha! For from his generous Resolution to revive and restore the ancient Order of Knight-Errantry, that was not only wholly neglected, but almost lost and abolish'd, our Age, barren in itself of pleasant Recreations, derives the Pleasure it reaps from his true History, and the various Tales and Episodes thereof, in some respects, no less pleasing, artful and authentic, than the History itself.

So begins the fourth book of *Don Quixote* (part 1, chap. 28).

In reality, the thread of action in Cervantes' work is fragile and tattered. The inset stories of *Don Quixote* may be divided into several categories in accordance with the way they are introduced into the novel. Before I proceed to classify these stories, though, I would like to describe them.

If we classify the stories by their "reality," then, above all, we meet with a whole array of pastoral ones. These tales begin with the Marcella episode in chapters 12, 13, and 14 of part 1. More correctly, the episode begins with Don Quixote's speech on the Golden Age (see my analysis above) and then continues under the guise of a poem, naively interpolated into the text: " 'Sir Knight,' said he, 'that you may be sure you are heartily welcome, we'll get one of our Fellows to give us a Song; he is just a coming' " (part 1, chap. 11).

This is followed by lines of verse. As you can see, the introduction of verse into the text is motivated in much the same way that racy, topical doggerel is interspersed in vaudeville acts or the way that poems are recited by the heroes of *A Thousand and One Nights* before evil spirits as well as beautiful ladies.

A little later, we encounter the Marcella episode itself. The story is introduced in the following way:

A Young Fellow, who us'd to bring 'em Provisions from the next Village, happen'd to come while this was doing, and addressing himself to the Goat-herds, "Hark ye, Friends," said he, "d'ye hear the News?" "What News," cry'd one of the Company? "That fine Shepherd and Scholar Chrysostome dy'd this Morning," answer'd the other; "and they say 'twas for Love of that devilish untoward Lass Marcella, rich William's Daughter, that goes up and down the Country in the Habit of a Shepherdess." (chap. 12)

In order to introduce this episode into the text, Cervantes makes use of a "courier-storyteller" that recalls, apparently, the "herald" of classical tragedy. Yet, his role is essentially different. The herald informs his audience about crucial events not depicted on stage. He thereby helps it to make sense of the basic plot of the tragedy. This courier, on the other hand, is used to motivate the interpolation of an inset story into the main plot.

The courier's story begins at the point in the narrative where everyone has left for the site of the murder.

In order to connect the inset story with the main plot of the novel, Cervantes involves Don Quixote himself in its plot. This boils down to the device of having the Knight of Woeful Figure emend the story as it unfolds: " 'We call it an Eclipse,' cry'd Don Quixote, 'and not a Clip, when either of those two great Luminaries are darken'd.' "

Yet Peter, not dwelling on such petty details, continues his story:

"He wou'd also" (continu'd Peter, who did not stand upon such nice Distinctions) "foretel when the Year wou'd be plentiful or 'estil.' " "You wou'd say 'steril,' " cry'd Don Quixote. "Steril or Estil," reply'd the Fellow, "that's all one to me: But this I say, that his Parents and Friends, being rul'd by him, grew woundy rich in a short Time; for he would tell 'em, 'This Year sow Barley, and no Wheat: In this you may sow Pease, and no Barley: Next Year will be a good Year for Oil: The three after that, you shan't gather a Drop': and whatsoever he said wou'd certainly come to pass." "That Science," said Don Quixote, "is call'd Astrology." "I don't know what you call it," answer'd Peter, "but I know he knew all this, and a deal more. But, in short, within some few Months after he had left the Versity, on a certain Morning we saw him come dress'd for all the World like a Shepherd, and driving his Flock, having laid down the long Gown, which he us'd to wear as a Scholar. At the same time one Ambrose, a great Friend of his, who had been his Fellow-Scholar also, took upon him to go like a Shepherd, and keep him Company, which we all did not a little marvel at. I had almost forgot to tell you how he that's dead was a mighty Man for making of Verses, insomuch that he commonly made the Carols which we sung on Christmas-Eve; and the plays which the young Lads in our Neighbourhood enacted on Corpus Christi Day, and every one wou'd say, that no body cou'd mend 'em. Somewhat before that time Chrysostome's Father died, and left him a deal of Wealth, both in Land, Money, Cattle, and other Goods, whereof the young Man remain'd dissolute Master; and in troth he deserv'd it all, for he was as good-natur'd a Soul as e'er trod on Shoe of Leather; mighty good to the Poor, a main Friend to all honest people, and had a Face like a Blessing. At last it came to be known, that the Reason of his altering his Garb in that Fashion, was only that he might go up and down after that Shepherdess Marcella, whom our comrade told you of before, for he was fallen mightily in love with her. And now I'll tell you such a thing you never heard the like in your born Days, and may'nt chance to hear of such another while you breathe, tho' you were to live as long as Sarnah." "Say Sarah," cry'd Don Quixote, who hated to hear him blunder thus. "The Sarna, or the Itch, (for that's all one with us, quoth Peter) lives long enough too; but if you go on thus, and make me break off my Tale at every Word, we an't like to have done this Twelve-month."

These interruptions become less and less frequent.

This method of linking the inset story with the novel itself by constantly reminding the reader of the presence of the leading characters of the main plot is often employed by Cervantes.

In *Tristram Shandy,* the speech about the Inquisition, drawn out by the author, is interrupted by Trim's emotional outbursts. Or else in other places the author interrupts himself by alluding to other motifs: either knots and buttonholes or Jenny or else he reminds the reader of the existence of the novel by resorting to repetition (i.e., by repeating the very phrase with which he had broken off his narrative in the first place). But of this I shall have more to say in my analysis of Sterne.

In Cervantes the story is linked with the main plot of *Don Quixote* in the following ways:

1) A principal character of the novel interrupts the action of the inset story. Using precisely this technique, Don Quixote interrupts the confused, tangled web of tales of the second volume with a speech comparing the fate of the student with the fate of the soldier. Even more typical is his interruption not by word or speech but by action. So, for example, Don Quixote's battle with the wineskins repeatedly interrupts the drawn-out story called "The Novel of the Curious Impertinent" (incorporated into the novel in accordance with the principle of the "found manuscript"):

> The Novel was come near a conclusion, when Sancho Panza came running out of Don Quixote's Chamber in a terrible Fright and crying out, "Help, Help, good People, Help my Master, he's just now at it, Tooth and Nail, with that same giant, the Princess Micomicona's Foe: I ne'er saw a more dreadful battle in my born-days. He has lent him such a Sliver, that whip, off went the Giant's head, as round as a Turnip." (part 1, chap. 35)

2) The leading characters of the story participate in the action of the main plot. This takes its most sophisticated form in the participation by Dorothea (the heroine of the most powerful inset tale in *Don Quixote*) in the hoax perpetrated on Don Quixote, where she is passed off as Princess Micomicona.

> ... and then turning to Cardenio and Dorothea, he informed 'em of the Design which he and the Barber had laid in order to his Cure, or at least to get him home to his House. Dorothea, whose Mind was much eas'd with the Prospect of better Fortune, kindly undertook to act the distressed Lady herself, which she said she thought wou'd become her better than the Barber, having a Dress very proper for that Purpose; besides she had read many Books of Chivalry, and knew how the

distress'd Ladies us'd to express themselves when they came to beg some Knight-Errant's Assistance. (part 1, chap. 29)

This is presented in a more naive form by Cervantes in the two episodes in which Don Quixote gets involved in a fight with the leading characters of the respective inset tales.

At last, after he had stood thus a considerable while, he rais'd his Head, and suddenly breaking Silence, "I am positively convinc'd," cry'd he, "nor shall any Man in the World ever perswade me to the contrary; and he's a Blockhead who says, that great Villain Mr. Elisabat, never lay with Queen Madasima."
" 'Tis false," cry'd Don Quixote, in a mighty Heat; "by all the Powers above, 'tis all Scandal and base Detraction to say this of Queen Madasima. She was a most noble and virtuous Lady; nor is to be presum'd that so great a Princess would ever debase her self so far as to fall in Love with a Quack. Whoever dares to say she did, lyes like an arrant Villain; and I'll make him acknowledge it either a-Foot or a-Horseback, arm'd or unarm'd, by Night or by Day, or how he pleases." Cardenio very earnestly fix'd his Eyes on Don Quixote, while he was thus defying him, and taking Queen Madasima's Part, as if she had been his true and lawful Princess; and being provok'd by these Abuses into one of his mad Fits, he took up a great Stone that lay by him, and hit Don Quixote such a Blow on his Breast with it, that it beat him down backwards. (part 1, chap. 24)

In precisely this way the relationship with the main novel is renewed in one of the pastoral episodes, in which the shepherd tells the story of the soldier who had captivated the proud shepherdess Leandra with his fancy attire.

The commentaries that Cervantes interpolates into the body of the story are most curious:

The Goat-herd's Story was mightily lik'd by the whole Company, especially by the Canon, who particularly minded the manner of his relating it, that had more of a Scholar and a Gentleman, than of a rude Goat-herd; which made him conclude the Curate had reason to say, that even the Mountains bred Scholars and Men of Sense. (part 1, chap. 52)

Here the author directly alludes to the bookishness of his story.

There is one extremely odd tale in Cervantes' oeuvre. It was written, if I am not mistaken, around 1613, during the interval between the publication of parts 1 and 2 of *Don Quixote.* Its title is "A Conversation between Two Dogs."

The structure of this story is quite banal, taking on the form of a newspaper article. The protagonists, two dogs, are, however, unusual, or more correctly, one of the two dogs, Berganza, since the other dog Scipion serves only as an audience for the former's life story. As is common in novels of the "thread" type, this work is sewn out of a whole series of episodes, at times existing only in outline form. They are linked to each other only by the fact that they occur to one and the same unemployed dog which changes hands from one day to the next.

This novella may be seen as a canine version of *Lazarillo* and *Gil Blas*. It is worth noting that the device of a job hunt has served as a motivating link between episodes to the present day. This is the structural pattern in Octave Mirbeau's *Diary of a Chambermaid* and of Maksim Gorky's *In the World.*

In his wanderings, the dog works for a time for a slaughterhouse, then for shepherds, for the police, for soldiers, for gypsies, for a Moor, for a poet, in the theater, and finally, in a hospital. Each new job of Berganza's is accompanied by a corresponding new tale. Still, on occasion a new job serves only as a motivation for a brief description of customs and mores.

Let us look, for instance, at what the dog saw in the world of the shepherds. Above all, Berganza was struck by the discrepancy between the real life shepherds lived and what she had learned about them from recitations by her first owner's mistress. Reality did not in the least correspond to the portrayal of shepherds in books. Shepherds did not play flutes or oboes and they never beat their sticks or pieces of pottery except when singing very simple country tunes. They spent their days not in dreaming about shepherdesses but in repairing their footwear and gathering insects. They called each other not Amorisa or Filida or Galathea or Lozarda or Hyacinthia, but Antonio, Dominique, Paul and Florentia. It would be worth comparing this realistically "grumbling" picture with how Cervantes described shepherds before and after his writing of "A Conversation between Two Dogs." Here, for purposes of comparison, is the conclusion of the story about Leandra (see above):

"There is not a hollow Place of a Rock, a bank of a Brook, or a shady Grove, where there is not some or other of these amorous Shepherds telling their doleful Stories to the Air and winds. Echo has learnt to repeat the Name of Leandra, Leandra all the Hills resound, the Brooks murmur Leandra, and 'tis Leandra that holds us all Inchanted, hoping without Hope, and fearing without knowing what we fear. Of all these foolish People, the person who shews the least, and yet has the most Sense, is my Rival Anselmo, who forgetting all other Causes of Complaint, complains only of her Absence; and to his Lute, which he touches to Admiration, he joins his Voice in Verses of his own composing, which declare the Greatness of his Genius. For my part, I take another Course, I think a better, I'm sure an easier, which is to say all the ill things I can of Women's Levity, Inconstancy, their broken Vows and vain deceitful Promises, their fondness of Show and Disregard of Merit. This, Gentlemen, was the Occasion of those Words, which, at my coming hither, I addrest to this Goat: for being a she, I hate her, tho' she is the best of my Herd. This is the Story which I promis'd to tell you; if you have thought it too long, I shall endeavor to requite your Patience in any thing I can serve you. Hard by is my Cottage, where I have some good fresh Milk and excellent Cheese, with several sorts of Fruits, which I hope you will find agreeable both to the Sight and Taste." (part 1, chap. 51)

The Leandra story is very naively introduced: the shepherd simply walks up to the stopping-place where Don Quixote was being deceitfully led away home by certain people and relates to them his tale. Let us, however, turn our attention to the way in which the story is interpolated into the novel.

This Cervantes does by resorting to the "fight" type (i.e., just as in the Cardenio episode). Don Quixote takes offense at the shepherd, who has mistaken him for a madman:

With that, snatching up a Loaf that was near him, he struck the Goat-herd so furious a Blow with it, that he almost level'd his Nose with his Face. T'other, not ac-custom'd to such Salutations, no sooner perceiv'd how scurvily he was treated, but without any Respect to the Table-cloth, Napkins, or to those who were eating, he leap'd furiously on Don Quixote, and grasping him by the Throat with both his Hands, had certainly strangl'd him, had not Sancho Panza come in that very nick of Time, and griping him fast behind, pull'd him backwards on the Table, bruising Dishes, breaking Glasses, spilling and overturning all that lay upon it. Don Quixote seeing himself freed, fell violently again upon the Goat-herd, who, all besmear'd with Blood, and trampl'd to pieces under Sancho's Feet, grop'd here and there for some Knife or Fork to take a fatal Revenge; but the Canon and Curate took care to prevent his Purpose, and in the mean while, by the Barber's Contrivance, the Goat-herd got Don Quixote under him, on whom he let fall such a Tempest of Blows, as caus'd as great a Shower of Blood to pour from the poor Knight's Face as he had stream'd from his own. (part 1, chap. 52)

Such is the second mode of reinforcing the relationship between the novel itself and the subordinate story set within it.

A few more words concerning this. Freeing himself from the shepherd's grip, Don Quixote launches immediately upon a new adventure without even bothering to wipe the blood from his face. This is the episode of the Penitents. He is beaten once again.

I am not surprised by this streak of coarseness in the novel. Still, these rows and battles belong to the world of the circus and fairy tale. Even the tears we shed for our hero are more artificial than real.

Now let's take up a more fundamental issue, that of the technical means by which Cervantes interpolates these stories into the main body of the novel.

As we have already noted, the Marcella episode is introduced by means of a story. The first part of the Cardenio–Lucinda–Dorothea–Don Fernando tale is similarly introduced. At first it is related by Cardenio to Don Quixote with an interruption occasioned by a fight. It is then told by Cardenio to the barber and the curate. Then everyone hears out Dorothea, too. Both Cardenio and Dorothea captivate the other members of the company with their singing:

While they quietly refresh'd themselves in that delightful Place, where they agreed to stay till Sancho's Return, they heard a Voice, which though unattended with any Instrument, ravish'd their Ears with its melodious Sound: And what increas'd their Surprize, and their Admiration, was to hear such artful Notes, and such delicate Musick, in so unfrequented and wild a Place, where scarce any Rusticks ever straggl'd, much less such skilful Songsters, as the Person whom they heard unques-tionably was; for though the Poets are pleas'd to fill the Fields and Woods with Swains and Shepherdesses, that sing with all the Sweetness and Delicacy imaginable, yet 'tis well enough known that those Gentlemen deal more in Fiction than in Truth, and love to embellish the Descriptions they make, with Things that have no Existence but in their own Brain. Nor could our two list'ning Travellers think it the Voice of a Peasant, when they began to distinguish the Words of the song, for they seem'd to relish more of a courtly Style than a rural Composition. These were the Verses. (part 1, chap. 27)

These lines of verse give way to the following discourse:

The Time, the Hour, the Solitariness of the Place, the Voice and agreeable Manner with which the unseen Musician sung, so fill'd the Hearers Minds with Wonder and Delight, that they were all Attention; and when the Voice was silent, they continu'd so too a pretty while, watching with list'ning Ears to catch the expected Sounds, expressing their Satisfaction best by that dumb Applause. At last, concluding the Person would sing no more, they resolv'd to find out the charming Songster; but as they were going so to do, they heard the wish'd-for Voice began another Air, which fix'd 'em where they stood till it had sung the following Sonnet:

A SONNET

O Sacred Friendship, Heaven's Delight,
Which tir'd with Man's unequal Mind,
Took to thy native Skies thy Flight,
    While scarce thy Shadow's left behind!

From thee, diffusive Good, below,
    Peace and her Train of Joys we trace;
But Falsehood with dissembl'd Show
    Too oft usurps thy sacred Face.

Bless'd Genius then resume thy Seat!
Destroy Imposture and Deceit,
    Which in thy Dress confound the Ball!
Harmonious Peace and Truth renew,
Shew the false Friendship from the true,
    Or Nature must to Chaos fall.

This Sonnet concluded with a deep Sigh, and such doleful Throbs, that the Curate and the Barber now out of Pity, as well as Curiosity before, resolv'd instantly to find out who this mournful Songster was.

In just this way the second leading character of this story (i.e., Dorothea) is introduced:

We told you that as the Curate was preparing to give Cardenio some seasonable Consolation, he was prevented by a Voice, whose doleful Complaints reach'd his Ears. "O Heavens," cry'd the unseen Mourner, "is it possible I have at last found out a Place that will afford a private Grave to this miserable body, whose Load I so repine to bear? Yes, if the Silence and Solitute of these Desarts do not deceive me, here I may die conceal'd from Human Eyes. Ah me! Ah wretched Creature! to what Extremity has Affliction driven me, reduc'd to think these hideous Woods and Rocks a kind Retreat! 'Tis true indeed, I may here freely complain to Heaven, and beg for that relief which I might ask in vain of false Mankind: For 'tis vain, I find to seek below either Counsel, Ease, or Remedy." (part 1, chap. 28)

At this juncture, necessity compels me to share with the reader the story line of that tale which Cervantes introduced into his novel, and which I am now introducing into my work.

Cardenio, an aristocrat, introduces his friend Don Fernando, the younger son of a certain Spanish grandee, to his fiancée Lucinda. Don Fernando falls in love with her and sends Cardenio away through chicanery. He then proceeds to woo Cardenio's fiancée himself. She notifies her beloved, who rushes to her defense. Arriving just in time for the wedding ceremony, Cardenio hears Lucinda say (mistakenly) "yes" to Fernando at the altar, whereupon he goes mad and flees to the mountains.

Meanwhile, Don Fernando has a fiancée himself, the rich and beautiful peasant girl Dorothea, whom he dumps for Lucinda. Grief-stricken, Dorothea flees to the mountains too. There she lands in Cervantes' novel. Subsequently, both Cardenio and Dorothea arrive at the inn, the same one in which Sancho was once tossed on a blanket.

This is indeed a remarkable inn. It was set up by Cervantes in accordance with a patent that was evidently issued with strictly literary purposes in mind. Dozens of tales and recognitions cross paths within its confines. This place constitutes the geometric center of the individual crisscrossing lines of the novel. To this "compositional" inn come Don Fernando and Lucinda. We see here a new mode of introducing stories by means of a "meeting." Here Dorothea recognizes Fernando, and Cardenio recognizes Lucinda. It turns out that when Lucinda fainted during the wedding ceremony, Don Fernando discovered a letter resting on Lucinda's breast. In this letter, written by Lucinda, she speaks of herself as Cardenio's wife. Lucinda enters a convent, from which Don Fernando abducts her. On the way, though, they meet Cardenio. Dorothea challenges him with a speech in which she proves point by point that he is under obligation to love her. This speech recalls the "suosaria" (or speeches of persuasion), examples of which we find in Ovid:

"I am that poor and humble Villager, whom your generous Bounty, I dare not say your Love, did condescend to raise to the Honour of calling you her own: I am she, who, once confin'd to peaceful Innocence, led a contented Life, till your Importunity, your Shew of Honour, and deluding Words, charm'd me from my Retreat, and made me resign my Freedom to your Power. How I am recompens'd, may be guess'd by my Grief, and my being found here in this strange Place, whither I was led, not through any Dishonourable Ends, but purely by Despair and Grief to be forsaken of You. 'Twas at your Desire I was bound to you by the strictest Tie, and whatever you do, you can never cease to be mine. Consider, my dear Lord, that my matchless Love may balance the Beauty and Nobility of the Person for whom You would forsake me; she cannot share your Love, for 'tis only mine; and Cardenio's Interest in her will not admit a Partner. 'Tis easier far, my Lord, to recall your wandring Desires, and fix them upon her that adores you, than to draw Her to love who hates you. Remember how you did sollicit my humble State, and conscious of my Meanness, yet paid a Veneration to my Innocence, which join'd with the honourable condition of my yielding to your Desires, pronounce me free from ill Design or

Dishonour. Consider these undeniable Truths: have some Regard to your Honour! Remember you're a Christian! Why should you then make her Life end so miserably, whose Beginning your Favour made so happy? If I must not expect the Usage and Respect of a Wife, let me but serve you as a Slave; So I belong to you, tho' in the meanest Rank, I never shall complain: Let me not be expos'd to the slandring Reflections of the Censorious World by so cruel a Separation from my Lord: Afflict not the declining Years of my poor Parents, whose faithful Services to You and Yours have merited a more suitable Return. If you imagine the Current of your noble Blood should be defil'd by mixing with mine, consider how many noble Houses have run in such a Channel; besides the woman's Side is not essentially requisite to enoble Descent: But chiefly think on this, that Virtue is the truest Nobility, which if you stain by basely wronging me, you bring a greater blot upon your Family than Marrying me could cause. In fine, my Lord, you cannot, must not disown me for your Wife: To attest which Truth, I call your own Words, which must be true, if you prize yourself for Honour, and that Nobility, whose want you so despise in Me; witness your Oaths and Vows, witness that Heaven which you so often invok'd to ratify your Promises; and if all these should fail, I make my last Appeal to your own Conscience, whose Sting will always represent my Wrongs fresh to your thoughts, and disturb your Joys amidst your greatest Pleasures."

These, with many such Arguments, did the mournful Dorothea urge, appearing so lovely in her Sorrow, that Don Ferdinand's Friends, as well as all the rest sympathiz'd with her, Lucinda particularly, as much admiring her Wit and Beauty, as mov'd by the Tears, the piercing Sighs and Moans that follow'd her Intreaties; and she wou'd have gone nearer to have comforted her, had not Ferdinand's Arms, that still held her, prevented it. He stood full of Confusion, with his eyes fix'd attentively on Dorothea a great while; at last, opening his Arms, he quitted Lucinda, "Thou has Conquered," cry'd he, "charming Dorothea, thou hast Conquer'd me, 'tis impossible to resist so many united Truths and Charms." (part 1, chap. 36)

While this interminable tale unfolds at a snail's pace, another story entitled "The Novel of the Curious Impertinent" is incorporated into the text. This second story, about eight manuscript pages in length (by Cervantes' own calculation), is incorporated into *Don Quixote* in the capacity of "a found manuscript" (i.e., it is read by the principal characters of the novel as an unknown manuscript which was found by them). The curate's remark is interesting at this point, since he is a sworn critic of the novel. (See the episode with Don Quixote's library, the conversation with the innkeeper, etc.) He says:

"I like this Novel well enough," said the Curate; "yet, after all, I cannot persuade myself, that there's any thing of Truth in it; and if it be purely Invention, the Author was in the wrong; for 'tis not to be imagin'd there cou'd ever be a Husband so foolish, as to venture on so dangerous an Experiment. Had he made his Husband and Wife, a Gallant and a Mistress, the Fable had appear'd more probable; but, as it is, 'tis next to impossible. However, I must confess, I have nothing to object against his manner of telling it." (part 1, chap. 35)

This comment recalls another maxim uttered by the selfsame curate concerning the style of another inset story, which I have already touched upon.

It seems to me that we may perceive here an "expressive" orientation, so typical in art. The writer himself comments on the various parts of his novel, first, as individual phenomena (the style of *this* particular story), and secondly, as literary phenomena in general (e.g., "the pastoral style is a good one").

The technique of introducing inset stories in accordance with the principle of the "found manuscript" became subsequently very popular. This was widely used by Sterne. The speeches of Yorick in *Tristram Shandy* represent such a "found manuscript," as does one episode in his *Sentimental Journey*. The same device was utilized by Dickens in *Pickwick Papers*, a work which was, generally speaking, written in accordance with the principle of the framing novel ("Diary of a Madman") along with an admixture of elements derived from the "threading" device. This is the source for the Pickwick type. The Cervantes connection serves as a basis, in all probability, for the Samuel Weller type, who, like Panza, also weaves many proverbs like a thread. But Sancho's sayings represent a different type than those of Samuel. The proverbs of Pickwick's servant are consciously enstranged. Their humor lies in the inappropriateness, in the discrepancy between their use and the situation at hand. Perhaps Dickens has here revealed in general one of the essential guidelines in the use of examples: a sense of irony should inform their use. Let me illustrate with two proverbs by Samuel:

> "There is nothin' so refreshin' as sleep, sir, as the servant-girl said afore she drank the egg-cupful o' laudanum." (chap. 16)

> "Poverty and oysters always seem to go together." (chap. 22)*

But I am already beginning to feel the influence of this novel: I'm allowing myself to be sidetracked by episode after episode, forgetting the main thrust of the essay. What did Cervantes do under similar circumstances? Why, he interrupted the action, reminding the reader of the protagonist of the novel by bringing on one of the knight's usual acts of madness. So, "The Novel of the Curious Impertinent," along with the Cardenio story in which it is implanted, is interrupted by Don Quixote's famous battle with the wineskins. As I have already said before, this episode is taken in all probability from Miletus through Apuleius' *Golden Ass*.

The inn where Cardenio meets Fernando and Lucinda later plays the role of a hovel in Shakespeare's *King Lear*. This is the crossroads for all of the leading characters in the novel, whose actions are therefore connected to each other only by the fact that they all take place in this inn at one and the same time. However, while in Shakespeare the principal characters belong

---

*After much searching, I was still unable to locate the Dickens original for Shklovsky's second quote, which reads something like this: " 'We all have to go sometime,' said the thrush, as the cat dragged him away by his tail." I have therefore substituted for it another of Samuel's innumerable sayings. [Trans. note]

to one complex of events, in Cervantes they are related only by their common locale and by the author's desire to introduce them into his novel. The relationship obtaining among them is limited to the fact that they are either surprised or enraptured by each other. In this they recall rather the linkage of the type represented by *A Thousand and One Nights* with the difference that in Cervantes' novel these characters coexist, as it were, while in *A Thousand and One Nights* they are co-narrated. But this is not a fundamental distinction, since the element of the storyteller's "yarn" does in fact exist in Cervantes, though perhaps only because the whole novel is incorporated within the feebly perceived framework of the "found manuscript" of one Cide Hamete Benengeli, an Arab storyteller.

Into this literary tavern walks a man of around forty years of age with a beautiful Moslem woman. After Don Quixote's introductory speech, the captive relates the story of his life and his adventures. This is the common type (or what later became a common type) of escape through the help of a beautiful native woman. In this story Cervantes expresses his strategic judgment concerning Fort Gol. One of the captive's comrades turns out to be the brother of Don Fernando, a faint allusion to its connection with the main plot. At this very moment, his brother's sonnets are being brought in. The reading of the sonnets is followed by the history of this captive, which is told in full detail. It occupies, at most, about five chapters.

A literary assessment, so characteristic in general of Cervantes, follows immediately on the heels of this inset tale. I don't know whether I have already told you that these inset lines of verse, for example, are always evaluated on the spot by one of the guests. So also now:

"Truly, Captain, the wonderful and surprizing turns of your Fortune are not only entertaining, but the pleasing and graceful manner of your Relation is as extraordinary as the Adventures themselves: We are all bound to pay you our Acknowledgments and I believe we could be delighted with a second Recital, though 'twere to last till to Morrow, provided it were made by You." (part 1, chap. 42)

The literary inn, however, continues to overflow with guests, as Cervantes introduces more and more leading characters, who in turn bring with them new stories into the world of the novel. A state prosecutor enters the inn with his beautiful sixteen-year-old daughter. However, the story's interpolation into the novel by gathering the protagonists under one roof is not the only device employed by Cervantes. Another new device, though new only in a relative sense, is introduced: The state prosecutor turns out to be the brother of the captive storyteller (he's one of three brothers—a traditional fairy-tale number—as is the motif of the father partitioning the family estate among three sons, each of whom chooses a different path: one chooses a career in the academy, another in the military, a third in commerce). The next chapter (part 1, chap. 43) introduces a new episode by means of the same old technique of a meeting. This is "The Pleasant Story of the Young Muleteer with Other Strange Adventures That Happen'd in the Inn."

A young man bursts in, dressed like a mule driver. This is Don Louis, who is in love with Clara, the daughter of the state prosecutor. He sings a song in her honor. But here Cervantes brings in Don Quixote once again. This is the episode in which the servants of the inn mock and scorn the Knight of the Woeful Figure, as they bind him by his hands to the grating of the dormer window. Then follows the conclusion of the Don Louis episode, and, at last, the action returns once more to the main plot.

The point is that the barber from whom Don Quixote had once taken the shaving basin (mistaking it for Mambrino's helmet as Sancho Panza was busy removing the harness from his mule) has also arrived at the inn, the magnetic qualities of which we have already explained. Well, it so happens that the barber recognizes his basin.

A curious argument breaks out in the tavern in which all the guests present take the side of Don Quixote, assuring him that the basin is indeed a helmet. This curious hoax is far from being the only hoax in the novel. The episodes in the early part of the novel are explained by the delusions of Don Quixote, who takes a strumpet for a princess, a merchant who is torturing Andre for a gallant knight, and his stick for a lance. But towards the end of the first part, the motivation of the episodes changes. Don Quixote is no longer deluded so much as he is a victim of hoaxes. The whole episode in the duke's palace with its magical wooden leg and with the exorcism from Dulcinea's spell is an example of such a grandiose hoax.

A series of hoaxes now begins, not to mention the innkeeper's hilarious consecration of Don Quixote into knighthood (here the innkeeper is not the author of the hoax, but merely supports the delusions of our hero). This series begins with the "helmet" episode and with the fictitious enchantment, by means of which Don Quixote is taken home in a cage. Along the way Don Quixote is let out of the cage on his word of honor, whereupon he enters into an argument with a canon concerning books on chivalry. The conversation between the canon and the curate constitutes a whole critical survey of the literature of chivalry, the introduction of which at the beginning of the novel was so well-motivated by the examination of Don Quixote's library before it was put to the flames. It is also related to the conversation on the same subject between the curate and the innkeeper. And it also resembles the answer given by the curate upon examining Don Quixote's library. In response to the passionate tirade by the innkeeper and his daughter concerning the entertaining and edifying attributes of books on chivalry, he counters with the following:

"I shall do as well with the Books," said the Barber, "for I can find the Way to the Back-yard, or the Chimney, there's a good Fire that will do their Business." "Business!" said the Inn-keeper, "I hope you wou'd not burn my Books." "Only two of them," said the Curate, "this same Don Cirongilio and his Friend Felixmarte." "I hope, Sir," said the Host, "they are neither Hereticks nor Flegmaticks." "Schismaticks you mean," said the Barber; "I mean so," said the Inn-keeper; "and if you must burn any, let it be this of Goncalo Hernandez and Diego Garcia, for you should sooner burn one of my Children than the others." "These Books, honest Friend," said the Curate, "that you appear so concern'd for, are senseless Rhapsodies of Falsehoods and Folly; and this which you so despise is a true History, and contains a true Account of two celebrated Men; the first by his Bravery and Courage purchas'd immortal Fame, and the Name of the great General, by the universal Consent of Mankind. The other, Diego Garcia de Paredes, was of Noble Extraction, and born in Truxillo, a Town of Estremadura, and was a Man of singular Courage, and such mighty Strength, that with one of his Hands he could stop a Mill-wheel in its most rapid Motion; and with his single Force defended the Passage of a Bridge against a great Army. Several other great Actions are related in the Memoirs of his Life, but all with so much Modesty and unbiass'd Truth, that they easily pronounce him his own Historiographer; and had they been written by any one else, with Freedom and Impartiality, they might have eclips'd your Hectors, Achilles's, and Orlando's, with all their Heroick Exploits." (part 1, chap. 32)

We see the same in this conversation with the canon:

The Curate was very attentive, and believ'd him a Man of a sound Judgment, and much in the right in all he had urg'd; and therefore told him, That being of the same Opinion, and an Enemy to Books of Knight-Errantry, he had burnt all that belong'd to Don Quixote, which were a considerable Number. Then he recounted to him the Scrutiny he had made among them, what he had condemn'd to the flames, and what spar'd. (part 1, chap. 47)

These reminders serve like internal braces to bind episodes of the same type within the framework of *Don Quixote.*

The canon, however, is not satisfied with discussing novels of chivalry and begins talking about art in general, especially about drama. This is followed by Don Quixote's speech which I've already touched upon briefly during my analysis of his speeches.

The first part of the novel concludes with an inset episode on stray sheep and with Don Quixote's attack on a religious procession.

I do not intend to analyze the second part of *Don Quixote* with the same degree of consistency with which I have tried to follow the course of the first part. I only wish to point out what's new in the structure of the second part.

I've already had occasion several times before to say that the second parts of novels, or, rather, their sequels, often reveal changes in their structures. The novel, breaking off suddenly, exists now only conditionally as it sets off along new paths. So, we find towards the end of Rabelais's novel a transition to a type of picaresque novel, where the individual island allegories are connected by the wanderings of the heroes. Structurally speaking, the concluding parts of *Gargantua and Pantagruel* anticipate, so to speak, the finale of *Gulliver's Travels.* Towards the end of Swift's novel, though, the satirical material begins to supplant the material devoted to adventure (this was noted by my pupil L. Lunts).

What distinguishes chiefly the second part of *Don Quixote* is its abundance of small inset anecdotes introduced into the novel from without. Another feature which distinguishes it is the fact that we are witness here to a deceived Don Quixote who is now everywhere the object of a hoax. The family of the duke with its retainers amuses itself at the expense of the poor knight, and Sancho Panza's tenure as governor is nothing but an out-and-out hoax. Furthermore the Bachelor dismisses the knight out of his house as a hoax, and his battles with the Knight of Mirrors and then with the Knight of the Moon also constitute a hoax. Don Quixote is also the butt of a practical joke in Barcelona, where an inscription bearing a nickname is attached to his cloak. So, too, in restoring Falstaff to the stage (by order of the queen, they say), Shakespeare had to make Falstaff an object of a hoax in his *Merry Wives of Windsor.*

It's worth noting that in part 2 of Cervantes' novel, Don Quixote shows that he is fully cognizant of the existence of part 1 by polemicizing against the spurious anonymous version of part 2 (circulating in Spain even before Cervantes' version). A curious situation emerges. The leading character of the novel feels himself to be real as such but does not come across as a living human being. This is motivated by the fact that Don Quixote considers his illegitimate twin to be crude and trivial, so that he seems to take offense at him not as Don Quixote, the literary character, but as Don Quixote the living human being:

"Then without Dispute," said Don Quixote, "you are the same Don Alvaro Tarfe, whose Name fills a Place in the second Part of Don Quixote de la Mancha's *History,* that was lately publish'd by a new Author?" "The very Man," answer'd the Knight; "and that very Don Quixote, who is the principal Subject of that book, was my intimate Acquaintance; I am the Person that intic'd him from his Habitation so far at least, that he had never seen the Tournament at Saragosa, had it not been through My Persuasions, and in My Company; and indeed, as it happen'd, I prov'd the best Friend he had, and did him a singular Piece of Service; for had I not stood by him, his intolerable Impudence had brought him to some shameful Punishment." "But pray, Sir," said Don Quixote, "be pleas'd to tell me one Thing; Am I any thing like that Don Quixote of yours?" "The farthest from it in the World, Sir," reply'd the other. "And had he," said our Knight, "one Sancho Pança for his Squire?" "Yes," said Don Alvaro, "but I was the most deceiv'd in him that could be; for by common Report that same Squire was a comical, witty Fellow, but I found him a very great Blockhead." (part 2, chap. 72)

What ensues is an appeal to the sojourners to certify in writing that they have seen the real Don Quixote.

It seems to me that we are dealing here with an emphasis, expressed in a rather low key, on the theatrical dimension, the conventionality and manipulativeness of art. To this type belongs King Lear's address to his daughters when they inform him that a retinue of fifty knights or even less should be more than adequate for his needs. King Lear turns to an elegantly dressed lady in the audience and asks:

> Thou art a lady;
> If only to go warm were gorgeous,
> Why, nature needs not what thou gorgeous wear'st,
> Which scarcely keeps thee warm. (2.4.262-65)

In Gogol, a governor of a town likewise destroys the fourth invisible wall of the theater, which makes the audience, as it were, invisible to the characters on stage, by uttering the words that are now known to everyone: "Whom are you laughing at? For God's sake, can't you see that you are laughing at nobody but yourselves?"

Meanwhile, in Ostrovsky's *A Family Affair,* Rispolozhensky rushes to the footlights of the stage, where he shows the worn-out soles of his shoes to the audience.

In Tieck and in Hoffmann (Princess Brambila) the principal characters are at times aware of the fact that they are the leading characters of a story or capriccio "which is at this very moment being written." This device is canonical for vaudeville with its racy topical verse addressed to the public.

As far as the theater is concerned, the illusion presented on the stage ought to have a "flickering" quality to it (i.e., it should alternate with the other, more realistic element in the play). As for the spectator, he must experience within himself a shift in his perception of the action onstage from the "contrived" to the "realistic" and back. The awareness of a flickering illusion serves as a basis for Leoncavallo's *Pagliacci* and for Schnitzler's *Green Cockatoo.* The action on the stage is perceived either as play or as life.

But it's time for us now to return to Don Quixote.

In his conversation with the Bachelor, Sancho Panza tells how his donkeys were stolen. This detail was neglected in the first part:

"Now," quoth he, "as to what Master Sampson wanted to know; that is, when, where, and by whom my Ass was stol'n: I answer, That the very Night that we march'd off to the Sierra Morena, to avoid the Hue and Cry of the Holy Brotherhood, after the rueful Adventure of the Galley Slaves, and that of the dead Body that was carrying to Segovia, my Master and I slunk into a Wood; where he leaning on his Lance and I, without alighting from Dapple, both sadly bruis'd and tir'd with our late Skirmishes, fell fast asleep, and slept as soundly as if we had had Four Featherbeds under us; but I especially was as serious at it as any Dormouse; so that the Thief, whoever he was, had Leisure enough to clap four Stakes under the four Corners of the Pack-Saddle, and then leading away the Ass from between my Legs, without being perceiv'd by me in the least, there he fairly left me mounted." "This is no new thing," said Don Quixote, "nor is it difficult to be done: With the same Stratagem Sacripante had his Steed stol'n from under him by that notorious Thief Brunelo at the Siege of Albraca." (part 2, chap. 4)

Here we see that Cervantes has made use in his novel of a nomadic plot. This phenomenon is common enough even in the most recent literature. For example, quite distinct "historical words" and actions make their way into the text for the most part by being anonymously ascribed to the hero of the novel. This device is common, for example, in the works of Alexandre Dumas. We encounter it, with a parodistic tinge, also in Leo Tolstoi (*War and Peace:* the conversation between Petruska, Andrei Balkonsky's aide, and Napoleon). We see the same thing in Gogol's *Dead Souls.* Recounting the prank played by the contrabandists, who had transported Brabant lace underneath sheepskins placed over their sheep, Gogol says at first: "We heard that . . ." And then, retelling the anecdote, he adds: "There's not a single Jew in the world who could have pulled this off without Chichikov." That is, Gogol adopts and assimilates a definite roving anecdote into his novel. I have already spoken in my chapter concerning plot deployment about and analogous phenomenon in Apuleius' *The Golden Ass* and in *Lazarillo of Tormes.*

In the following chapter (chap. 5), Cervantes puts into the words of Sancho such highly complex sentences that he himself considers them apocryphal ". . . because it introduces Sancho speaking in another Style than could be expected from his slender Capacity, and saying things of so refin'd a Nature, that it seems impossible he cou'd do it."

After his speech on glory, Don Quixote goes on the road, where Sancho Panza plays a hoax on him by passing off a peasant passerby as Dulicinea Toboso. Episodes featuring Don Quixote's meeting with itinerant actors, another battle motivated by a hoax, and an encounter with a forest knight bring us to the famous battle in which the Knight of the Woeful Figure takes on the lions. This episode interrupts a long series of deliberations which Don Quixote carries on with a certain member of the gentry of La Mancha. In the opening of chapter 19, we find ourselves in an inset pastoral on cunning, with the aid of which a shepherd had wrested a fiancée from her rich peasant. This pastoral includes a description of the allegorical play performed at the wedding. As always in Cervantes, this play is immediately subjected to a literary assessment by those present:

When all was over, Don Quixote ask'd one of the Nymphs, who it was that compos'd the Entertainment? She answer'd, that it was a certain Clergyman who liv'd in their Town, that had a rare Talent that way. "I dare lay a Wager," said Don Quixote, "he was more a Friend to Basil than to Camacho, and knows better what belongs to a ̄ Play than a Prayer-Book: He has express'd Basil's Parts and Camacho's Estate very naturally in the Design of your Dance."

We shall not follow in the footsteps of Don Quixote. Let us instead move on to the set episodes. In chapter 24 we find an anecdote about a page who was walking along the road without his pants on in order not to soil them, while in chapters 25 through 27 we come across an anecdote concerning two villagers quarreling over the fact that one of them had teased the other by mimicking a donkey's bray. This little story is connected with the novel only by the fact that its leading characters end up beating Don Quixote. Later on, the novel turns into a fairy ballet given at the home of the duke. Analogous to the "donkey's bray" type of anecdote, we find interpolated into the novel an episode in which two young people discuss whether it is necessary to learn the art of fencing and how to equalize the weight of two fat men who are intent on competing in a race.

Sancho Panza's governorship is a complex inset episode of major scope.

Its origin is sufficiently understood. In "framing novels" it is common to select material in accordance with a unifying principle, at times of a very superficial nature. For example, in *A Thousand and One Nights* the stories are often selected because of the identical injury entailed by their denouements. This is the basis for the story about the three imperial beggars (each having lost an eye for a different reason). Often, on the other hand, these stories are selected because of their identical denouements, as, for example, where an enemy among the sheiks is converted by blood-redeeming stories like those early in *A Thousand and One Nights*. This type of character did not so much endure as insistently burst upon the scene. We see this in the eighteenth-century Georgian *Book of Wisdom and Lies*. The tales in Boccaccio's *Decameron* are partially arranged in this way. This was the same device that Voltaire made use of in *Candide* (chap. 26), where we see a *fortuitous* gathering of six retired monarchs in the same inn:

All the servants having disappeared, the six foreigners, Candide, and Martin remained in deep silence. Finally Candide broke it:

"Gentlemen," he said, "this is a singular jest. Why are you all kings? For myself, I admit that neither Martin nor I am."

Cacambo's master then spoke up gravely and said in Italian:

"I am not jesting, my name is Ahmed III. I was Grand Sultan for several years; I dethroned my brother; my nephew dethroned me; my viziers had their heads cut off; I am ending my days in the old seraglio. My nephew, the Grand Sultan Mahmud, allows me to travel sometimes for my health, and I have come to spend the Carnival in Venice."

A young man who was next to Ahmed spoke after him and said:

"My name is Ivan; I was Emperor of all the Russias; I was dethroned in my cradle; my father and mother were locked up; I was brought up in prison; I sometimes have permission to travel, accompanied by those who guard me, and I have come to spend the Carnival in Venice."

The third said:

"I am Charles Edward, King of England; my father ceded me his rights to the kingdom. I fought to maintain them; they tore the hearts out of eight hundred of my supporters and dashed them in their faces. I was put in prison; I am going to Rome to pay a visit to the King my father, who is dethroned like my grandfather and me; and I have come to spend the Carnival in Venice."

The fourth then took the floor and said:

"I am King of the Poles; the fortunes of war have deprived me of my hereditary states; my father underwent the same reverses; I resign myself to Providence like Sultan Ahmed, Emperor Ivan, and King Charles Edward, whom God give long life; and I have come to spend the Carnival in Venice."

The fifth said:

"I too am King of the Poles; I have lost my kingdom twice; but Providence has given me another state, in which I have done more good than all the kings of the Sarmatians together have ever been able to do on the banks of the Vistula; I too resign myself to Providence; and I have come to spend the Carnival in Venice."

It remained for the sixth monarch to speak.

"Gentlemen, I am not as great a lord as you; but even so I have been a King like anyone else. I am Theodore; I was elected King of Corsica; I have been called Your Majesty, and at present I am hardly called Sir. I have coined money, and I do not have a penny; I have had two secretaries of state, and I have scarcely a valet. I was once on a throne, and I was in prison for a long time in London, on the straw. I am much afraid I shall be treated the same way here, although I have come, like Your Majesties, to spend the Carnival in Venice."

The five other Kings listened to this speech with noble compassion. Each of them gave King Theodore twenty sequins to get clothes and shirts; and Candide presented him with a diamond worth two thousand sequins.

"Who is this man," said the five Kings, "who is in a position to give a hundred times as much as each of us, and who gives it? Are you a King too, sir?"

"No, gentlemen, and I have no desire to be."

At the moment when they were leaving the table, there arrived in the same hotel four Most Serene Highnesses, who had also lost their states by the fortunes of war, and who were coming to spend the rest of the Carnival in Venice. But Candide did not even take note of these newcomers; he was preoccupied only with going to find his dear Cunégonde in Constantinople.

CHAPTER 27

The faithful Cacambo had already obtained an agreement with the Turkish captain who was about to take Sultan Ahmed back to Constantinople that he would take Candide and Martin on his ship. Both came on board after having prostrated themselves before his miserable Highness. On the way, Candide said to Martin:

"But those were six dethroned Kings that we had supper with, and besides, among those six Kings there was one to whom I gave alms. Maybe there are many other princes still more unfortunate. As for me, I have lost only a hundred sheep, and I am flying to Cunégonde's arms. My dear Martin, once again, Pangloss was right, all is well."

"I hope so," said Martin.

"But," said Candide, "that was a most implausible adventure we had in Venice. No one ever saw or heard of six dethroned Kings having supper together in an inn." (Frame translation)

What we see here may be less a motivation for the device than an attempt to interpret it or at the very least to specify it. It would be interesting to point to one passage from Conan Doyle as an analogous attempt to motivate another "technical convention," that is, the convention of the adventure novel with its favorable confluence of circumstances:

"For this is pure coincidence Holmes, fate itself smiles upon you!"

"My dear Watson, I view this in an entirely different light. Any man who pursues something with stubbornness, whose thoughts are fixed on one and only one thing, and whose desire is urgently directed to bring this about come what may, involuntarily furthers his cause in everything that he undertakes. Call this hypnosis, the inflexible force of the will, but that's the way it is! Precisely the way that a magnet attracts to itself iron and steel filings from everywhere, so does this will power bend all of the petty affairs and circumstances in its path into a chain which must lead to a revelation of the crime."*

The principle of selecting material in accordance with some external criterion is widely applied in the novel. Sometimes, especially in a more limited novel, the inset parts interact in a definite way. For example, they represent a parallel structure. Panza's governorship represents a summary of folkloric episodes concerning the trials of wisdom. Here we also hear an echo of the trials of Solomon and of the Talmud (the episode with the money in the cane). Sancho himself points out the important nature of this wisdom:

All the Spectators were amaz'd, and began to look on their Governor as a second Solomon. They ask'd him how he could conjecture that the ten Crowns were in the Cane? He told 'em, that having observ'd how the Defendant gave it to the Plaintiff to hold while he took his Oath, and then swore he had truly return'd him the Money in his own Hands, after which he took his Cane again from the Plaintiff; this consider'd, it came into his Head, that the Money was lodg'd within the Reed. From whence may be learn'd, that though sometimes those that govern are destitute of Sense, yet it often pleases God to direct 'em in their Judgments. Besides, he had heard the Curate of his Parish tell of such another Business; and he had so special a Memory, that were it not that he was so unlucky as to forget all he had a mind to remember, there could not have been a better in the whole Island. (part 2, chap. 45)

The other episodes, for instance, the episode with the woman who had falsely accused the swineherd of rape, have many parallels elsewhere in accordance with the laws of plot formation.

Certain episodes from Sancho's governorship include picaresque proverbs and fables incorporated into the novel.

Apart from this type of interpolated episode and the different "tasks" of folkloric type, Cervantes introduces into his description of Sancho's governorship (as he had done earlier in Don Quixote's speeches) various administrative considerations of his own. Sometimes, these speeches of Sancho differ radically from what we have become accustomed to hear from Don Quixote's armor-bearer. In that case, Cervantes himself points out the incongruity and thereby lays bare the device:

"Now," said he, "do I find in good earnest that Judges and Governors must be made of Brass, or ought to be made of Brass, that they may be proof against the Importunities of those that pretend Business, who at all Hours, and at all Seasons would be heard and dispatch'd, without any Regard to any body but themselves, let what will come of the rest, so their turn is serv'd. Now if a poor Judge does not hear and dispatch them presently, either because he is otherways busy and cannot, or because they don't come at a proper Season, then do they grumble, and give him their Blessing backwards, rake up the Ashes of his Forefathers, and would gnaw his very Bones. But with your Leave, good Mr. Busy-Body, with all your Business you are too hasty, pray have a little Patience, and wait a fit Time to make your Application. Don't come at Dinner-time, or when a Man is going to sleep, for we

*From "The Dancer's Knife," not by Conan Doyle but a pastiche of uncertain origin. [Trans. note]

Judges are Flesh and Blood, and must allow Nature what she naturally requires; unless it be poor I, who am not to allow mine any food. Thanks to my Friend, Master Doctor Pedro Rezio Tirteafuera here present, who is for starving me to Death, and then swears 'tis for the preservation of my Life. Heaven grant him such a Life, I pray, and all the Gang of such Physickmongers as he is; for the good Physicians deserve Palms and Laurels."

All that knew Sancho wonder'd to hear him talk so sensibly, and began to think that Offices and Places of Trust inspir'd some Men with Understanding, as they stupify'd and confounded others. (part 2, chap. 49)

In the description of Sancho's governorship, Cervantes has inserted a short story, poorly executed, about a woman who had run away from her parents' home dressed in a man's outfit.

All of these episodes are integrated in one compact and motley kaleidoscope, which is more than just an accumulation of episodes delivered by Sancho upon his renunciation of the governorship. What is evident here is a new interpretation of old material. This is already a step forward in the direction of a new novel. The writer is conscious at this point of his option of presenting his hero not merely as a victim of a variety of jokes and pranks but also as a man who had felt them to the quick.

The humanity of the novel is introduced (for example, in Cervantes' condemnation of the mockery heaped on Don Quixote by the duke and duchess) as material for new structures.

Here the effect consists of a change in Don Quixote's two masks and in a reinterpretation of old material.

On the way from the island of Barataria, Sancho Panza meets his friend and neighbor Ricote the Moor, who, under the guise of a pilgrim, has been making his way home, where he had once buried a treasure (chap. 54). After a brief chat, the friends part. This episode has no independent significance but is introduced into the novel in order to connect the story about the Mauritanian woman more firmly to the novel (chap. 63). In this chapter we discover that during their assault, the Mauritanian galleys take into custody a young Moor, who turns out later to be a Christian woman and the daughter of Ricote. By sheer coincidence, Ricote himself appears on the scene. The fact is that we have met this Ricote earlier, though Sancho draws the inset tale somehow closer to the main plot. The description of Don Quixote's meeting with Roque, the bandits' ringleader, represents a separate story, or rather a story within a story. In the picturesque description of the noble highwayman, Cervantes has inserted a tale about a senselessly jealous woman by the name of Claudia Geronima, who had killed her suitor on false grounds of suspicion. These stories are connected to the novel only by the fact that Don Quixote is present at their telling. This is an almost perfect type of threading. In order to include episodes in this manner, it has always been especially appropriate to have the characters go on a journey. This journey has served as a motivation for bringing about contact between them and the hero.

The hero integrates these episodes in exactly the same way that an observer integrates the pictures of an art gallery in his mind.

To this type belong also the examination of houses by Don Cleophaus and Asmodeus (Le Sage's *Devil on Two Sticks*) by raising their roofs. Asmodeus's remarks, accompanying as they do his inspection of the paintings, play a role analogous to the hero's attitude towards the episodes strung together on his journey or to the astonishment shown by the princesses at the tales related to them in *A Thousand and One Nights.*

Sometimes we encounter in stories of the framing type not anecdotes but collections of scientific knowledge. In this way, arithmetic problems have been incorporated into the Georgian *Book of Wisdom and Lies,* while in the novels of Jules Verne we discover reference books on scientific matters and lists of geographical discoveries. The poem called *The Dove Book,* drawing entirely upon a body of learning considered scientific in its own time, is incorporated into a story about "the heavenly book."* Similarly, Aeschylus introduces into his tragedy a description of an optical telegraph.

I have already noted on innumerable occasions the interspersing of this type of material in Cervantes. Don Quixote's encounter in chapter 58 of part 2 with the people carrying the statues of the saints immediately after delivering his famous speech on freedom is a case in point.

In similar fashion, Cervantes interpolates into the novel the description of the talking head, with details galore concerning its structure. This happens in chapter 62, in which is related the "Adventure of the Inchanted Head with Other Impertinences Not to Be Omitted."

Elsewhere, during a conversation on the baselessness of omens, which includes parallels from ancient history and an explanation of the battle cry of the Spanish and so on, Don Quixote unexpectedly notes that he had become entangled in a net made of silk. It turns out that close by several young men and women have decided to create their own Arcadia. This game of shepherds and shepherdesses is in fact the source for all of the pastoral scenes in the novel. Cervantes himself wrote pastoral novels in this same conventional spirit. Pastoral scenes are numerous throughout *Don Quixote* and at times we are led to believe that the whole novel is about to take off on a new tangent that will turn into a pastoral. In fact, after his defeat at the hand of the Knight of the White Moon, Don Quixote goes home, intent upon becoming a shepherd.

But approaching death removes from Don Quixote, the Knight of the Woeful Figure, the mask of madness. In its place, he puts on the new mask of the meek Christian, Alonso the Brave.

--------

*My thanks to Prof. Oinas of Indiana University for his explanation of the strange name: Originally called the Book of Depths (*Glubokaya Kniga*), it became known in time as the Blue Book (*Golubaya Kniga*) and, more importantly, the Dove Book (*Golubinaya Kniga*), symbolizing, of course, the Holy Ghost. [Trans. note]

# Chapter 5

# Sherlock Holmes and the Mystery Story

1) A story may be told in such a way that the reader sees the unfolding of events, how one event follows another. In such a case, such a narration commonly adheres to a temporal sequence without any significant omissions. We may take as an example of this type of narration Tolstoi's *War and Peace.*

2) A story may also be told in such a way that what is happening is incomprehensible to the reader. The "mysteries" taking place in the story are only later resolved.

As an example of the latter type of narration let me mention "Knock! Knock! Knock!" by Turgenev, the novels of Dickens and detective stories, of which I shall have more to say.

Characteristic of this second type of narration is temporal transposition. As a matter of fact, a single temporal transposition such as the omission of a particular incident and its appearance after the consequences of this incident have already been revealed is often quite sufficient to create such a mystery. The mysterious appearance of Svidrigailov at the bedside of the ailing Raskolnikov in *Crime and Punishment* is a case in point, though, admittedly, it had already been prepared for by Dostoevsky, who had pointed out in passing that a certain man had been eavesdropping at the time the address was given. Still, the mystery is renewed by Raskolnikov's dream. By the mere omission of the fact that Svidrigailov had found out the address, the author achieves a mystery in the second meeting.

In an adventure novel built on several parallel lines of narration, the effects of surprise are achieved by the fact that while one plot line progresses, the other one may proceed at the same or even quicker tempo, during which we cross over to another narrative line, preserving all the while the time of the first line; that is, we find ourselves among consequences whose causes are unknown to us.

Thus does Don Quixote come upon Sancho in a mountain gorge.

This device seems perfectly natural, but it is in fact a definite accomplishment, utterly unknown to the Greek epic. Zelinsky has demonstrated that simultaneity of action is not admissible in the *Odyssey.* Although parallel narrative lines do exist in the story line (Odysseus and Telemachus), yet the events unfold alternately in each line. Transposition in time, as we see, may serve as a basis for a "mystery." However, we ought not to think that the mystery is in the transposition itself. For example, Chichikov's childhood, related after he had already been introduced by the author, would have ordinarily been found in the opening part of a classic adventure novel, and yet even in its transposed form it cannot make our hero mysterious.

The late works of Leo Tolstoi are frequently constructed *without special resort* to this device. That is, this device is presented in such a way that the center of gravity shifts from the temporal transposition to the denouement.

In *The Kreutzer Sonata* we find the following:

"Yes, no doubt, married life is filled with crises," the attorney said, wishing to put an end to the indecently passionate conversation.

"I see that you have found out who I am," silently and calmly said a grey-haired gentleman.

"No, I have not had that pleasure."

"It's a small pleasure. My name is Pozdnishev, the man who has gone through this crisis that you have just alluded to, the crisis which ended when he killed his wife," he said glancing quickly at each and every one of us.

In *Hadji-Murad* a cossack shows Butler the hacked-off head of Hadji-Murad, whereupon the drunken officers look it straight in the eye and kiss it. Later we are present at the scene of the last battle of Hadji-Murad. Apart from this, the destiny of Hadji-Murad, his entire history, is given in the image of the broken, crushed burdock, which nevertheless yearns stubbornly to live.

"The Death of Ivan Ilych" begins in the following way:

In a large building attached to the institutes of jurisprudence, during the intermission between the sessions concerning the Melovinsky case, the prosecutor and a member of the court gather in the study of Ivan Yegorovich Shchebek. A conversation had started concerning the famous Krasinsky case . . . Pyotr Ivanovich, on the other hand, who had kept silent throughout the proceedings, was examining the documents that had just been submitted.

In the examples above taken from *The Kreutzer Sonata, Hadji-Murad* and "The Death of Ivan Ilych" we witness a struggle with the story line rather than a complication of it.

Apparently, Tolstoi found it necessary to eliminate the plot interest of his novels. In its stead, he laid great stress on analysis, on the "details," as he used to say.

We know the death date of Ivan Ilych and the fate of Pozdnishev's wife, even the result of his trial. We know the fate of Hadji-Murad and we even know how people will judge him.

Curiosity concerning this aspect of a literary work is thereby removed.

What Tolstoi needed here was a new understanding of what a literary work is, a change in the usual categories of thought. And so he renounced plot, assigning to it a merely perfunctory role.

I have tried in this digression to show the difference between temporal transposition, which may, in certain cases, be used as a basis for the construction of "mysteries," and the mystery itself as a definite plot device.

I believe that even the most careless reader of adventure novels can cite the number of mysteries that figure in it.

Titles with the word "mystery" are exceedingly common in literature, as in, for example, *The Mystery of Madrid Court, The Mysterious Island, The Mystery of Edwin Drood,* etc.

Mysteries are usually introduced into adventure novels or stories for the purpose of heightening the reader's interest in the action, thereby making possible an ambiguous interpretation of the action.

Detective novels, a subspecies of the "crime novel," have come to overshadow the "cops and robbers novel" in importance. This is due, most probably, to the very convenience afforded by the mystery motivation. At first, the crime is presented as a riddle. Then, a detective appears on the scene as a professional riddle-solver.

*Crime and Punishment* similarly makes broad use of the device represented by Raskolnikov's preparations (the ax's noose, the change of hat and so on are described before we learn their purpose). The motives for the crime in this novel are revealed after the crime, which serves as its effect.

In novels of the Arsène Lupin type the main hero is not a detective but a "gentleman criminal." Still, there is a detective, a "discloser" of the mystery, whose presentation is motivated only by a lapse in time. Yet even Arsène Lupin often works as a detective.

To illustrate this story built on a mystery let us look closely at one of the stories by Conan Doyle devoted to the adventures of Sherlock Holmes.

For my analysis I have selected the story entitled "The Adventure of the Speckled Band." I shall point out parallels from time to time, taken, for the most part, from the *Collected Works of Conan Doyle* (St. Petersburg: Sojkin, 1909-11), vol. 4. My purpose in doing so is to make it easier for the reader, if he should choose to do so, to follow my analysis with the book in his hands.

Conan Doyle's stories begin on a rather monotonous note. A Sherlock Holmes story will often begin with Watson's enumeration of the famous detective's adventures and exploits. After this, Watson selects a story for the occasion.

Meanwhile, hints are dropped concerning certain little-known matters, with some details thrown in for good measure.

More commonly, a story will begin with the appearance of a "client." The situation that serves as the basis for his or her appearance is quite prosaic. For example:

He had risen from his chair, and was standing between the parted blinds, gazing down into the dull, neutral-tinted London street. Looking over his shoulder I saw that on the pavement opposite there stood a large woman with a heavy fur boa around her neck, and a large curling red feather in a broad-brimmed hat which was tilted in a coquettish Duchess-of-Devonshire fashion over her ear. From under this great panoply she peeped up in a nervous, hesitating fashion at our windows, while her body oscillated backwards and forwards, and her fingers fidgeted with her glove buttons. Suddenly, with a plunge, as of the swimmer who leaves the bank, she hurried across the road, and we heard the sharp clang of the bell.

"I have seen those symptoms before," said Holmes, throwing his cigarette into the fire. "Oscillation upon the pavement always means an *affaire du cœur.* She would like advice, but is not sure that the matter is not too delicate for communication. And yet even here we may discriminate. When a woman has been seriously wronged by a man she no longer oscillates, and the usual symptom is a broken bell wire. Here we may take it that there is a love matter, but that the maiden is not so much angry as perplexed, or grieved. But here she comes in person to resolve our doubts." ("A Case of Identity")

Here is another example:

"Holmes," said I, as I stood one morning in our bow-window looking down the street, "here is a madman coming along. It seems rather sad that his relatives should allow him to come out alone."

My friend rose lazily from his arm-chair, and stood with his hands in the pockets of his dressing-gown, looking over my shoulder. It was a bright, crisp February morning, and the snow of the day before still lay deep upon the ground, shimmering brightly in the wintry sun. Down the centre of Baker Street it had been ploughed into a brown crumbly band by the traffic, but at either side and on the heaped-up edges of the footpaths it still lay as white as when it fell. The grey pavement had been cleaned and scraped, but was still dangerously slippery, so that there were fewer passengers than usual. Indeed, from the direction of the Metropolitan station no one was coming save the single gentleman whose eccentric conduct had drawn my attention.

He was a man of about fifty, tall, portly, and imposing, with a massive, strongly marked face and a commanding figure. He was dressed in a sombre yet rich style, in black frock-coat, shining hat, neat brown gaiters, and well-cut pearl-grey trousers. Yet his actions were in absurd contrast to the dignity of his dress and features, for he was running hard, with occasional little springs, such as a weary man gives who is little accustomed to set any tax upon his legs. As he ran he jerked his hands up and down, waggled his head, and writhed his face into the most extraordinary contortions. ("The Adventure of the Beryl Coronet")

As you can see, there is precious little variety in these excerpts. And let's not forget that both passages come from the same volume.

Before reproaching Conan Doyle, however, let us devote a little time to the question: what does Doyle need Dr. Watson for?

Dr. Watson plays a dual role.

First, as the narrator, Watson tells us about Sherlock Holmes and conveys to us his expectation of the latter's decision, while he himself is not privy to the detective's mental process. Only from time to time does Sherlock Holmes share some of his tentative decisions with his friend.

In this way, Watson serves to retard the action while at the same time directing the flow of events into separate channels. He could have been replaced in this case by a special arrangement of the story in the form of chapters.

Secondly, Watson is necessary as the "eternal fool" (this term is, of course, rather crude, and I do not insist on making it a permanent part of the theory of prose). In this respect, he shares the fate of Inspector Lestrade, about whom more later.

Watson misconstrues the meaning of the evidence presented to him by Sherlock Holmes, allowing the latter to correct him.

Watson also serves as a motivation for a false resolution.

In addition, Watson carries on a dialogue with Holmes, answers the latter's queries, etc., that is, he plays the role of a servant boy who picks up after his master.

When a client pays a visit to Sherlock Holmes, he or she usually relates to him, in great detail, the full circumstances of the case. However, when such a storyteller is absent, that is, when, for example, Holmes is out on a call, then Holmes himself relates the details of the case to Watson.

Holmes loves to dumbfound his visitors (and Watson too) with his omniscience.

Holmes's devices of analysis hardly ever vary: in three out of the twelve stories under consideration, Sherlock Holmes singles out the sleeve:

"There is no mystery, my dear madam," said he, smiling. "The left arm of your jacket is spattered with mud in no less than seven places. The marks are perfectly fresh. There is no vehicle save a dog-cart which throws up mud in that way, and then only when you sit on the left-hand side of the driver." ("The Adventure of the Speckled Band")

Elsewhere Holmes adds:

"My first glance is always at a woman's sleeve. In a man it is perhaps better first to take the knee of the trouser. As you observe, this woman had plush upon her sleeves, which is a most useful material for showing traces. The double line a little above the wrist, where the typewritist presses against the table, was beautifully defined. The sewing-machine, of the hand type, leaves a similar mark, but only on the left arm, and on the side of it farthest from the thumb, instead of being right across the broadest part, as this was. I then glanced at her face, and observing the dint of a pince-nez at either side of her nose, I ventured a remark upon short sight and type-writing, which seemed to surprise her." ("A Case of Identity")

In another story, "The Red-Headed League," Holmes astounds his client by pointing out that he, the client, had been doing a lot of writing recently:

"Ah, of course, I forgot that. But the writing?"
"What else can be indicated by that right cuff so very shiny for five inches, and the left one with the smooth patch near the elbow where you rest it upon the desk."

This monotonous technique is explained, most likely, by the fact that these stories appeared in print in succession. The author could not clearly remember, apparently, that he had already used this device before. Yet, we must state as a generalization that self-repetition is far more common in literature than is commonly supposed.

The mystery device is sometimes implanted in the body of a novel in the way leading characters express themselves and in the author's comments on them. I will endeavor to demonstrate this in Dickens.

Conan Doyle's Sherlock Holmes expresses himself mysteriously on occasion. This mysteriousness is sometimes achieved by obliqueness (i.e., by a simple indirection).

The Inspector asks Holmes whether he plans to visit the scene of the crime:

"It was very nice and complimentary of you," Holmes answered. "It is entirely a question of barometric pressure."

Lestrade looked startled. "I do not quite follow," he said. ("The Boscombe Valley Mystery")

This indirection means: "If it doesn't rain."

Conan Doyle thought this passage important enough to be included in the story, even though it has no significance in the unfolding plot. Yet, in order to make use of this device, the author leaves Sherlock Holmes in the hotel. Holmes, therefore, has even more reasons than before to feel angry: " 'Oh, how simple it would all have been had I been here before they came like a herd of buffalo, and wallowed all over it' " (ibid.).

Apart from Doyle's desire to show off Sherlock Holmes's wit and to demonstrate his prudence, the awkward delay in the hotel also enables the author to introduce certain analytical conversations into his story.

In "The Adventure of the Speckled Band" the story is told in two parts. The first part tells of the cause of the crime. This is, so to speak, a summary. In the second part we are given the crime itself, and in great detail, at that.

I shall now tell the beginning of this story in excerpts. This is the story of the death of a woman as told by her sister. Since I am not writing a mystery story myself in these pages, I shall provide a preface to the deposition.

In the excerpts below you will find certain clues, whose purpose in each case is clearly to create a false resolution. Other instructions are given not directly but in passing (i.e., in subordinate clauses, on which the storyteller does not dwell, but which are nonetheless of major importance). And so a word of caution.

Excerpt 1: Material for a false resolution.

Excerpt 2: A vague clue as to the method used by the culprit to commit the crime.

Excerpt 3: The beginning of this passage includes an important clue concerning the circumstances of the crime. This clue is intentionally placed in the oblique form of a subordinate clause.

Excerpt 4: Details of the murder.

Excerpt 5: Same.

Excerpt 6: The words of the deceased are given in such a way as to support a false resolution (as if the woman were killed by gypsies).

In the opening of the story we discover certain pieces of information pointing, it seems, to the stepfather as the culprit. This part is fully motivated.

(1) "He had no friends at all save the wandering gipsies, and he would give these vagabonds leave to encamp upon the few acres of bramble-covered land which represent the family estate, and would accept in return the hospitality of their tents, wandering away with them sometimes for weeks on end."

(2) "He has a passion also for Indian animals, which are sent over to him by a correspondent, and he has at this moment a cheetah and a baboon, which wander freely over his grounds, and are feared by the villagers almost as much as their master."

(3-4) "The windows of the three rooms open out upon the lawn. That fatal night Dr. Roylott had gone to his room early, though we knew that he had not retired to rest, for my sister was troubled by the smell of the strong Indian cigars which it was his custom to smoke. She left her room, therefore, and came into mine, where she sat for some time, chatting about her approaching wedding. At eleven o'clock she rose to leave me but she paused at the door and looked back.

" 'Tell me, Helen,' said she, 'have you ever heard anyone whistle in the dead of night?'

" 'Never,' said I.

" 'I suppose that you could not possibly whistle yourself in your sleep?'

" 'Certainly not. But why?'

" 'Because during the last few nights I have always, about three in the morning, heard a low clear whistle. I am a light sleeper, and it has awakened me. I cannot tell where it came from—perhaps from the next room, perhaps from the lawn. I thought that I would just ask you whether you had heard it.'

" 'No, I have not. It must be those wretched gipsies in the plantation.' "

(5) "As I opened my door I seemed to hear a low whistle, such as my sister described, and a few moments later a clanging sound, as if a mass of metal had fallen."

(6) "At first I thought that she had not recognized me, but as I bent over her she suddenly shrieked out in a voice which I shall never forget, 'Oh, my God! Helen! It was the band! The speckled band!' . . . It is certain, therefore, that my sister was quite alone when she met her end. Besides, there were no marks of any violence upon her."

The point is that in English the word "band" is a homonym (i.e., it has two meanings: a "ribbon" and a "gang"). The existence of two possible interpretations of this word are evident from the subsequent dialogue.

"Ah, and what did you gather from this allusion to a band—a speckled band?"

"Sometimes I have thought that it was merely the wild talk of delirium, sometimes that it may have referred to some band of people, perhaps to these very gipsies in the plantation. I do not know whether the spotted handkerchiefs which so many of them wear over their heads might have suggested the strange adjective which she used."

Holmes shook his head like a man who is far from being satisfied.

This use of a homonym is common in Conan Doyle. The following passage from "The Boscombe Valley Mystery" is built on the same principle:

"The Coroner: Did your father make any statement to you before he died?
"Witness: He mumbled a few words, but I could only catch some allusion to a rat. . . ."

Holmes suggests quite a different meaning for this word:

"What of the rat, then?"
Sherlock Holmes took a folded paper from his pocket and flattened it out on the table. "This is a map of the Colony of Victoria," he said. "I wired to Bristol for it last night." He put his hand over part of the map. "What do you read?" he asked.
"ARAT," I read.
"And now?" He raised his hand.
"BALLARAT."
"Quite so. That was the word the man uttered, and of which his son only caught the last two syllables. He was trying to utter the name of his murderer. So-and-so of Ballarat."

It would be easy to cite several such examples from Conan Doyle alone. The device is common enough. Jules Verne makes use of the semantic differences between languages in *Children of Captain Grant.* A mysterious document, hidden in a bottle and partially effaced by the water, is interpreted in several very different ways, depending upon the meaning that is assigned to the words jotted down by the traveler in his native tongue. The correct resolution of this puzzle is complicated by the fact that this traveler refers to the sight of the shipwreck by a geographic synonym (the island of Tabor).

Those of you who care to can easily find parallels elsewhere.

As you can see, it all comes down to this: Is it possible to lower two perpendiculars from one point onto the same line?

The writer looks for a case where two incongruous things overlap, at least in one respect. Of course, even in detective stories this coincidence often takes the form of something quite other than a word. In *The Innocence of Father Brown,* Chesterton employs as a device the coincidence of a gentleman's dress coat with the uniform of a valet.

But I digress.

Such hints, warning of a possible resolution and investing it with greater verisimilitude when it does take place, are quite common in mystery novels. In Conan Doyle's "The Man with the Twisted Lip," a man dons the attire of a beggar in order to collect alms. A series of none-too-complicated coincidences leads to St. Clair's arrest in his professional disguise. The beggar is charged with his own murder.

Sherlock Holmes investigates the case but comes up with a false resolution. The point is that St. Clair has been declared missing, while in the canal not far from the site of the alleged murder, a dress coat is found, whose pockets are crammed with coins.

Sherlock Holmes constructs a new hypothesis:

"No, sir, but the facts might be met speciously enough. Suppose that this man Boone had thrust Neville St. Clair through the window, there is no human eye which could have seen the deed. What would he do then? It would of course instantly strike him that he must get rid of the tell-tale garments. He would seize the coat then, and be in the act of throwing it out when it would occur to him that it would swim and not sink. He has little time, for he had heard the scuffle downstairs when the wife tried to force her way up, and perhaps he has already heard from his Lascar confederate that the police are hurrying up the street. There is not an instant to be lost. He rushes to some secret hoard, where he has accumulated the fruits of his beggary, and he stuffs all the coins upon which he can lay his hands into the pockets to make sure of the coat's sinking. He throws it out, and would have done the same with the other garments had not he heard the rush of steps below, and only just had time to close the window when the police appeared."

This is a false resolution.

Meanwhile, the identity of St. Clair and Boone is alluded to in the following manner: During their search of Boone's apartment, the police discover traces of blood on the windowsill as well as on the wooden floor. At the sight of blood Mrs. St. Clair faints, and the police send her home in a cab, since her presence is of no help in the investigation. Inspector Barton searches the premises thoroughly and finds nothing. He has made a mistake in not arresting Boone on the spot, thereby giving him the opportunity to talk the matter over with the Malaysian. Remembering their error in time, the police rectify it by arresting Boone and searching him. However, no incriminating evidence is found on his person. True, they find bloodstains on the right sleeve of his shirt, but he shows them a finger sporting a prominent cut. In all probability, he explains, those bloodstains on the windowsill came from this cut. After all he was walking towards the window when his finger started to bleed.

We see that the cut on Boone's finger is established indirectly. The main focus is on the windowsill with its bloodstains.

On the other hand, Mrs. St. Clair, speaking of her deep feelings for her husband, says:

"There is so keen a sympathy between us that I should know if evil came upon him. On the very day that I saw him last he cut himself in the bedroom, and yet I in the dining-room rushed upstairs instantly with the utmost certainty that something had happened."

The author lays stress on the fact that Mrs. St. Clair sensed that her husband had injured himself rather than on the injury itself. Meanwhile, a motive for identifying St. Clair with Boone is established, since both have cuts on their fingers.

These elements of coincidence, however, are given in incongruous forms. Here the author's purpose is not so much to supply a "recognition" as to give it verisimilitude after the fact: Chekhov says that if a story tells us that there is a gun on the wall, then subsequently that gun ought to shoot.

This motif, presented forcefully, changes over into what is called "inevitability" (Ibsen). This principle in its usual form corresponds in reality to the general principle of art. In a mystery novel, however, the gun that hangs on the wall does not fire. Another gun shoots instead.

It is very curious to observe the artist as he gradually prepares his material for just such a denouement. Let us take a distant example: In *Crime and Punishment*, Svidrigailov listens in on Raskolnikov's confession but does not inform on him. Svidrigailov represents a threat of a different nature.

However, it is quite uncomfortable for me to speak of Dostoevsky as a footnote to a chapter on Conan Doyle.

Before digressing, I had observed that the word "band" (by virtue of its dual meaning) as well as the reference to the gypsies prepare us for a false denouement. Sherlock Holmes says:

"When you combine the ideas of whistles at night, the presence of a band of gipsies who are on intimate terms with this old doctor, the fact that we have every reason to believe that the doctor has an interest in preventing his stepdaughter's marriage, the dying allusion to a band, and finally, the fact that Miss Helen Stoner heard a metallic clang, which might have been caused by one of those metal bars which secured the shutters falling back into their place, I think that there is good ground to think that the mystery may be cleared along those lines."

Obviously, the person responsible for this particular "false resolution" is Sherlock Holmes himself. This is explained by the fact that an official detective who usually constructs the false resolution is absent from "The Adventure of the Speckled Band" (precisely in this way Watson invariably misconstrues the evidence). Since this is so, it falls to Sherlock Holmes himself to commit the blunder.

The same holds for "The Man with the Twisted Lip."

One critic has explained the perennial failure on the part of the state investigator and the eternal victory of Conan Doyle's private detective by the confrontation existing between private capital and the public state.

I do not know whether Conan Doyle had any basis for pitting the English state against the English bourgeoisie. Yet I believe that if these stories were written by a writer living in a proletarian state, then, though himself a proletarian writer, he would still make use of an unsuccessful detective. Most likely, it is the state detective who would be victorious in such a case, while the private detective would no doubt be floundering in vain. In such a hypothetical story Sherlock Holmes would no doubt be working for the state while Lestrade would be engaged in private practice, but the structure of the story (the issue at hand) would not change. Let us now return to it.

Sherlock Holmes and his friend Watson, having traveled to the scene of the alleged crime, inspect the house.

They inspect the room of the deceased, where her sister, frightened for her life, now resides.

"Where does that bell communicate with?" he asked at last, pointing to a thick bell-rope which hung down beside the bed, the tassle actually lying upon the pillow.

"It goes to the housekeeper's room."

"It looks newer than the other things?"

"Yes, it was only put there a couple of years ago."

"Your sister asked for it, I suppose?"

"No, I never heard of her using it. We used always to get what we wanted for ourselves."

"Indeed, it seemed unnecessary to put so nice a bell-pull there. You will excuse me for a few minutes while I satisfy myself as to this floor." He threw himself down upon his face with his lens in his hand, and crawled swiftly backwards and forwards, examining minutely the cracks between the boards. Then he did the same with the woodwork with which the chamber was panelled. Finally he walked over to the bed, and spent some time in staring at it, and in running his eye up and down the wall. Finally he took the bell-rope in his hand and gave it a brisk tug.

"Why, it's a dummy," said he.

"Won't it ring?"

"No, it is not even attached to a wire. This is very interesting. You can see now that it is fastened to a hook just above where the little opening of the ventilator is."

"How very absurd! I never noticed that before."

"Very strange!" muttered Holmes, pulling at the rope. "There are one or two very singular points about this room. For example, what a fool a builder must be to open a ventilator into another room, when, with the same trouble, he might have communicated with the outside air!"

"That is also quite modern," said the lady.

"Done about the same time as the bell-rope," remarked Holmes.

"Yes, there were several little changes carried out about that time."

"They seem to have been of a most interesting character—dummy bell-ropes, and ventilators which do not ventilate."

We have three objects before us: (1) the bell, (2) the floor, (3) the ventilator. I would like to point out that Sherlock Holmes is speaking here only of a one in three chance, and the third one appears more in the form of a hint. See the first story concerning the crime, that is, the subordinate clause of the first point.

There follows an examination of the adjacent room belonging to the doctor.

Sherlock Holmes examines the room and asks, pointing to the safe that has survived the fire:

"There isn't a cat in it, for example?"

"No. What a strange idea!"

"Well, look at this!" He took up a small saucer of milk which stood on the top of it.

"No; we don't keep a cat. But there is a cheetah and a baboon."

"Ah, yes, of course! Well, a cheetah is just a big cat, and yet a saucer of milk does not go very far in satisfying its wants, I daresay. There is one point which I should wish to determine." He squatted down in front of the wooden chair, and examined the seat of it with the greatest attention.

"Thank you. That is quite settled," said he, rising and putting his lens in his pocket.

As you can see, Holmes's findings are not made known. He then examines the bed.

The results of this examination are also not immediately revealed, while our attention is first drawn to a plinth: "The object which had caught his eye was a small dog lash hung on one corner of the bed."

Sherlock Holmes's conversation with Watson follows.

Sherlock Holmes brings out the as-yet-unemphasized details concerning the ventilator and says what he had not said earlier, that is, that the bed is screwed down.

"I saw nothing remarkable save the bell-rope [says Watson], and what purpose that could answer I confess is more than I can imagine."

"You saw the ventilator, too?"

"Yes, but I do not think it is such a very unusual thing to have a small opening between two rooms. It was so small that a rat could hardly pass through."

"I knew that we should find a ventilator before ever we came to Stoke Moran."

"My dear Holmes!"

"Oh, yes, I did. You remember in her statement she said that her sister could smell Dr. Roylott's cigar. Now, of course that suggests at once that there must be a communication between the two rooms. It could only be a small one, or it would have been remarked upon at the coroner's inquiry. I deduced a ventilator."

"But what harm can there be in that?"

"Well, there is at least a curious coincidence of dates. A ventilator is made, a cord is hung, and a lady who sleeps in the bed dies. Does not that strike you?"

"I cannot as yet see any connection."

"Did you observe anything very peculiar about that bed?"

"No."

"It was clamped to the floor. Did you ever see a bed fastened like that before?"

"I cannot say that I have."

"The lady could not move her bed. It must always be in the same relative position to the ventilator and to the rope—for so we may call it, since it was clearly never meant for a bell-pull."

In this way, the new detail is first suggested and then connected to the other details of the story.

Ventilator, bell, bed. What remains unknown is what Holmes saw on the table and what is the significance of the rope.

Watson, as usual slow on the uptake, still does not understand. Holmes tells him nothing and consequently, tells us, who are separated from him by the narrator, nothing.

Sherlock Holmes in general does not bother to explain. He simply ends the matter with a flourish. But this flourish is preceded by our anticipation.

The detective and his friend are sitting in a room where a crime is anticipated. They have been waiting for a long time.

How shall I ever forget that dreadful vigil? I could not hear a sound, not even the drawing of a breath, and yet I knew that my companion sat open-eyed, within a few feet of me, in the same state of nervous tension in which I was myself. The shutters cut off the least ray of light, and we waited in absolute darkness. From outside came the occasional cry of a night-bird, and once at our very window a long drawn, cat-like whine, which told us that the cheetah was indeed at liberty. Far away we could hear the deep tones of the parish clock, which boomed out every quarter of an hour. How long they seemed, those quarters! Twelve o'clock, and one, and two, and three, and still we sat waiting silently for whatever might befall.

Suddenly there was the momentary gleam of a light up in the direction of the ventilator . . .

I don't want to criticize Conan Doyle. However, I must point out his custom of repeating not only plot schemata but also elements of their execution.

Let me adduce a parallel from "The Red-Headed League":

What a time it seemed! From comparing notes afterwards it was but an hour and a quarter, yet it appeared to me that the night must have almost gone, and the dawn be breaking above us. My limbs were weary and stiff, for I feared to change my position, yet my nerves were worked up to the highest pitch of tension, and my hearing was so acute that I could not only hear the gentle breathing of my companions, but I could distinguish the deeper, heavier in-breath of the bulky Jones from the thin sighing note of the bank director. From my position I could look over the case in the direction of the floor. Suddenly my eyes caught the glint of a light.

In both cases the waiting (an obvious case of the use of the device of retardation of action) ends with the commission of the crime.

The criminal lets loose a snake. The snake crawls along the string from the ventilator. Holmes strikes at the snake, and shortly afterwards a scream is heard. Holmes and his assistants run into the adjacent room:

It was a singular sight which met our eyes. On the table stood a dark lantern with the shutter half open, throwing a brilliant beam of light upon the iron safe, the door of which was ajar. Beside this table, on the wooden chair, sat Dr. Grimesby Roylott, clad in a long grey dressing-gown, his bare ankles protruding beneath, and his feet thrust into red heelless Turkish slippers. Across his lap lay the short stock with the long lash which we had noticed during the day. His chin was cocked upwards, and his eyes were fixed in a dreadful rigid stare at the corner of the ceiling. Round his brow he had a peculiar yellow band, with brownish speckles, which seemed to be bound tightly round his head. As we entered he made neither sound nor motion.

"The band! the speckled band!" whispered Holmes.

The pieces all begin to fall into place: the band on the face and finally the lash improvised from the loop that had been used. Here is Holmes's analysis:

"I had," said he, "come to an entirely erroneous conclusion, which shows, my dear Watson, how dangerous it always is to reason from insufficient data. The presence of the gipsies, and the use of the word 'band,' which was used by the poor girl, no doubt, to explain the appearance which she had caught a horrid glimpse of by the light of her match, were sufficient to put me upon an entirely wrong scent. I can only claim the merit that I instantly reconsidered my position when, however, it became clear to me that whatever danger threatened an occupant of the room could not come either from the window or the door. My attention was speedily drawn, as I have already remarked to you, to this ventilator, and to the bell-rope which hung down to the bed. The discovery that this was a dummy, and that the bed was clamped to the floor, instantly gave rise to the suspicion that the rope was there as a bridge for something passing through the hole, and coming to the bed. The idea of a snake instantly occurred to me, and when I coupled it with my knowledge that the Doctor was furnished with a supply of creatures from India, I felt that I was probably on the right track. The idea of using a form of poison which could not possibly be discovered by any chemical test was just such a one as would occur to a clever and ruthless man who had had an Eastern training. The rapidity with which such a poison would take effect would also, from his point of view, be an advantage. It would be a sharp-eyed coroner indeed who could distinguish the two little dark punctures which would show where the poison fangs had done their work. Then I thought of the whistle. Of course, he must recall the snake before the morning light revealed it to the victim. He had trained it, probably by the use of the milk which we saw, to return to him when summoned. He would put it through the ventilator at the hour that he thought best, with the certainty that it would crawl down the rope, and land on the bed. It might or might not bite the occupant, perhaps she might escape every night for a week, but sooner or later she must fall a victim.

"I had come to these conclusions before ever I had entered his room. An inspection of his chair showed me that he had been in the habit of standing on it, which, of course, would be necessary in order that he should reach the ventilator. The sight of the safe, the saucer of milk, and the loop of whipcord were enough to finally dispel any doubts which may have remained. The metallic clang heard by Miss Stoner was obviously caused by her father hastily closing the door of his safe upon its terrible occupant."

Of course all these devices are masked to one degree or another. Every novel assures us of its reality. It is a common practice for every writer to compare his story with "literature."

In Pushkin's *Ruslan and Lyudmila,* Lyudmila not only eats the fruits in Chernomor's garden, but she eats them while violating literary tradition: "She thought about it and began eating."

All the more so is this applicable to a detective novel, which tries to pass itself off as a document.

Watson says:

I walked down to the station with them, and then wandered through the streets of the little town, finally returning to the hotel, where I lay upon the sofa and tried to interest myself in a yellow-backed novel. The puny plot of the story was so thin, however, when compared to the deep mystery through which we were groping, and I found my attention wander so constantly from the fiction to the fact, that I at last flung it across the room, and gave myself up entirely to a consideration of the events of the day. ("The Boscombe Valley Mystery")

To this device of "make-believe" also belong (a) an allusion to other matters not ordinarily part of fiction and (b) suggestions that the publication of a given novel has been made possible due to the death of a certain woman.

The range of types in Conan Doyle is very limited. Of course, if we are to judge by the author's world renown, then perhaps he had no need for such diversity. From the standpoint of technique, the devices employed by Conan Doyle in his stories are, of course, simpler than the devices we find in other English mystery novels. On the other hand, they show greater concentration.

Crime and its consequences all but dominate the detective novel, while in Radcliffe and Dickens we always find descriptions of nature, psychological analyses, and so on. Conan Doyle rarely gives us a landscape and, when he does offer it, it is usually to remind us that nature is good while man is evil.

The general schema of Conan Doyle's stories is as follows:

1. Anticipation, conversation concerning previous cases, analysis.

2. The appearance of the client. The business part of the story.

3. Clues introduced into the story. The most important clues take the form of secondary facts, which are presented in such a way that the reader does not notice them. In addition, the author supplies us with material for a false resolution.

4. Watson misinterprets these clues.

5. A trip to the site of the crime, which very frequently has not even been committed yet. By this device, the story attains narrative vigor. The crime story is thereby incorporated into the detective novel. Evidence gathered at the scene of the crime.

6. The official detective offers a false resolution. If there is no official detective, then the false resolution is furnished by a newspaper, by a victim, or by Sherlock Holmes himself.

7. The interval is filled in by the reflections of Watson, who has no idea what is going on. Sherlock Holmes is smoking or else listening to music. Sometimes he classifies the facts by groups without hazarding a definitive conclusion.

8. The denouement is for the most part unexpected. For the denouement, Doyle makes frequent use of an attempted crime.

9. Analysis of the facts made by Sherlock Holmes.

This schema was not created by Conan Doyle, although it was not stolen by him, either. It is called forth by the very essence of the story. Let us compare it briefly with "The Gold Bug" by Edgar Allan Poe. (I assume this work is well known. If one of you readers does not know of it, then I congratulate you on the prospect of reading another good story.) I myself shall analyze this story so as not to miss out on the pleasure:

1. Exposition: a description of a friend.

2. A chance discovery of a document. The friend calls the protagonist's attention to its *reverse* side. (A common enough device even for Sherlock Holmes.)

3. Mysterious actions committed by friends, related by a Negro (Watson).

4. A search for the treasure. Failure due to an error on the part of the

Negro. (The usual device of braking the pace of the action. Compare the false resolution.)

5. The discovery of the treasure.

6. The friend's story with an analysis of the facts.

Everyone intent on studying the role of plot structures in Russian literature should pay close attention to Conan Doyle's use of clues and to the way the denouement emerges out of them.

# Chapter 6

# Dickens and the Mystery Novel

Everyone who has ever worked on riddles has probably had occasion to notice that a riddle usually allows not one but several solutions.

*A riddle is not merely a parallelism, one part of which has been omitted. Rather, it plays with the possibility of establishing a number of parallel structures.*

This is especially noticeable in erotic riddles.

In erotic riddles, play is evident in the displacement of an indecent image by a decent one. In this process, the first image is not eliminated but simply repressed.

D. Savodnikov makes the following observation concerning his riddle number 102:

Nearly all of the riddles having to do with a lock and a key are very ambiguous, and certain ones could not be admitted into this anthology. The number of such riddles is quite large, and we may boldly state that they are among those that are most widely known. Children tell these riddles without inhibitions. Young lads tell them with laughter, women and girls tell them in a whisper only. The latter case, however, is rare except for the kind of riddle where everything is called by its own name but from which, as in a song, the word has not been discarded. Instead, the storyteller warns his audience that the riddle is poorly told. The foundation for many of those riddles is most likely formed by mythic concepts and parallels, which have lost today their significance and meaning.

I'm in total disagreement with the latter assertion. At any rate, the necessity for such a hypothesis is not evident from the examples above.

A special type of riddle is represented by a riddle with a single solution of the Samson type: "From a poisonous thing emerges poison and from the strong emerges a sweet thing."

In these riddles the solution is usually provided by a single object known only to the storyteller. In fairy tales such a riddle, being the most difficult, is usually posed as the third in a series, or else it serves as an antiphonal riddle. At times it is resolved not by a verbal response but with a showing of the object. In Andersen for example, the queen's first question as to "what am I thinking about" is answered by the suitor when he shows her the chopped-off head of a troll.

Sometimes the riddle process begins with just such a riddle. Ivan the Fool poses the following riddle:

"I was riding on my father, sitting on my mother, directing my brother, and chasing my sister." The solution to the riddle: "My father gave me a horse, and so I rode my father. The saddle was paid for with my mother's money and the bridle was paid with my brother's money, and the riding crop was paid for with my sister's money." (*Belozero Tales,* no. 78)

A similar type of story about a single episode is presented by the riddle of Solomon's wife: "I'm sitting on the emperor but looking at the king."

In the well-known nomadic plot "The Emperor and the Abbot," the king asks the third question, "What am I thinking about?" to which the respondent (a teacher, worker, or psalm-reader) says: "You think you're addressing someone, but in reality you are talking to some *thing.*" Of the three tasks, the third has a single solution (false substitution).

Such a riddle, by its very essence, does not admit a solution. There's no way to guess at its meaning. There is no false riddle in it. It is interpreted against the background of the usual riddle.

One riddle of this type is already known to us. This is the riddle about the horse that was bought with papa's money.

Let me offer a second riddle:

Well, after spending the night at home, Ivan resolved to tell riddles again. Before doing so, Ivan, son of a peasant, washed himself with the sweat of a horse, dried himself with the mane of a horse and went off to meet her. She asks: "So why did you come, to tell riddles or to solve them?" "To tell riddles," said Ivan: "I sat on a horse, washed myself but not with the dew nor with water, and then dried myself but not with silk nor with a piece of cloth." Martha the queen was at a loss for words.

The second part follows with riddles of a totally different nature.

I would like to call your attention to the unique character of the first part of the riddle above. It is not to be found in riddle books. Such riddles remind us of Armenian riddles, which also do not admit of a solution and which have survived in the contemporary oral tradition. These riddles are understood against the background of the conventional riddle with a solution.


## Story Based on Error

As I've already said, the simplest form of plot construction is based on a progressive or step-by-step development. In such a development, each succeeding step is distinguished from the preceding one both in quality and quantity. Step-by-step construction usually results in a circular structure.

Let us take, for example, *Around the World in Eighty Days* by Jules Verne. Built on degrees of adventure, it is a circular story involving an error of one day lost when crossing the international date line.

In adventure novels the circular story is very often built on recognition.

In *Gil Blas,* one of the stories serves as a denouement. It is not distinguished in its structure from the others. Rather, the sense of the end is achieved in this novel by the change in the writer's attitude towards his hero. At the end of the novel we see Gil Blas (as was true of Lazarillo in the earlier picaresque novel *Lazarillo of Tormes*) married, settled, and evidently deceived. The author introduces a note of irony into his relationship with his hero.

Much more frequently, an error, such as the one at the heart of Jules Verne's novel above, becomes the basis for a framing story. For the sake of simplicity, let us first examine the "error" in the story, and then the "error" in the novel.

A great number of stories are built on "errors."

Let us take an example from the story of Chekhov:

*Given:* Both priests and socialists wear their hair long.

*Task:* Confuse their identities.

*Motivation:* The bathhouse.

In Maupassant, genuine precious stones become mixed up with counterfeit ones. Two possibilities arise:

(1) The counterfeit jewelry is mistaken for genuine. This is the story of "The Necklace." A young woman borrows a necklace from her female friend only to lose it. She purchases a similar necklace on credit and returns it. She then squanders her youth in an attempt to pay off the debt. It turns out that the necklace that she had borrowed from her friend was counterfeit.

(2) The genuine precious stones are mistaken for counterfeit ones. This is the case of "Jewels." A man and his wife are living happily. The wife suffers from one defect: a love for costume jewelry. The wife dies. Needing them, the husband decides to sell the jewelry for a song. They turn out to be the real thing. She was paid for her infidelities with them.

In folklore we often find that a son mistakes his mother and father, whom he has found in his bed, for his wife and her lover. He then kills them (the legend of Julian). In Chekhov, a husband lands in someone else's room and mistakes the sleeping residents for his wife and her lover.

Elsewhere, a brother, a son, or a husband are taken for lovers.

In love one seeks to conquer while another resists. The same holds for the battlefield, from which we get the usual image of the battle of the sexes:

> Oh staircase! You shall be the path,
> Along which my Romeo, handsome and fair,
> Intends to walk in the night to our marriage bed.
> Give me counsel! How am I to win this battle,
> In which I must lose my chastity.

This very same motif appears in Lucretius' *De rerum natura* and in Apuleius' *The Golden Ass.*

A reverse metaphor is common in folk poetry: the battlefield is compared to love or to a wedding (see *The Song of Igor's Campaign*).

People quarrel whether in love or war. It is possible to create parallels. In Maupassant, a parallel is given as a mistake. This is the short story "The

Crime of Good Uncle Bonnard." The old man mistakes the quarreling newlyweds for murderers.

A woman might find herself asleep with her own children. This is the basis for the following case of non-recognition:

> He arrives at his dwelling. He looks through the little windows located at the edge of the piece of land. A woman is sleeping with two young ones by her side next to a friend. He takes out a sword and is intent on cutting their heads off. "Threaten all you want but do not strike me." He raises his hand threateningly but without striking and enters his dwelling. He wakes up his wife and son, but she does not recognize him. He says: "Honey-dove, how many husbands do you have?" She says, "These are my sons." (from the same Onchukov 155, "Ivan the Unfortunate One")

Coming home to his wife, the husband sees her asleep with some young man. It is his own son.

In this way, the stories founded on error are similar to stories founded on puns. A pun is built on the customary meaning of a word, to which is added a new meaning and a justification for jumbling them up.

The motivation for both consists in the presence of a verbal sign that is shared by two distinct concepts.

In the story based on error the confusion of two given concepts is motivated by an external resemblance in circumstance that involves an ambiguous interpretation.

At bottom this is a mystery story and is therefore to be distinguished from the story based on parallelism.

The latter variety is typical, as I've already said, of Maupassant.

## Story Based on Parallelism

In a story built on parallel structure, we are dealing with a comparison of two objects.

For example, the destiny of a woman is compared with the destiny of a female dog or with the destiny of a doe that's been beaten, etc. This comparison is usually developed in two segments, in two independent stories, as it were, united often only by the presence of a single narrator or by the place of action.

There is no need for examples. Nearly the entire body of Maupassant's shorter fiction clearly illustrates this principle of construction.

In the mystery story and mystery novel, on the other hand, we're dealing not with a comparison of objects but with the displacement of one object by another.

When a story is expanded into a novel, the moment of denouement increasingly loses its meaning. Parallel structure holds dominance over the structure built on intersecting plot lines.

The possibility of extending the denouement while sustaining the mystery has led to the fact that mystery stories, in contrast to stories built on puns, are often chosen as a framing device.

In the history of the mystery novel, the denouement has gradually lost its significance, becoming awkward, hardly noticed and superfluous.

This technique of the mystery novel is opposed by the novel based on a purely parallel structure, where the author does not resort to the device of entanglement.

While Dostoevsky had recourse in his plots to the technique of the mystery novel, Tolstoi preferred pure parallelism.

Even in choosing a framing story, Tolstoi adopted a parallel structure based on a paradoxical correlation between one member of a parallelism and another. For example, let us look at *Hadji-Murad.*

The tale begins with a description of a field. The narrator is gathering flowers for a bouquet. The tempo is leisurely on purpose:

> I had gathered a large bouquet of flowers of all sorts and was now walking home when I noticed a wonderful crimson burdock in full bloom at the bottom of a ditch. It belonged to the species called amongst us the *Tartar,* which people go to great pains to cut down. When it is inadvertently cut down, it is thrown out of the hay wagon by the mowers lest they prick their fingers on it. Well, it occurred to me that I might want to pick this flower and place it in the very center of my bouquet. I lowered myself into the ditch and chased away a furry bumblebee which had fallen into a sweet and sluggish sleep within the arms of a flower. I then set out to get at the flower. However, this wasn't easy. As if it weren't enough that the stalk pricked and stabbed my hand on all sides after I had wrapped it in a handkerchief—it was so incredibly strong that even after five whole minutes and many a filament ripped off, I was still struggling with it. When I had finally managed to pluck the flower, the stalk was literally in pieces, and the flower no longer seemed that fresh and beautiful. Besides, on account of its coarse and disfigured state, it was no longer suitable for a bouquet of delicate flowers. I felt sorry that I had unjustly destroyed this flower which had looked so handsome in its place, so I threw it away. "And yet, what energy, what sheer tenacity," I thought to myself, as I recalled the efforts which I had expended in plucking this flower. How fiercely it defended itself, how dearly it made me pay for its life.

The narrator sees the shrub once again on his way home.

> When I approached nearer, I recognized in the little shrub that same Tartar whose flower I had so unjustly plucked and abandoned. The Tartar shrub consisted of three shoots. One had been torn off, with the disabled bough protruding from its base like an arm whose hand has been hacked off. One lonely flower remained standing on each of the other shoots. These flowers had once been red and were now black. One stalk, broken, drooped towards the ground, and the soiled flower hanging on its tip bent along with it. The third stalk, although smeared with rich black mud, still managed to protrude upward. You could see that the whole shrub had been run over by a wheel and had afterwards risen up and, for that reason, was presently lying twisted on its side. And yet it stood—as if a piece of its body had been ripped out of it, as if its insides had been ripped open, as if its hand had been cut off, as if its eyes had been gouged. And still it stands, refusing to surrender to the human being who had snuffed out the life of its siblings all around him.

"What energy," I thought to myself. "Man has conquered everything. He has laid low and destroyed millions of shrubs and yet this shrub refuses to surrender to him." And I recalled a recent incident from the Caucasus, part of which I had witnessed with my own eyes, part of which I had gathered from an eyewitness and part of which sprang out of my own imagination . . . Here is that story and how it came to be.

What follows is the story of Hadji-Murad covering approximately three hundred printed pages and followed by the concluding half of the framing device: "His death reminded me of the burdock crushed in the middle of the plowed field."

The correlation between the parts forming this particular parallel structure is most unusual. This parallelism is nevertheless very much felt thanks to Tolstoi's description of the burdock and thanks also to the play on words (burdock = Tartar). The concluding part of the parallel is deliberately simple. Yet, it effectively recapitulates the principal elements of the parallel: one burdock stubbornly holding out amidst a plowed field, one last uncompromising Circassian amidst his pacified compatriots. The stubborn struggle for existence is not repeated, but its presence can be felt.

# The Mystery Novel

In Ann Radcliffe, one of the founders of the mystery novel, the mysteries are constructed in the following way:

The heroine lands in a castle where she finds a half-decomposed corpse behind a curtain. While apparitions roam through the castle, someone speaks through the conversations of drunken cutthroats, etc. At the end of the novel, at the denouement. we discover that the corpse was really made of wax and had been placed there by the count's predecessor, the proprietor, by order of the pope, as a form of penance. The mysterious voice turns out to belong to a prisoner, who had been wandering through the castle by making use of secret passageways, etc.

As you can see, these explanations are only partially satisfactory, as one of Radcliffe's contemporaries said.

In the second part of the novel, the story begins all over again. A new castle, new mysterious voices. Subsequently, we learn that these are the voices of smugglers. The castle is engulfed in music. It turns out that this music was played at the time by a nun, etc.

I shall not attempt to list all of Radcliffe's secrets, since I do not have her book at hand.

Curiously, these mysteries initially present false resolutions (as in Dickens, for instance). We often suspect something far more horrible than we actually find. For example, in the second part of the novel, the author suggests in no uncertain terms the idea of incest. The whole affair unfolds by means of indecent songs with their indecent rhymes, taking the form, for instance, of the celebrated but rarely cited song entitled "In Knopp's Shop," and so on, concluding with the solution: "Don't think the worst . . . yellow gloves."

I would like to remind the reader that this device, as I've already pointed out, is canonical for Russian folk riddles of the type: "It hangs, swings back and forth. Everybody tries to get his hands on it." The solution: "It's a towel."

When solving these riddles, the storyteller usually introduces a pause suggesting the "false," obscene solution. Let me offer an example of how such a riddle evolves into a plot (from *Tales and Songs of the Belozero Region,* recorded by Boris and Yuri Sokolov).

The "bylitsa" or true story presented below was recorded by an old woman, recording no. 131. This bylitsa is of interest to us because the moment of false resolution is clearly observable in it. Its content is a game of riddles:

> There once was a young tailor who posed the following riddle: "A crow has lived two years. So what happens next?" I answer him: "He'll live another year." The tailor bursts out laughing at my guess. I then pose my own riddle to the tailor: "A man has no trade or occupation, a woman is covered with vegetation." The young tailor thinks of the worst case possible. No one seems to guess. So I tell them: "On the strip of land even bushes quickly grow, on the strip of land, on Mother Earth."

And so we see that the false solution is a very common element in the mystery story or mystery novel. The false solution is a true solution and provides the technique organizing the mystery. The moment of transition from one solution to another is the moment of the denouement. The inter-relationship of the parts composing the mystery is similar to that in plots founded on puns.

Characteristic of the mystery type is its kinship with the device of inversion, that is, rearrangement.

This type of mystery novel is usually represented by a story in reverse (i.e., in which the exposition of the present state of affairs is followed by an account of what has preceded it). We have a good example of this in the secret of the clocks in *Little Dorrit,* the mystery of the double, and so on.

On the other hand, the secret of the house and the secret of Dorrit's love for Clennam and of Clennam's love for Minnie is constructed without the use of inversion. Here the mystery is created by means of the exposition. A factual leitmotif and a metaphorical leitmotif form a parallel. Where, however, the mysteries are built on a transposition of cause and effect, such a parallel is achieved by introducing a false solution.

The organization of the mystery is very curious in Dickens's last novel, *Our Mutual Friend.*

The first secret is the secret of John Rokesmith. The author pretends to conceal from us the fact that John Rokesmith is none other than John Harmon. The second secret is Boffin's secret. We see how wealth has spoiled the "Golden Dustman," and we do not know that Boffin is pulling our leg. Dickens himself says that he never intended to conceal Rokesmith's real name from the reader.

The mystery of John Harmon is a dead end. It does not lead us to a solution of the mystery or even help us to notice Boffin's secret. The technical apparatus of this novel is exceedingly complex.

A direct heir of the mystery novel is represented by the detective novel in which the detective is none other than a professional solver of mysteries. A mystery is presented (e.g., a crime). This is followed usually by a false solution, for example, investigation by the police. Then, the murder is exposed in its true light. In a work of this type, inversion is mandatory, involving at times, in its more complex forms, the omission of individual elements.

Such is the structure (sans detective) of the mystery in *The Brothers Karamazov.* For a more detailed analysis of the technique of the mystery, I have chosen *Little Dorrit* by Dickens.

## Little Dorrit

Structurally, Dickens's novel moves simultaneously on several planes of action. The connection between the parallels is established either by involving the characters of one plot line in the actions of another plot line or by stationing them in the same place. Thus, we discover that the protagonists live within proximity to each other. So for example Clennam lives in the housing area called Bleeding Heart Yard, the home also of "the patriarch" and the Italian John Baptist. The story line of *Little Dorrit* consists of the following: (1) the love between Dorrit and Clennam, (2) the coming into wealth and the subsequent ruin of the Dorrits, and (3) the blackmail attempt by Rigaud, who threatens to expose Mrs. Clennam.

But a novel of this sort can only be told from the end. While we're reading the novel, we have before us a whole series of mysteries, not the least of which are the relationships among the protagonists which are also presented as mysteries. These mysteries are then interwoven with each other. We may distinguish the following mysteries which run through the entire work:

1. The mystery of the clock.

2. The mystery of the dreams.

These are the fundamental mysteries. They frame the plot but are in essence unresolved.

3. The mystery of Pancks (inheritance). This mystery is of a partial nature, that is, it does not run through the entire novel. It brings about an inequality between Clennam and Dorrit. It is based on an inversion.

4. The mystery of Merdle playing a similarly subsidiary role.

5. The mystery of noises in the house. It prepares the denouement of the first two secrets.

6. The mystery of the love of Dorrit and Clennam. It belongs to the central plot, but in its technique it represents the deployment of a negative parallelism.

## 1. The Secret of the Watch

*Chapter 3, "Home":* Arthur Clennam makes an appearance at his mother's house. Before us we see two or three books, a handkerchief, steel-rimmed glasses, a massive old-fashioned gold watch with a double case. Both mother and son are staring simultaneously at the gold watch:

"I see that you received the packet I sent you on my father's death, safely, mother."

"You see."

"I never knew my father to show so much anxiety on any subject, as that his watch should be sent straight to you."

"I keep it here as a remembrance of your father."

"It was not until the last, that he expressed the wish. When he could only put his hand upon it, and very indistinctly say to me 'your mother.' A moment before, I thought him wandering in his mind, as he had been for many hours—I think he had no consciousness of pain in his short illness—when I saw him turn himself in his bed and try to open it."

"Was your father, then, not wandering in his mind when he tried to open it?"

"No. He was quite sensible at that time."

Mrs. Clennam shook her head; whether in dismissal of the deceased or opposing herself to her son's opinion, was not clearly expressed.

"After my father's death I opened it myself, thinking there might be, for anything I knew, some memorandum there. However, as I need not tell you, mother, there was nothing but the old silk watch-paper worked in beads, which you found (no doubt) in its place between the cases, where I found and left it."

*Chapter 5, "Family Affairs":* We find the following:

"I want to ask you, mother, whether it ever occurred to you to suspect—"

At the word Suspect, she turned her eyes momentarily upon her son, with a dark frown. She then suffered them to seek the fire, as before; but with the frown fixed above them, as if the sculptor of old Egypt had indented it in the hard granite face, to frown for ages.

"—that he had any secret remembrance which caused him trouble of mind—remorse? Whether you ever observed anything in his conduct suggesting that; or ever spoke to him upon it, or ever heard him hint at such a thing?"

"I do not understand what kind of secret remembrance you mean to infer that your father was a prey to," she returned, after a silence. "You speak so mysteriously."

"Is it possible, mother," her son leaned forward to be the nearer to her while he whispered it, and laid his hand nervously upon her desk, "is it possible, mother, that he had unhappily wronged any one, and made no reparation?"

Looking at him wrathfully, she bent herself back in her chair to keep him further off, but gave him no reply.

"I am deeply sensible, mother, that if this thought has never at any time flashed upon you, it must seem cruel and unnatural in me, even in this confidence, to breathe it. But I cannot shake it off. Time and change (I have tried both before breaking silence) do nothing to wear it out. Remember, I was with my father. Remember, I saw his face when he gave the watch into my keeping, and struggled to express that he sent it, as a token you would understand, to you. Remember, I saw him at the last with the pencil in his failing hand, trying to write some word for you to read, but to which he could give no shape. The more remote and cruel this vague suspicion that I have, the stronger the circumstances that could give it any semblance of probability to me. For Heaven's sake, let us examine sacredly whether there is any wrong entrusted to us to set right. No one can help towards it, mother, but you."

Towards the end of the chapter, Dickens hints that this mystery may have something to do with the little seamstress of *Little Dorrit.*

*Chapter 29, "Mrs. Flintwinch Goes on Dreaming":* The riddle of the watch continues to be tangled up with the riddle of Little Dorrit. Little Dorrit tells the story of her life to Arthur's mother:

"Yes, ma'am; indeed it is. I have been here many a time when, but for you and the work you gave me, we should have wanted everything."

"We," repeated Mrs. Clennam, looking towards the watch, once her dead husband's . . .

*Chapter 30, "The Word of a Gentleman":* Rigaud appears at the house, obviously intent on blackmail. He doesn't say anything directly, but takes the watch into his hands. " 'A fine old-fashioned watch,' he said, taking it in his hand," and so forth.

*Chapter 8, "The Lock":* Clennam imagines that his mother is speaking to him: "He has decayed in his prison; I in mine. I have paid the penalty."

*Chapter 15, "Mrs. Flintwinch Has Another Dream":*

"None of your nonsense with me," said Mr. Flintwinch, "I won't take it from you."
Mrs. Flintwinch dreamed that she stood behind the door, which was just ajar, and most distinctly heard her husband say these bold words.
"Flintwinch," returned Mrs. Clennam, in her usual strong low voice, "there is a demon of anger in you. Guard against it."

*Chapter 23, "Machinery in Motion":* "Alone, again, Clennam became a prey to his old doubts in reference to his mother and Little Dorrit, and revolved the old thoughts and suspicions."

Naturally, the riddles are interspersed throughout the novel rather than being developed throughout. In addition, the novel includes "chapters descriptive of manners and life," in which secrets are used for the purpose of binding the parts.

So, for example, chapters 6 and 7, containing a description of the Dorrit household, introduce no new secrets. The compositional role of these chapters is to impede the progress of the novel. If we insist on seeing these chapters as the core of the novel, then we must insist also that they bear the full brunt of the plot when squeezed by the framing vise of the riddle. The descriptive chapters conclude with Dickens's usual recapitulating images, for example, the image of "the shadow of the wall."

The Circumlocutions Office and the Polips family are similarly described. These parts of the novel would have been called by Tolstoi "details."

Let us now turn to the following riddles.

## 2. The Riddle of the Dreams

*Chapter 4, "Mrs. Flintwinch Has a Dream":*

Having got her mistress into bed, lighted her lamp, and given her good-night, Mrs. Flintwinch went to roost as usual, saving that her lord had not yet appeared. It was her lord himself who became—unlike the last theme in the mind, according to the observation of most philosophers—the subject of Mrs. Flintwinch's dream.

It seemed to her that she awoke, after sleeping some hours, and found Jeremiah not yet abed. That she looked at the candle she had left burning, and, measuring the time like King Alfred the Great, was confirmed by its wasted state in her belief that she had been asleep for some considerable period. That she arose thereupon, muffled herself up in her wrapper, put on her shoes, and went out on the staircase, much surprised, to look for Jeremiah.

The staircase was as wooden and solid as need be, and Affery went straight down it without any of those deviations peculiar to dreams. . . . She expected to see Jeremiah fast asleep or in a fit, but he was calmly seated in a chair, awake, and in his usual health. But what—hey?—Lord forgive us!—Mrs. Flintwinch muttered some ejaculation to this effect, and turned giddy.

For Mr. Flintwinch awake was watching Mr. Flintwinch asleep. . . . "And all friends round Saint Paul's." He [i.e., the double] emptied and put down the wine-glass half-way through this ancient civic toast, and took up the box.

In this way, two mysteries are introduced: (1) the mystery of the double and (2) the mystery of the box.

The end of the scene is very curious: Affery remains standing on the staircase, frightened to such an extent that she cannot resolve to enter the room:

Consequently, when he came up the staircase to bed, candle in hand, he came full upon her. He looked astonished, but said not a word. He kept his eyes upon her, and kept advancing; and she, completely under his influence, kept retiring before him. Thus, she walking backward and he walking forward, they came into their own room. They were no sooner shut in there, than Mr. Flintwinch took her by the throat, and shook her until she was black in the face.

"Why, Affery, woman—Affery!" said Mr. Flintwinch. "What have you been dreaming of? Wake up, wake up! What's the matter?"

Subsequently, Flintwinch tries to convince his wife that she has had a dream.

Compositionally speaking, this is the heart of the matter. Some of the mysterious scenes are presented by Dickens with the special motivation of eavesdropping at night. Since the dream resembles reality, a double construction is therefore possible, that is, "It's not reality. It's a dream."

Meanwhile, the true situation is given in a negative form. I could better demonstrate this situation to you by excerpting about twenty pages from the novel. But the expense of paper holds me back. This construction, utilizing the motivation of a dream, is quite common in literature. In folklore, for example, it takes the following form: A young girl lands in the house of hoodlums, sees them commit a murder and carries off the chopped-off hand of the victim. The ringleader of this gang later proposes to the young girl. During the wedding, she tells everything she knows. Everyone is convinced that she is describing a dream, but finally she shows the chopped-off hand in her possession. This motif also appears in parodic form in Zhukovsky's "Svetland," where the dream really turns out to be a dream.*

Subsequently, Affery confirms the first part of Dickens's negative parallel, that is, that the "dream" was "reality." The role of the "cut-off hand" serves as evidence for Rigaud.

*Chapter 15, "Mrs. Flintwinch Has Another Dream":* Her dream records a conversation between Clennam's mother and her servant, Mr. Flintwinch. This conversation concerns certain secrets.

In *chapter 30, "The Word of a Gentleman,"* the riddle is confirmed by the fact that Rigaud takes Mr. Flintwinch for someone else.

## 3. The Riddle of the Inheritance

*Chapter 23, "Machinery in Motion":* Most riddles are prepared for by some form of motivation. For example, in Edgar Allan Poe's "The Gold Bug" we encounter a man who loves to study codes. Generally speaking, the introduction of the character does not coincide with the beginning of the action. In this case, at the first appearance of Pancks, we discover that he has an interest in locating the heirs to escheated estates:

*Compare "The Priest's Wife and the Highway Robbers" (Onchukov, no. 83). A similar story, but recognition is achieved by revealing a chopped-off finger with a ring on it: "And it's as if she has a finger with a ring on it under her bed." "No! No! My sweet lady," says one of the brigands. She takes out the finger with the ring from her pocket and shows it to them. At this point the robber tries to flee but is seized by the people. Onchukov, "The Merchant's Daughter and the Highway Robbers," no. 13: The brigands were sitting in the chamber. The young girl describes everything that had happened to her in a dream that night as well as her encounter with the brigands. She reveals everything, and the brigands listen. At each word they say: "How wonderful, my lass. Your dream has turned into reality." The whole affair ends with a recognition that is brought about by a chopped-off ear.

"Mr. Clennam," he then began, "I am in want of information, sir."

"Connected with this firm?" asked Clennam.

"No," said Pancks.

"With what then, Mr. Pancks? That is to say, assuming that you want it of me."

"Yes, sir; yes, I want it of you," said Pancks, "if I can persuade you to furnish it. A, B, C, D. DA, DE, DI, DO. Dictionary order. Dorrit. That's the name, sir?"

Pancks poses a number of questions to Clennam without revealing his purpose (*chap. 24, "Fortune-Telling"*). Pancks arrives at the house of Clennam's mother and speaks with Little Dorrit. He tells her fortune by examining her hand, speaks to her about her past, about her father and about her uncle. He tells her that he sees himself involved in her destiny and calls himself a gypsy and a fortune-teller.

Such predictions and presentiments extend throughout the novel.

Compare, for instance, the presentiments in Stendhal and in *David Copperfield*. The riddle surrounding the inheritance is developed with sufficient consistency and continuity, in contrast to the riddle of the framing story (the secret identity of Arthur's mother). The subsequent chapter, *"Conspirators and Others,"* offers us a glimpse of a consultation by Rugg, a solicitor:

"There's a Church in London; I may as well take that. And a Family Bible; I may as well take that, too. That's two to me. Two to me," repeated Pancks, breathing hard over his cards. "Here's a Clerk at Durham for you, John, and an old seafaring gentleman at Dunstable for you, Mr. Rugg," etc.

Pancks appears momentarily in chapter 29 and utters, at most, just a few words: " 'Pancks the gipsy, fortune-telling.' "

The mystery surrounding the inheritance is resolved in *chapter 32, "More Fortune-Telling":*

"You are to understand"—snorted Pancks, feverishly unfolding papers, and speaking in short high-pressure blasts of sentences. "Where's the Pedigree? Where's Schedule number four, Mr. Rugg? Oh! all right! Here we are. — You are to understand that we are this very day virtually complete. We shan't be legally for a day or two. Call it at the outside a week. We've been at it, night and day, for I don't know how long. Mr. Rugg, you know how long? Never mind. Don't say. You'll only confuse me. You shall tell her, Mr. Clennam. Not till we give you leave. Where's that rough total, Mr. Rugg? Oh! Here we are! There, sir! That's what you'll have to break to her. That man's your Father of the Marshalsea!"

The excerpt above is preceded by a storm of joy which breaks upon Pancks, the source of which is not yet known to us.

The purpose of this secret is to create an inequality between Clennam and Little Dorrit: Dorrit is rich, Clennam is, relatively speaking, poor. The role of the secret in the unfolding of the details of the novel lies in this, that the descriptions of the Marshalsea Prison are interwoven with it.

## 4. Merdle's Secret

*Chapter 33, "Mrs. Merdle's Complaint":* Mr. Merdle is filthy rich. The novel unfolds in his shadow. He inspires a passion both in Dorrit, who has recently come into a fortune, and also in the hearts of the indigent residents of Bleeding Heart Yard. We find Merdle suffering from a certain mysterious illness. At first, the matter seems to be rather simple, but gradually a mystery emerges:

"Do I ever say I care about anything?" asked Mr. Merdle.

"Say? No! Nobody would attend to you if you did. But you show it."

"Show what? What do I show?" demanded Mr. Merdle hurriedly.

*Chapter 12 (book 2), "In Which a Great Patriotic Conference Is Holden":* "Mr. Merdle, his eyes fixed cowardly on the Chief Butler's boots and hesitating to look into the mirror of this terrifying creature's soul, informs him of his intention."

*Chapter 16, "Getting On":* " 'You know we may almost say we are related, sir,' said Mr. Merdle, curiously interested in the pattern of the carpet, 'and, therefore, you may consider me at your service.' "

*Chapter 24, "The Evening of a Long Day":* We again hear Merdle's enigmatic phrases. Fanny asks him whether her governess will receive anything at all from her father's will: " '*She* won't get anything,' said Mr. Merdle." He asks Fanny to hand him the penknife:

"Edmund," said Mrs. Sparkler, "open (now, very carefully, I beg and beseech, for you are so very awkward) the mother of pearl box on my little table there, and give Mr. Merdle the mother of pearl penknife."

"Thank you," said Mr. Merdle; "but if you have got one with a darker handle, I think I should prefer one with a darker handle."

"Tortoise-shell?"

"Thank you," said Mr. Merdle; "yes. I think I should prefer tortoise-shell." . . .

"I will forgive you, if you ink it."

"I'll undertake not to ink it," said Mr. Merdle.

The subsequent *chapter 25* bears the title *"The Chief Butler Resigns the Seals of Office."* The chapter is taken up with Merdle's suicide. His secret is revealed: he was a speculator, a bankrupt who had brought thousands of people to ruin:

The room was still hot, and the marble of the bath still warm; but, the face and figure were clammy to the touch. The white marble at the bottom of the bath was veined with a dreadful red. On the ledge at the side, were an empty laudanum-bottle and a tortoise-shell handled penknife—soiled, but not with ink.

And so the little mystery of the knife, soiled not with ink but with blood— a negative parallelism—closes the circle of Merdle's secret.

Merdle's secret serves the following purpose: by means of it, the author succeeds in comparing the circumstances of his protagonists. Dorrit is just as poor as Clennam. Her role in relation to the details of the novel consists of "tightening" the descriptive passages.

## 5. A Noise in the House

*Chapter 15, "Mrs. Flintwinch Has Another Dream":*

On a wintry afternoon at twilight, Mrs. Flintwinch, having been heavy all day, dreamed this dream:

She thought she was in the kitchen getting the kettle ready for tea, and was warming herself with her feet upon the fender and the skirt of her gown tucked up, before the collapsed fire in the middle of the grate, bordered on either hand by a deep cold, black ravine. She thought that as she sat thus, musing upon the question, whether life was not for some people a rather dull invention, she was frightened by a sudden noise behind her. She thought that she had been similarly frightened once last week, and that the noise was of a mysterious kind—a sound of rustling, and of three or four quick beats like a rapid step; while a shock or tremble was communicated to her heart, as if the step had shaken the floor, or even as if she had been touched by some awful hand. She thought that this revived within her, certain old fears of hers that the house was haunted; and that she flew up the kitchen stairs, without knowing how she got up, to be nearer company.

*Chapter 15, "Mrs. Flintwinch Has Another Dream":* " 'There, Jeremiah! Now! What's that noise!' " Afterwards the noise, if indeed it was a noise, comes to a stop.

*Chapter 29, "Mrs. Flintwinch Goes on Dreaming":* Rigaud enters the house:

"Now, my dear madam," he said, as he took back his cloak and threw it on, "if you'll have the goodness to— what the devil's that!"

The strangest of sounds. Evidently close at hand from the peculiar shock it communicated to the air, yet subdued as if it were far off. A tremble, a rumble, and a fall of some light dry matter.

*Chapter 17 (book 2), "Missing":*

At that moment, Mistress Affery (of course, the woman with the apron) dropped the candlestick she held, and cried out, "There! O good Lord! there it is again. Hark, Jeremiah! Now!"

If there were any sound at all, it was so slight that she must have fallen into a confirmed habit of listening for sounds; but, Mr. Dorrit believed he did hear a something, like the falling of dry leaves.

*Chapter 23 (book 2), "Mistress Affery Makes a Conditional Promise Respecting Her Dreams":* " 'I'll tell you then,' said Affery, after listening, 'that the first time he [Rigaud] ever come he heard the noises his own self.' "

On the following page, we're given a hint, though as yet we don't understand it, to the effect that the door to the house will not open, as if someone were holding it back.

Like the majority of secrets, the mystery of the house at first has a false resolution. The mystery of the watch is just now becoming clear. It turns out that Mrs. Clennam is most definitely not Arthur's mother. Arthur is the illegitimate son of his father's mistress, who was subsequently put away in a mental institution by Mrs. Clennam and her husband's uncle. The watch served as a reminder of the need for rectifying a wrong. Affery thinks that it was Arthur's mother who was put away in the madhouse. She says in *Chapter 30 (book 2), "Closing In":*

"Only promise me, that, if it's the poor thing that's kept here secretly, you'll let me take charge of her and be her nurse. Only promise me that, and never be afraid of me."

Mrs. Clennam stood still for an instant, at the height of her rapid haste, saying in stern amazement:

"Kept here? She has been dead a score of years and more. Ask Flintwinch—ask *him.* They can both tell you that she died when Arthur went abroad."

"So much the worse," said Affery, with a shiver, "for she haunts the house, then. Who else rustles about it, making signals by dropping dust so softly? Who else comes and goes, and marks the walls with long crooked touches, when we are all a-bed? Who else holds the door sometimes?"

As you can see, the scene having to do with the "noises" has already been set up. We are now close to the real solution of the secret: The house, slowly subsiding to the ground, threatens to collapse. But the reader doesn't know that as yet.

## Denouements

The chief mystery of the novel, that is, the mystery of the watch, has already been revealed. Likewise, the secret of Arthur's birth has also been disclosed. The secondary mysteries are now being resolved one by one. First on the agenda is the mystery of the house. In one stroke the novelist eliminates Rigaud, who has essentially been playing the auxiliary role of the man who knows the secret. When the secret is exposed, Rigaud is no longer needed.

Mrs. Clennam runs home with Little Dorrit. They enter the gate. *Chapter 31 (book 2), "Closed":*

They were in the gateway. Little Dorrit, with a piercing cry, held her back.

In one swift instant, the old house was before them, with the man lying smoking in the window; another thundering sound, and it heaved, surged outward, opened asunder in fifty places, collapsed, and fell. Deafened by the noise, stifled, choked, and blinded by the dust, they hid their faces and stood rooted to the spot. The dust storm, driving between them and the placid sky, parted for a moment and showed them the stars. As they looked up, wildly crying for help, the great pile of chimneys which was then alone left standing, like a tower in a whirlwind, rocked, broke, and hailed itself down upon the heap of ruin, as if every tumbling fragment were intent on burying the crushed wretch deeper. . . . The mystery of the noises was out now;

Affery, like greater people, had always been right in her facts, and always wrong in the theories she deduced from them.

It is curious that the device of the secret is prolonged by Dickens throughout *Little Dorrit.* This device is even extended to the events, the beginning of which take place in our presence. They too are given as mysteries.

Dorrit's love for Clennam and Clennam's love for Minnie are not presented in the form of simple description. Rather, they are presented as "mysteries."

Dickens speaks of this love, and yet he also seems to deny it.

Clennam is overjoyed at the fact that he is not in love at the very same time that he is, in fact, in love.

*Chapter 16, "Nobody's Weakness":* the following chapter utilizes the same device.

*Chapter 17, "Nobody's Rival,"* concludes in the following way:

> The rain fell heavily on the roof, and pattered on the ground, and dripped among the evergreens, and the leafless branches of the trees. The rain fell heavily, drearily. It was a night of tears.
>
> If Clennam had not decided against falling in love with Pet; if he had had the weakness to do it; if he had, little by little, persuaded himself to set all the earnestness of his nature, all the might of his hope, and all the wealth of his matured character, on that cast; if he had done this, and found that all was lost; he would have been, that night, unutterably miserable. As it was—
>
> As it was, the rain fell heavily, drearily.

The technique in this excerpt consists of the following: a false interpretation of Clennam's action is provided by Dickens. He is not in love, and his true attitude is given through the metaphor of the rain.

*Chapter 24, "Fortune-Telling":* Little Dorrit's love for Arthur Clennam is also presented in the form of a riddle. Little Dorrit tells Maggy a tale about a tiny little woman, who loved the shadow and who died without ever revealing the secret.

Dickens connects the riddle of Dorrit's love with the riddle of Pancks by the very title of the chapter:

> "Who's he, Little Mother?" said Maggy. She had joined her at the window and was leaning on her shoulder. "I see him come in and out often."
>
> "I have heard him called a fortune-teller," said Little Dorrit. "But I doubt if he could tell many people, even their past or present fortunes."
>
> "Couldn't have told the Princess hers?" said Maggy.
>
> Little Dorrit, looking musingly down into the dark valley of the prison, shook her head.
>
> "Nor the tiny woman hers?" said Maggy.
>
> "No," said Little Dorrit, with the sunset very bright upon her. "But let us come away from the window."

This device is similar to the one in the previous excerpt: the "sunset flush" on Little Dorrit's face is presented as if it meant "blushing with the excitement of hope." And the quote "let's move away from the window" is a false solution. "Flush" really means "turning red" because of the change in the light.

Maggy recalls the princess's secret in the presence of Clennam in *chapter 32, "More Fortune-Telling."* Clennam is conversing with Little Dorrit:

"So you said that day, upon the bridge. I thought of it much afterwards. Have you no secret you could entrust to me, with hope and comfort, if you would!"

"Secret? No, I have no secret," said Little Dorrit in some trouble.

They had been speaking in low voices: more because it was natural to what they said, to adopt that tone, than with any care to reserve it from Maggy at her work. All of a sudden Maggy stared again, and this time spoke:

"I say! Little Mother!"

"Yes, Maggy."

"If you an't got no secret of your own to tell him, tell him that about the Princess. *She* had a secret, you know."

Clennam understands nothing and tortures Little Dorrit by telling her that someday she will fall in love:

"It was the little woman as had the secret, and she was always a-spinning at her wheel. And so she says to her, why do you keep it there? And so, the t'other one says to her, no I don't; and so the t'other one says to her, yes you do; and then they both goes to the cupboard, and there it is. And she wouldn't go into the Hospital, and so she died. *You* know, Little Mother; tell him that. For it was a reg'lar good secret, that was!" cried Maggy, hugging herself.

Clennam is at a loss to understand. We're dealing here with a game that resembles the game of peripeteia in classical tragedy. The resolution of the mystery has already been prepared, but is not yet recognized by the protagonists.

Of real interest to us is the recognition utilized in *The Cricket on the Hearth.* The first hint at the old man's change of clothes after the hostess's fainting spell is given in the incoherent words of the nanny and of Momma:

"Did its mothers make it up a Beds then!" cried Miss Slowboy to the Baby; "and did its hair grow brown and curly, when its caps was lifted off, and frighten it, a precious Pets, a-sitting by the fires!"

With that unaccountable attraction of the mind to trifles, which is often incidental to a state of doubt and confusion, the Carrier, as he walked slowly to and fro, found himself mentally repeating even these absurd words, many times. So many times that he got them by heart, and was still conning them over and over, like a lesson, when Tilly, after administering as much friction to the little bald head with her hand as she thought wholesome (according to the practice of nurses), had once more tied the Baby's cap on.

"And frighten it, a precious Pets, a-sitting by the fires. What frightened Dot, I wonder!" mused the Carrier, pacing to and fro.

Here the resolution (change of dress) is presented, but not recognized. The incoherence of form (the plural number, etc.) serves as the motivation for the non-recognition.

On the stage and in the novel, it is the usual practice, indeed, it is always the practice, for the secret or recognition to be first alluded to in the form of a hint. For example, in *Our Mutual Friend,* the presence of the Boffin couple at the wedding of John Harmon and Bella is intimated by Dickens when he speaks of a certain noise in the annex to the church.

It is the custom in the theater for the man who has had a change of dress to reveal himself first to the audience and only then to the stage characters.

Very curious indeed is Chaplin's reversal of this device.

A crowd of people had been waiting for his appearance on stage, where he had promised to perform. One of the acts on the program called for a young man in tails to read a certain banal poem. A certain gentleman read the poem with impeccable taste and aplomb. Only when he turned his back to the audience and moved off stage, shuffling his feet in his inimitable way, did the audience recognize Chaplin.

This is very much analogous to the device of the spurious resolution.

A resolution is offered in the conversation carried on between John, who is in love with Dorrit, and Clennam, who has landed in debtors' prison.

*Chapter 27 (book 2), "The Pupil of the Marshalsea";*

"Mr. Clennam, do you mean to say that you don't know?"

"What, John?"

"Lord," said Young John, appealing with a gasp to the spikes on the wall. "He says, What!"

Clennam looked at the spikes, and looked at John; and looked at the spikes, and looked at John.

"He says What! And what is more," exclaimed Young John, surveying him in a doleful maze, "he appears to mean it! Do you see this window, sir?"

"Of course, I see this window."

"See this room?"

"Why, of course I see this room."

"That wall opposite, and that yard down below? They have all been witnesses of it, from day to day, from night to night. from week to week, from month to month. For, how often have I seen Miss Dorrit here when she has not seen me!"

"Witnesses of what?" said Clennam.

"Of Miss Dorrit's love."

"For whom?"

"You," said John.

But the semantic resolution does not yet unlock the verbal riddle:

The equation: Dorrit–Clennam (little woman–shadow) has not yet been solved. The "shadow" theme reappears in the words of Maggy.

Love has been openly declared, but Clennam rejects it. The inequality between them (as in the case of Eugene Onegin–Tatiana) has tilted in favor of Dorrit:

Maggy, who had fallen into very low spirits, here cried, "Oh get him into a hospital; do get him into a hospital, Mother! He'll never look like hisself again, if he an't got into a hospital. And then the little woman as was laways a-spinning at her wheel, she can go to the cupboard with the Princess and say, what do you keep the Chicking there for? (book 2, chap. 29)

Here the theme is complicated by Dickens's introduction of Maggy's delirium (she had been undergoing treatment in the hospital, and both the hospital and the chickens are her paradise). A similar device is used in *The Cricket on the Hearth*.

The resolution of the plot line, which may be called "The Love of Arthur and Dorrit and the Obstacles to Their Marriage," is presented, as you can see, in a rather trivial way by means of Merdle's secret. Old Man Dorrit had entrusted his entire fortune to this Merdle, and now Little Dorrit is ruined. And so by means of this turn of events their positions in society have become equal. And herein lies the resolution. What still remains to be solved is the framing mystery of the watch.

In Turgenev's *A Nest of the Gentry,* the inequality is expressed in the following way: Lavretsky cannot love Liza, because he's already married. He is released from his vows by the newspaper's report of his wife's death. His wife's return (the rumor of her death was false) restores the complication to the plot. Since the composition is not resolved, a spurious ending is required. An ending is spurious, in my opinion, when it introduces a new concluding motif as a parallel to the old one. The spurious ending of *A Nest of the Gentry* lies in the fact that Lavretsky is sitting on a bench, while "the young tribe is growing up."

In the case of Knut Hamsun, failure at love is presented entirely within the context of a psychological motivation. Lieutenant Glahn and Edvarda in *Pan* truly love each other, but whenever one says "yes," the other says "no." I do not mean to say, of course, that Hamsun's motivation or even that his entire composition is superior or more expertly done than that of Ariostovsky or Pushkin. It is simply different. Perhaps Hamsun's device will appear ludicrous with the years. Just as today, for instance, the attempt on the part of certain artists of the nineteenth century to conceal their technique appears equally odd to us.

## The Relationship among Members of a Parallelism As a Mystery

The device of several simultaneous planes of action, the relationship among which is not given immediately by the author, may be understood as a complication, as a peculiar continuation of the technique of the mystery.

So begins *Little Dorrit.* We are immediately confronted by two plot lines in this novel, the line of Rigaud and the line of Clennam, each of which is developed into a full chapter.

In the first chapter, entitled "Sun and Shadow," we encounter Mr. Rigaud and the Italian John Baptist. They are in prison—Rigaud on a charge of murder and John for smuggling. Rigaud is led out to face trial. The crowd, gathered around the prison house, is in an uproar and wants to tear him to pieces. Like his prison-mate, Rigaud himself is not a principal character in the novel.

This manner of beginning a novel with a minor character instead of with the chief protagonist is quite common in Dickens, and can be found in *Nicholas Nickleby, Oliver Twist, Our Mutual Friend,* and *Martin Chuzzlewit.*

Perhaps this device is connected with the technique of the riddle.

The second group of characters is given in the second chapter, entitled "Fellow-Travellers." This chapter is connected with the first chapter by the following phrase: " 'No more of yesterday's howling, over yonder, to-day, sir; is there?' "

*Little Dorrit* is a novel built on multiple levels. In order to connect these various planes, it was necessary for Dickens to connect the protagonists in some contrived way at the outset of the novel. Dickens selects for this purpose a place of quarantine. This quarantine corresponds to the tavern or monastery of story anthologies (see the *Heptameron* of Margaret of Navarre and the inn in *The Canterbury Tales*). At this quarantine we find gathered together Mr. and Mrs. Meagles, their daughter Minnie (Pet) and the servant Tattycoram (her story is about to be told), Mr. Clennam and Miss Wade.

The same holds for *Our Mutual Friend.* We have before us the first chapter, entitled "On the Look-out." Dickens introduces us here to Gaffer and to his daughter, who are towing a corpse attached to their boat. This chapter makes use of the device of the mystery, that is, we do not know precisely what these people on the boat are searching for, and the description of the corpse is presented obliquely:

> Lizzie shot ahead, and the other boat fell astern. Lizzie's father, composing himself into the easy attitude of one who had asserted the high moralities and taken an unassailable position, slowly lighted a pipe, and smoked, and took a survey of what he had in tow. What he had in tow lunged itself at him sometimes in an awful manner when the boat was checked, and sometimes seemed to try to wrench itself away, though for the most part it followed submissively. A neophyte might have fancied that the ripples passing over it were dreadfully like faint changes of expression on a sightless face; but Gaffer was no neophyte, and had no fancies.

It is worth comparing this description with the fishing scene in *A Tale of Two Cities.*

In the second chapter, "The Man from Somewhere," Dickens describes the home of the Veneerings and introduces us to the attorney Mortimer and to a whole social circle, which serves as a Greek chorus throughout the novel. Anna Pavlovna's salon does the same for *War and Peace.*

At the end of the second chapter, we discover its connection with the first: we discover that a certain person who is heir to a huge fortune has drowned, and we therefore connect his fate with the corpse towed by the boat.

In the third chapter, entitled "Another Man," Dickens introduces a new character by the name of Julius Handford. In the fifth chapter he brings in the Boffin family, and in the sixth chapter the Wilfer family. These plot lines are maintained all the way to the end of the novel, and they do not so much intersect as occasionally touch each other.

The plot lines of *A Tale of Two Cities* intersect even less. We perceive in this novel a transition from one plot line to another that is evidently foreign to it, as if it were a kind of riddle. The identification of the characters of the various plot lines is deferred to the middle of the novel.

At the present time, we're on the eve of a revival of the mystery novel. Interest in complex and entangling plot structures has grown greatly. For an example of a peculiarly distorted technique of the mystery, let us look at Andrei Bely.

It is interesting to observe in Andrei Bely a novel reincarnation of the technique of the riddle. I shall limit myself here to an example from *Kotik Letaev*.

This work presents the two planes of "swarm" and "form." While "swarm" stands for the effervescent *coming*-into-being of life, "form" stands for the actual life that has *already* "come into being."

This swarm is formed either by a series of metaphor leitmotivs or by puns. We begin first with swarm and proceed on to form, that is, we're dealing here with an inversion. The pun is presented as a riddle. At times we also find in Bely the technique of the mystery in its pure form.

See for example, "The Lion":

Among the strangest illusions which have passed like a haze before my eyes, the strangest one of all is the following: a shaggy mug of a lion looms before me, as the howling hour strikes. I see before me yellow mouths of sand, from which a rough woolen coat is calmly looking at me. And then I see a face, and a shout is heard: "Lion is coming."

In this strange incident, all of the sullenly flowing images are condensed for the first time: like a shaft of light, illuminating my labyrinths, they cut through the illusoriness of the darkness that had loomed over me. In the midst of the yellow areas of sunlight I recognize myself. It's a circle; along its edges are benches; on them are dark images of women, like the images of night. It's nannies, and around them in the light are children, hands clasped to the dark hems of their dresses. There is a curiosity of many noses in the air, and in midst of it all there is Lion. (Subsequently, I saw the yellow circle of sand between Arbat and Dog Square, and to this day you will see a circle of greenery, as you pass from Dog Square. You'll see nannies sitting in silence while children frolic all over the place.)

This is Bely's first hint of a resolution. Lion's image appears once again: "The huge head of a wild beast, a lion, starts crawling towards us from one circle of light to another. And once again everything has disappeared."

And now the resolution. Twenty years later, the author is talking to a friend at the university:

"I am describing my childhood: the old woman and the reptilian monsters. I am speaking of the little circle and of the lion and of his yellow mug . . ."

"Come on, now. This lion's mug of yours is pure fantasy." My friend laughs.

"Well, yes. It was a dream."

"No, it's not a dream. It's a fantasy. It's a cock and bull story . . ."

"But I *did* see this in a dream," I insisted.

"The point is that you *didn't* have the dream. What you saw, simply, was a St. Bernard."

"No, I saw 'Lion,' " I insisted again.

"Well, all right, so you saw a lion. But don't you mean Lion, the St. Bernard?" my friend pressed on.

"What do you mean?" I asked.

"I remember Lion. I remember that yellow mug . . . It wasn't a lion, but a dog," he hesitated. "Your lion's mug was a fantasy," he launched on an explanation. "It belonged to a St. Bernard by the name of Lion."

"But how do you know?" I asked.

"When I was a child," he recollected, "I used to live around Dog Square. They used to take me for a walk. There I saw Lion. . . . He was a good, kind dog. Sometimes he would run onto the playground, carrying a stick in his mouth. We were afraid of him and ran in all directions, screaming."

"And do you remember that shout, 'Lion is coming'?"

"Of course I do."

Later, Bely confirms the mystical sense of "Lion." That device is also not so extraordinary.

Bely commonly states the metaphorical or the fantastic leitmotiv after first bringing out the story line.

Sometimes this is followed by a second, definitive resolution.

Let me illustrate with two examples from Turgenev.

The resolutions of "Clara Milich" are constructed along the first type (a lock of hair in the hand): this is an irreducible remnant. The denouement's self denial.

The second case is represented by "Knock! Knock! Knock!" The first riddle of the "knock" is explained, but the riddle of the "name" remains unsolved.*

In Andrei Bely, we are dealing with the technique of the mystery in its purest form, as for example, in his *St. Petersburg*.

In the successors and imitators of Bely, particularly in Boris Pilnyak, we find the device of parallelism widely employed. However in this type of parallelism the relationship between the parallel planes is toned down and/or suppressed. These novels produce an impression of complex structure,

---

*One of the protagonists has heard someone's voice calling him. Then follows a second resolution, where Ilya, the peddler, a namesake of the protagonist, hears the voice of his girlfriend calling him from the kitchen garden, i.e., the mysterious "call" to Ilya, the officer now dead, from the woman he had once jilted, turns out to be pure fantasy. [Trans. note]

while in fact they're quite elementary. The relationship among the parts is presented either through the most elementary of devices (the kinship bond among the leading characters) or through an episodic participation of a leading character of one plane in the action of another plane. See "A Tale of Petersburg," "Ryazan-Apple," "The Blizzard." It is interesting to follow in Pilnyak the coalescence of the individual stories into a novel.

I am planning to write a separate work concerning contemporary Russian prose, and at this point I wish only to assert that in all probability the technique of the mystery will occupy an outstanding role in the novel of the future, since it already has made deep inroads into those novels that are constructed on the principle of parallelism.

The interest in plot keeps growing. The time when a Leo Tolstoi could begin a story with the device of death ("The Death of Ivan Ilyich") and not tell the reader "what happens next" is evidently over.

Tolstoi himself loved the works of Alexandre Dumas and understood the business of plot very well indeed, but his literary orientation was elsewhere.

In the mystery novel, the solution is as important as the riddle itself.

The riddle makes it possible for the writer to manipulate the exposition, to enstrange it, to capture the reader's attention. The main thing is not to allow the reader to find out what is in fact going on, because, once recognized, such a situation loses its horror. For this reason, in Maturin's novel *Melmoth the Wanderer,* we are kept in the dark throughout the exposition about Melmoth's secret proposals to various people in dire straits: to prisoners of the Inquisition, to people who, to stave off death from starvation, sell their own blood, to inmates of an insane asylum, to people who had strayed into subterranean caves, and so on. Every time the action approaches the actual moment of the proposal, the text comes to an abrupt halt (the novel consists of several sections, confusedly connected with each other).

For many novelists, the duty of solving the mystery is a burdensome tradition, but for the most part they do not resort to fantastic resolutions. If fantasy is introduced, then it is only at the very end, as the denouement unravels. The fantastic is then presented as a direct or, on rare occasions, as an attendant cause of the action. And, if so, then in a special form, for example, as a prediction that permits the novel to develop against the backdrop of a necessity thus posited.

We encounter the device of the fantastic in Lewis's *The Monk.* Among its protagonists are a devil accompanied by a lieutenant spirit and the apparition of a nun. In the last part of the book, the devil carries off the monk and reveals the entire intrigue to him.

This revelation of the intrigue is no accident in the novel. With his complex plot structures, not unraveled by action, Dickens has recourse all the time to these devices.

Thus is the secret of the watch exposed in *Little Dorrit.* In addition, it is again very typical that in order to elucidate it, Dickens gathers everyone in one room. This device is common to many novelists and has been parodied by Veniamin Kaverin in his "The Chronicle of the City of Leipzig for the Year 18—."

In Dickens, the protagonists are brought together quite literally against their will. So, for example, Rigaud is dragged before Clennam's mother, Pancks and John Baptist in *chapter 30 (book 2), "Closing In":*

"And now," said Mr. Pancks, whose eye had often stealthily wandered to the window-seat, and the stocking that was being mended there, "I've only one other word to say before I go. If Mr. Clennam was here—but unfortunately, though he has so far got the better of this fine gentleman as to return him to this place against his will, he is ill and in prison—ill and in prison, poor fellow—if he was here," said Mr. Pancks, taking one step aside towards the window-seat, and laying his right hand upon the stocking; "he would say, 'Affery, tell your dreams!'"

The denouement is brought about by having Affery tell her dreams. Dreams are a new ironic motivation with an enstrangement of the old device of eavesdropping.

In Dickens, eavesdropping is carried on by clerks (*Nicholas Nickleby*), and occasionally by the leading characters.

In Dostoevsky's *The Adolescent,* eavesdropping is presented as fortuitous. This is a renewal of the device.

The artificiality of the denouement in *Little Dorrit* lies in this, that it takes place without any outside witnesses. Characters tell each other what they already know all too well. We cannot consider Affery to be an audience for the other characters.

The denouement in *Our Mutual Friend* is more successfully organized. Again, everyone is brought together here. They all reveal a secret, the secret of the bottle. They throw Wegg out, and then they tell the story to John Harmon's wife all over again from the beginning.

The denouement of *Martin Chuzzlewit* is similarly organized. All the leading characters are assembled. Old man Martin (a hoaxer and director of his own novel) explains all the riddles he himself has been responsible for.

Let me now present the denouement of *Little Dorrit,* also from *chapter 30, "Closing In":*

The determined voice of Mrs. Clennam echoed "Stop!" Jeremiah had stopped already.
"It is closing in, Flintwinch."

The process of disposing of the riddles now begins.

First of all, we do not know what Rigaud needs from Clennam's house and why he had disappeared when he did, forcing everybody to search for him. It turns out that he had a secret, imposed a price on the secret, and when he was not paid for it he left the household for purposes of blackmail.

Rigaud takes Mrs. Clennam by the wrist and tells her the secret about a certain house. Unfortunately, Rigaud's story and Mrs. Clennam's revelation of the secrets of the house take approximately twenty-four pages of printed text and cannot be quoted in their entirety.

Mrs. Clennam's story is motivated by the fact that she does not want to hear her story from the mouth of a scoundrel.

Let me now turn to the analysis of the denouement.

First to be resolved are the dreams of Mrs. Flintwinch.

Rigaud tells the story of "a certain strange marriage, a certain strange mother," and so on.

Flintwinch is interrupted by Affery:

"Jeremiah, keep off from me! I've heerd in my dreams, of Arthur's father and his uncle. He's a-talking of them. It was before my time here; but I've heerd in my dreams that Arthur's father was a poor, irresolute, frightened chap, who had everything but his orphan life scared out of him when he was young, and that he had no voice in the choice of his wife even, but his uncle chose her."

Rigaud continues. A happy union is concluded . . .

"Soon, the lady makes a singular and exciting discovery. Thereupon full of anger, full of jealousy, full of vengeance, she forms—see you, madame!—a scheme of retribution, the weight of which she ingeniously forces her crushed husband to bear himself, as well as execute upon her enemy. What superior intelligence!"

"Keep off, Jeremiah!" cried the palpitating Affery, taking her apron from her mouth again. "But it was one of my dreams that you told her, when you quarrelled with her one winter evening at dusk—there she sits and you looking at her—that she oughtn't to have let Arthur when he came home, suspect his father only; . . ."

You see now the technique of interruption. Several secrets are woven together into one and resolved as one.

Mrs. Clennam speaks first. It turns out that Arthur is not her son, but the son of her husband's mistress. The mystery of the watch is revealed:

She turned the watch upon the table, and opened it, and, with an unsoftening face, looked at the worked letters within.
"They did *not* forget."

She "did not forget."
Simultaneously Little Dorrit's secret is revealed.

It turns out that the watch was sent to Mrs. Clennam as a reminder. Arthur's father's uncle repented on his deathbed and left, Rigaud says, " 'One thousand guineas to the little beauty you slowly hunted to death. One thousand guineas to the youngest daughter her patron might have at fifty, or (if he had none) brother's youngest daughter, on her coming of age, . . .' "

This brother was Frederick Dorrit, Little Dorrit's uncle.

I shall not continue to retell the novel and shall limit myself only to pointing out that the secret of the double is also resolved. The double turns out to be Mr. Flintwinch's brother.

We can now make the following observations.

As you can see, Little Dorrit's connection with Arthur's secret is tenuous at best. She is the niece of the protector of Arthur's mother. Her participation in the secret was purely formal, and not an active one. The very will and testament was counterfeit.

The secret in essence does not form a part of the plot. It is a supplement to the plot. The question of who Arthur is is, of course, very important to Arthur, but he never finds out about it.

*Chapter 34 (book 2), "Gone":* Mrs. Clennam hands over to Little Dorrit documents containing information that would reveal the secret.

Little Dorrit burns them by way of her husband:

"I want you to burn something for me."

"What?"

"Only this folded paper. If you will put it in the fire with your own hand, just as it is, my fancy will be gratified."

"Superstitious, darling Little Dorrit? Is it a charm?"

"It is anything you like best, my own," she answered, laughing with glistening eyes and standing on tiptoe to kiss him, "if you will only humour me when the fire burns up." . . .

"Does the charm want any words to be said?" asked Arthur, as he held the paper over the flame. "You can say (if you don't mind) 'I love you!' " answered Little Dorrit. So he said it, and the paper burned away.

The secret is woven into the entire novel, but it does not serve as a basis for the action itself. In essence, it is not revealed to the one person who is most uniquely concerned with it, that is, Arthur Clennam.

In essence, what Dickens needs here is not a secret but something mysterious to slow down the action.

Rigaud's secret is interwoven with the fundamental secret of "birth." Rigaud is the bearer of a secret. In accordance with the author's designs, he is involved in all the action. Yet even this is more a case of intention than realization.

Rigaud appears in the novel in the most varied situations, and it is interesting to see how Dickens emphasizes his connection with all of the leading characters.

*Chapter 1 (book 2), "Fellow-Travellers":*

Throwing back his head in emptying his glass, he cast his eyes upon the travellers' book, which lay on the piano, open, with pens and ink beside it, as if the night's names had been registered when he was absent. Taking it in his hand, he read these entries:

| William Dorrit, Esquire | |
|---|---|
| Frederick Dorrit, Esquire | And suite. |
| Edward Dorrit, Esquire | From |
| Miss Dorrit | France |
| Miss Amy Dorrit | to Italy. |
| Mrs. General | |

Mr. and Mrs. Henry Gowan. From France to Italy.

To which he added, in a small complicated hand, ending with a long lean flourish, not unlike a lasso thrown at all the rest of the names:

Blandois. Paris. From France to Italy.

And then, with his nose coming down over his moustache, and his moustache going up under his nose, repaired to his allotted cell.

This grimace is none other than a "superscription" made by the writer.

Rigaud simply adopted a new surname. Bringing him onto the stage, the author continues each time to apply the technique of the secret in every passage of the novel. It is as if he were applying makeup to the novel. But we recognize Rigaud either by the little ditty that he had picked up in prison, "Who Passes by This Road So Late?" or by his smile. The song is introduced in the first chapter of book 1:

> Who passes by this road so late?
> Compagnon de la Majolaine!
> Who passes by this road so late?
> Always gay!

At first this song is sung by the prison-keeper to his young daughter. John Baptist joins in:

> Of all the king's knights 'tis the flower,
> Compagnon de la Majolaine!
> Of all the king's knights 'tis the flower,
> Always gay!

Later, this song becomes Rigaud's song. We recognize him by it. The author has selected this song because it was "childlike" and at the same time "boastful." The braggadocio of the content corresponds to Rigaud's character, while the childlike character of the song, emphasized still further by the fact that it is first sung to a child, is necessary for contrast.

I fear making this analysis of the novel too exacting, of interest only to specialists. It is difficult for a nonspecialist (like myself) to illustrate the general laws of art in such minute detail. For I am not a showman but a *shower.*

Nonetheless, I will tell you one more detail. When Rigaud appears in his new role, the author at first shows his "secondary sign." No one can say whether he is handsome or ugly, and it is only later that the second sign is deployed, and it is at this moment of the second sign that recognition takes place (chapter 11).

Here we see the expression of the customary law of step-by-step construction in art.

Much the same can be said for the "noises in the house." By not allowing us time for a real resolution and confusing us with Affery's purposefully misleading resolution, Dickens produces new details: at first, simply a noise, then in succession the noise of something fragile falling, the rustling of dry material and the "noise of something reminiscent of falling leaves" (book 2). Subsequently, when the door fails to open, Affery offers her a false resolution: "They're hiding someone in the house." At the same time, though, new technical instructions are given in her own words that are very precise: ". . . who is . . . drawing lines on the wall?" This passage has to do with a description of the cracks on the wall.

Let us return to Rigaud, whom we have forgotten in our analysis of the novel's step-by-step construction. Rigaud himself is nothing more than a thief of documents. He is a passive bearer of a secret. He does not have "his own plot," as does Svidrigailov, who plays a similar role in *Crime and Punishment.*

An even more subsidiary role is played by Miss Wade.

What is the explanation for the success of the mystery novel, from Ann Radcliffe to Dickens?

This is the way I see the matter. The adventure novel had become obsolete. It was revived by satire. There are elements of the adventure novel in Swift (*Gulliver's Travels*) that play a purely ancillary role in the novel.

A time of crisis followed.

Fielding parodied the old novel in *Tom Jones* by presenting a hero of amoral character. Instead of the traditional loyalty expressed by the lover embarking on his adventures, we witness the merry escapades of Tom Jones.

Sterne composed a parody that was even more radical. He parodied the very structure of the novel by reviewing all of its devices. Simultaneously, a new, younger generation, aspiring to canonization, began its ascent.

It was Richardson who canonized the latter. According to legend, Richardson wanted to write a new manual of letter writing but ended up writing an epistolary novel instead.

At the same time, horror stories emerge on the scene, along with the Pinkertons of that age. We also meet with Ann Radcliffe and the mystery novel (Maturin).

The old novel tried to increase the range of its devices by introducing parallel intrigues.

In order to connect several intrigues, it was found convenient to use the technique of the mystery novel.

The final result was the complex plot structures of Dickens. The mystery novel allows us to interpolate into the work large chunks of everyday life, which, while serving the purpose of impeding the action, feel the pressure of the plot and are therefore perceived as a part of the artistic whole. Thus are the descriptions of the debtors' prison, the Circumlocution Office, and Bleeding Heart Yard incorporated into *Little Dorrit.* That is why the mystery novel was used as a "social novel."

At the present time, as I've indicated, the mystery technique is used by such young Russian writers as Pilnyak, Slonimsky (*Warsaw*), and by Veniamin Kaverin. In Kaverin we witness a "Dickensian" denouement with a list of all of the principal characters. However, this is not so much reminiscence as parody:

"Enough," I said, entering, at long last, into the shop. "What nonsense are you babbling here. I can't make heads or tails. And is there any sense in getting so excited over such a petty thing?"

I picked up a large lamp with a dark blue lampshade and lit its bright flame, so that I could look intently at those present one last time before saying good-bye.

"You'll get what you deserve for this! you hack!" Frau Bach grumbled. "What gives you the idea that you can act as if you were at home?!"

"Pipe down, Frau Bach!" I said with full composure. "I need to say a few words to all of you before bidding farewell."

I got up on the chair, waved my arms and said: "Attention, please!" Instantly, the faces of all present turned to me:

"Attention! This is the final chapter, my dear friends. Soon we shall have to part. I have come to love each and every one of you, and this separation shall be very hard on me. But time goes on, the plot is used up, and nothing could be more boring than to revive the statue, to turn it around, and then to marry him to the virtuous . . ."

"May I be so bold as to observe," a stranger interrupted me, "that it would be very helpful, my dear writer, to explain a number of things first."

"Yes?" I said, lifting my eyebrows in surprise. "Did anything seem unclear to you at the end?"

"If I may be so bold as to inquire," the stranger continued with a courteous but cunning smile. "I mean, what about the charlatan, who . . ."

"Tsh!" I interrupted him with a cautious whisper. "Please, not a word about the charlatan. Mum is the word. In your place, my dear friend, I would have asked why the professor fell silent."

"You threw into the envelope some kind of a poisonous drug," said Bor.

"How silly!" I replied, "You are a tedious young man, Robert Bor. The professor fell silent, because . . ." At this very instant, Bach's old wife put out the lamp. In the darkness I carefully climbed down from the chair, shook tenderly the hands of all present and walked out. ("The Chronicle of the City of Leipzig for the Year 18—")

We see here the laying bare of the Dickensian device. As in the case of the English writer, all of the protagonists are brought together. It is not, however, the characters who explain the action but the author himself. What we have before us is not a denouement, as such. Instead, the device for its resolution is pointed out. There is no real denouement because the source of motivation here is parody.

## Chapter 7

# The Novel as Parody:
# Sterne's *Tristram Shandy*

I do not intend in this chapter to analyze Laurence Sterne's novel. Rather, I shall use it in order to illustrate the general laws governing plot structure. Sterne was a radical revolutionary as far as form is concerned. It was typical of him to lay bare the device. The aesthetic form is presented without any motivation whatsoever, simply as is. The difference between the conventional novel and that of Sterne is analogous to the difference between a conventional poem with sonorous instrumentation and a Futurist poem composed in transrational language (*zaumnyi yazyk*). Nothing has as yet been written about Sterne, or if so, then only a few trivial comments.

Upon first picking up Sterne's *Tristram Shandy,* we are overwhelmed by a sense of chaos.

The action constantly breaks off, the author constantly returns to the beginning or leaps forward. The main plot, not immediately accessible, is constantly interrupted by dozens of pages filled with whimsical deliberations on the influence of a person's nose or name on his character or else with discussions of fortifications.

The book opens, as it were, in the spirit of autobiography, but soon it is deflected from its course by a description of the hero's birth. Nevertheless, our hero, pushed aside by material interpolated into the novel, cannot, it appears, get born.

*Tristram Shandy* turns into a description of one day. Let me quote Sterne himself:

> I will not finish that sentence till I have made an observation upon the strange state of affairs between the reader and myself, just as things stand at present——an observation never applicable before to any one biographical writer since the creation of the world, but to myself——and I believe will never hold good to any other, until its final destruction——and therefore, for the very novelty of it alone, it must be worth your worships attending to.
>
> I am this month one whole year older than I was this time twelve-month; and having got, as you perceive, almost into the middle of my fourth volume——and no farther than to my first day's life——'tis demonstrative that I have three hundred and sixty-four days more life to write just now, than when I first set out; so that instead of

advancing, as a common writer, in my work with what I have been doing at it——on the contrary, I am just thrown so many volumes back—— (285-86)*

But when you examine the structure of the book more closely, you perceive first of all that this disorder is intentional. There is method to Sterne's madness. It is as regular as a painting by Picasso.

Everything in the novel has been displaced and rearranged. The dedication to the book makes its appearance on page 25, even though it violates the three basic demands of a dedication, as regards content, form, and place.

The preface is no less unusual. It occupies nearly ten full printed pages, but it is found not in the beginning of the book but in volume 3, chapter 20, pages 192-203. The appearance of this preface is motivated by the fact that

All my heroes are off my hands; —— 'tis the first time I have had a moment to spare, —— and I'll make use of it, and write my preface.

Sterne pulls out all the stops in his ingenious attempt to confound the reader. As his crowning achievement, he transposes a number of chapters in *Tristram Shandy* (i.e., chapters 18 and 19 of volume 9 come after chapter 25). This is motivated by the fact that: "All I wish is, that it may be a lesson to the world, '*to let people tell their stories their own way*' " (633).

However, the rearrangement of the chapters merely lays bare another fundamental device by Sterne which impedes the action.

At first Sterne introduces an anecdote concerning a woman who interrupts the sexual act by asking a question (5).

This anecdote is worked into the narrative as follows: Tristram Shandy's father is intimate with his wife only on the first Sunday of every month, and we find him on that very evening winding the clock so as to get his domestic duties "out of the way at one time, and be no more plagued and pester'd with them the rest of the month" (8).

Thanks to this circumstance, an irresistible association has arisen in his wife's mind: as soon as she hears the winding of the clock, she is immediately reminded of something different, and vice versa (20). It is precisely with the question "*Pray, my dear, . . . have you not forgot to wind up the clock?*" (5) that Tristram's mother interrupts her husband's act.

This anecdote is preceded by a general discussion on the carelessness of parents (4-5), which is followed in turn by the question posed by his mother (5), which remains unrelated to anything at this point. We're at first under the impression that she has interrupted her husband's speech. Sterne plays with our error:

Good G---! cried my father, making an exclamation, but taking care to moderate his voice at the same time, —— "*Did ever woman, since the creation of the world,*

*Page references are to James A. Work's edition (Odyssey Press, 1940). Shklovsky used a Russian translation of *Tristram Shandy* that appeared in the journal *Panteon literatury* in 1892.

*interrupt a man with such a silly question?* Pray, what was your father saying?
——Nothing. (5)

This is followed (5-6) by a discussion of the homunculus (fetus), spiced up with anecdotal allusions to its right of protection under the law.

It is only on pages 8-9 that we receive an explanation of the strange punctuality practiced by our hero's father in his domestic affairs.

So, from the very beginning of the novel, we see in *Tristram Shandy* a displacement in time. Causes follow effects, the possibilities for false resolutions are prepared by the author himself. This is a perennial device in Sterne. The paronomastic motif of coitus, associated with a particular day, pervades the entire novel. Appearing from time to time, it serves to connect the various parts of this unusually complex masterpiece.

If we were to represent the matter schematically, it would take on the following form: the event itself would be symbolized by a cone, while the cause would be symbolized by its apex. In a conventional novel, such a cone is attached to the main plot line of the novel precisely by its apex. In Sterne, on the contrary, the cone is attached to the main plot line by its base. We are thus immediately thrust into a swarm of allusions and insinuations.

Such temporal transpositions are frequently met with in the poetics of the novel. Let us recall, for example, the temporal rearrangement in *A Nest of the Gentry,* which is motivated by Lavretsky's reminiscence. Or then again "Oblomov's Dream." Similarly, we encounter temporal transpositions without motivation in Gogol's *Dead Souls* (Chichikov's childhood and Tentetnikov's upbringing). In Sterne, however, this device pervades the entire work.

The exposition, the preparation of a given character comes only after we have already puzzled long and hard over some strange word or exclamation already uttered by this same character.

We are witnessing here a laying bare of the device. In *The Belkin Tales* (e.g., "The Shot"), Pushkin makes extensive use of temporal transposition. At first we see Silvio practicing at the shooting range, then we hear Silvio's story about the unfinished duel, then we meet the count, Silvio's adversary, and this is climaxed by the denouement. The various segments are given in the following sequence: 2 – 1 – 3. Yet this permutation is clearly motivated, while Sterne, on the contrary, lays bare the device. As I have already said, Sterne's transposition is an end in itself:

What I have to inform you, comes, I own, a little out of its due course; ——for it should have been told a hundred and fifty pages ago, but that I foresaw then 'twould come in pat hereafter, and be of more advantage here than elsewhere. (144)

In addition, Sterne lays bare the device by which he stitches the novel out of individual stories. He does so, in general, by manipulating the structure of his novel, and it is the consciousness of form through its violation that constitutes the content of the novel.

In my chapter on *Don Quixote* I have already noted several canonical devices for integrating tales into a novel.

Sterne makes use of new devices or, when using old ones, he does not conceal their conventionality. Rather, he plays with them by thrusting them to the fore.

In the conventional novel an inset story is interrupted by the main story. If the main story consists of two or more plots, then passages from them follow alternately, as in *Don Quixote,* where scenes of the hero's adventures at the duke's court alternate with scenes depicting Sancho Panza's governorship.

Zelinsky points out something completely contrary in Homer. He never depicts two simultaneous actions. Even if the course of events demands simultaneity, still they are presented in a causal sequence. The only simultaneity possible occurs when Homer shows us one protagonist in action, while alluding to another protagonist in his inactive state.

Sterne allows for simultaneity of action, but he parodies the deployment of the plot line and the intrusion of new material into it.

In the first part of the novel we are offered, as material for development, a description of Tristram Shandy's birth. This description occupies 276 pages, hardly any of which deals with the description of the birth itself. Instead, what is developed for the most part is the conversation between the father of our hero and Uncle Toby.

This is how the development takes place:

—— I wonder what's all that noise, and running backwards and forwards for, above stairs, quoth my father, addressing himself, after an hour and a half's silence, to my uncle Toby,——who you must know, was sitting on the opposite side of the fire, smoking his social pipe all the time, in mute contemplation of a new pair of black-plush-breeches which he had got on;——What can they be doing brother? quoth my father,——we can scarce hear ourselves talk.

I think, replied my uncle Toby, taking his pipe from his mouth, and striking the head of it two or three times upon the nail of his left thumb, as he began his sentence, ——I think, says he: ——But to enter rightly into my uncle Toby's sentiments upon this matter, you must be made to enter first a little into his character, the out-lines of which I shall just give you, and then the dialogue between him and my father will go on as well again. (63)

A discussion concerning inconstancy begins immediately thereafter. This discussion is so whimsical that the only way to convey it would be to literally transcribe it verbatim. On page 65 Sterne remembers: "But I forget my uncle Toby, whom all this while we have left knocking the ashes out of his tobacco pipe."

Conversations concerning Uncle Toby, along with a brief history of Aunt Dinah follow. On page 72 Sterne remembers: "I was just going, for example, to have given you the great out-lines of my uncle Toby's most whimsical character;——when my aunt Dinah and the coachman came a-cross us, and led us a vagary. . . ."

Unfortunately I cannot quote all of Sterne and shall therefore leap over a large part of the text:

> ... from the beginning of this, you see, I have constructed the main work and the adventitious parts of it with such intersections, and have so complicated and involved the digressive and progressive movements, one wheel within another, that the whole machine, in general, has been kept a-going;——and, what's more, it shall be kept a-going these forty years, if it pleases the fountain of health to bless me so long with life and good spirits. (73-74)

So ends chapter 22. It is followed by chapter 23: "I have a strong propensity in me to begin this chapter very nonsensically, and I will not balk my fancy.——Accordingly I set off thus."

We have before us new digressions.

On page 77 the author reminds us that: "If I was not morally sure that the reader must be out of all patience for my uncle Toby's character, . . ."

A page later begins a description of Uncle Toby's "Hobby-Horse" (i.e., his mania). It turns out that Uncle Toby, who was wounded in the groin at the siege of Namur, has a passion for building model fortresses. Finally, however, on page 99, Uncle Toby finishes the task he had started on page 63:

> I think, replied my uncle Toby,——taking, as I told you, his pipe from his mouth, and striking the ashes out of it as he began his sentence;——I think, replied he,——it would not be amiss, brother, if we rung the bell.

This device is constantly used by Sterne and, as is evident from his facetious reminders of Uncle Toby, he's not only aware of the hyperbolic nature of such development but plays with it.

This method of developing the action is, as I've already said, the norm for Sterne. Here's an example from page 144: "I wish, . . . you had seen what prodigious armies we had in Flanders." This is immediately followed by a development of the material concerned with the father's mania. The following manias are woven into the character of Tristram Shandy's father: the subject of the harmful effect of the pressure exerted on the baby's head by the mother's contractions during labor (149-54), the influence of a person's name on his character (this motif is developed in great detail), and the effect of the size of the nose on a person's faculties (this motif is developed with unusual magnificence from page 217 on). After a brief pause begins the development of the material concerned with the curious stories about noses. Especially remarkable is the story of Slawkenbergius. Tristram's father knows a full ten dozen stories by this man. The development of the theme of noseology concludes on page 272.

Mr. Shandy's first mania also plays a role in this development. That is, Sterne digresses in order to speak about it. The main plot returns on page 157:

"I wish, Dr. Slop," quoth my uncle Toby (repeating his wish for Dr. Slop a second time, and with a degree of more zeal and earnestness in his manner of wishing, than he had wished it at first)——"I wish, Dr. Slop," quoth my uncle Toby, *"you had seen what prodigious armies we had in Flanders."*

Again, the developmental material intrudes.

On page 163 we again find: " 'What prodigious armies you had in Flanders!' "

This conscious, exaggerated development often takes place in Sterne even without the use of a repetitive, connective phrase:

The moment my father got up into his chamber, he threw himself prostrate across his bed in the wildest disorder imaginable, but at the same time, in the most lamentable attitude of a man borne down with sorrows, that ever the eye of pity dropp'd a tear for. (215-16)

There follows a description of a bodily posture, very characteristic of Sterne:

The palm of his right hand, as he fell upon the bed, receiving his forehead, and covering the greatest part of both his eyes, gently sunk down with his head (his elbow giving way backwards) till his nose touch'd the quilt;——his left arm hung insensible over the side of the bed, his knuckles reclining upon the handle of the chamber pot, which peep'd out beyond the valance,——his right leg (his left being drawn up towards his body) hung half over the side of the bed, the edge of it pressing upon his shin-bone.

Mr. Shandy's despair is called forth by the fact that the bridge of his son's nose was crushed during delivery by the midwife's tongs. This occasions (as I have already said) a whole epic on noses. On page 273 we return once more to the bedridden father: "My father lay stretched across the bed as still as if the hand of death had pushed him down, for a full hour and a half, before he began to play upon the floor with the toe of that foot, which hung over the bed-side."

I cannot restrain myself from saying a few words about Sterne's postures in general. Sterne was the first writer to introduce a description of poses into the novel. They're always depicted by him in a strange manner, or rather they are enstranged.

Here is another example: "Brother Toby, replied my father, taking his wig from off his head with his right hand, and with his *left* pulling out a striped India handkerchief from his right coat pocket. . . " (158).

Let us move right on to the next page: "It was not an easy matter in any king's reign, (unless you were as lean a subject as myself) to have forced your hand diagonally, quite across your whole body, so as to gain the bottom of your opposite coat-pocket."

Sterne's method of depicting postures was inherited by Leo Tolstoi (Eikhenbaum), but in a weaker form and with a psychological motivation.

Let us now return to the development. I shall offer several examples of development in Sterne, and I shall select a case in which the device turns upon itself, so to speak, that is, where the realization of the form constitutes the content of the work:

> What a chapter of chances, said my father, turning himself about upon the first landing, as he and my uncle Toby were going down stairs——what a long chapter of chances do the events of this world lay open to us! (279)

A discussion with an erotic tinge, of which I shall speak more later:

> Is it not a shame to make two chapters of what passed in going down one pair of stairs? for we are got no farther yet than to the first landing, and there are fifteen more steps down to the bottom; and for aught I know, as my father and my uncle Toby are in a talking humour, there may be as many chapters as steps. (281)

This entire chapter is dedicated by Sterne to a discussion of chapters.

> *Vol. 4, chap. 11:* We shall bring all things to rights, said my father, setting his foot upon the first step from the landing. . . . (283)

> *Chap. 12:* ——And how does your mistress? cried my father, taking the same step over again from the landing, . . . (284)

> *Chap. 13:* Holla!——you chairman!——here's sixpence——do step into that bookseller's shop, and call me a *day-tall* critick. I am very willing to give any one of 'em a crown to help me with his tackling, to get my father and my uncle Toby off the stairs, and to put them to bed. . . .
> I am this month one whole year older than I was this time twelve-month; and having got, as you perceive, almost into the middle of my fourth volume——and no farther than to my first day's life——'tis demonstrative that I have three hundred and sixty-four days more life to write just now, than when I first set out; so that instead of advancing, as a common writer, in my work with what I have been doing at it——on the contrary, I am just thrown so many volumes back. . . . (285-86)

This orientation towards form and towards the normative aspect of that form reminds us of the octaves and sonnets which were filled with nothing but a description of the fact of their composition.

I would like to add one final example of Sterne's development:

> My mother was going very gingerly in the dark along the passage which led to the parlour, as my uncle Toby pronounced the word *wife.* ——'Tis a shrill, penetrating sound of itself, and Obadiah had helped it by leaving the door a little a-jar, so that my mother heard enough of it, to imagine herself the subject of the conversation: so laying the edge of her finger across her two lips——holding in her breath, and bending her head a little downwards, with a twist of her neck——(not towards the door, but from it, by which means her ear was brought to the chink)——she listened with all her powers:——the listening slave, with the Goddess of Silence at his back, could not have given a finer thought for an intaglio.
> In this attitude I am determined to let her stand for five minutes: till I bring up the affairs of the kitchen (as Rapin does those of the church) to the same period. (357-58)

*Vol. 5, chap. 11:* I am a Turk if I had not as much forgot my mother, as if Nature had plaistered me up, and set me down naked upon the banks of the river Nile, without one.

However, these reminders are followed again by digressions. The reminder itself is necessary only in order to renew our awareness of the "forgotten mother," so that its development would not fade from view.

Finally, on page 370, the mother changes her posture: "Then, cried my mother, opening the door, . . ."

Here Sterne develops the action by resorting to a second parallel story. Instead of being presented discursively, time in such novels is thought to have come to a stop or, at least, it is no longer taken into account. Shakespeare uses inset scenes in precisely this way. Thrust into the basic action of the plot, they deflect us from the flow of time. And even if the entire inset conversation (invariably, with new characters) lasts for only a few minutes, the author considers it possible to carry on the action (presumably without lowering the proscenium curtain which in Shakespeare's theater most likely did not exist), as if hours had passed or even an entire night (Silverswan). By mentioning them and by reminding us of the fact that his mother has been left standing bent over, Sterne fulfills the device and compels us to experience it.

It is interesting in general to study the role of time in Sterne's works. "Literary" time is pure conventionality whose laws do not coincide with the laws of ordinary time. If we were to examine, for example, the plethora of stories and incidents packed into *Don Quixote,* we would perceive that the day as such hardly exists at all, since the cycle of day and night does not play a compositional role in the alternation of events. Similarly in Abbé Prévost's narration in *Manon Lescaut:* the Chevalier de Grieux relates the first part of the novel in one fell swoop, and then after taking a breather, he relates the remainder. Such a conversation would last about sixteen hours, and only if the Chevalier read them through quickly.

I have already spoken about the conventionality of time onstage. In Sterne this conventionality of "literary" time is consciously utilized as material for play.

Volume 2, chapter 8:

It is about an hour and a half's tolerable good reading since my uncle Toby rung the bell, when Obadiah was order'd to saddle a horse, and go for Dr. Slop the man-midwife;——so that no one can say, with reason, that I have not allowed Obadiah time enough, poetically speaking, and considering the emergency too, both to go and come;——tho', morally and truly speaking, the man, perhaps, has scarce had time to get on his boots.

If the hypercritic will go upon this; and is resolved after all to take a pendulum, and measure the true distance betwixt the ringing of the bell, and the rap at the door;——and, after finding it to be no more than two minutes, thirteen seconds, and three fifths,——should take upon him to insult over me for such a breach in the unity, or rather probability, of time;——I would remind him, that the idea of duration and of its simple modes, is got merely from the train and succession of our ideas,——and is the true scholastic pendulum,——and by which, as a scholar, I will be tried in this matter,——abjuring and detesting the jurisdiction of all other pendulums whatever.

I would, therefore, desire him to consider that it is but poor eight miles from Shandy-Hall to Dr. Slop, the man mid-wife's house;——and that whilst Obadiah has been going those said miles and back, I have brought my uncle Toby from Namur, quite across all Flanders, into England:——That I have had him ill upon my hands near four years;——and have since travelled him and Corporal Trim, in a chariot and four, a journey of near two hundred miles down into Yorkshire;—— all which put together, must have prepared the reader's imagination for the entrance of Dr. Slop upon the stage,——as much, at least (I hope) as a dance, a song, or a concerto between the acts.

If my hypercritic is intractable, alledging, that two minutes and thirteen seconds are no more than two minutes and thirteen seconds,——when I have said all I can about them;——and that this plea, tho' it might save me dramatically, will damn me biographically, rendering my book, from this very moment, a profess'd ROMANCE, which, before, was a book apocryphal:——If I am thus pressed——I then put an end to the whole objection and controversy about it all at once,——by acquainting him, that Obadiah had not got above threescore yards from the stable-yard before he met with Dr. Slop. (103-4)

From the old devices, and with hardly a change, Sterne made use of the device of the "found manuscript." This is the way in which Yorick's sermon is introduced into the novel. But the reading of this found manuscript does not represent a long digression from the novel and is constantly interrupted mainly by emotional outbursts. The sermon occupies pages 117-41 but it is vigorously pushed aside by Sterne's usual interpretations.

The reading begins with a description of the corporal's posture, as depicted with the deliberate awkwardness so typical of Sterne:

He stood before them with his body swayed, and bent forwards just so far, as to make an angle of 85 degrees and a half upon the plain of the horizon;——which sound orators, to whom I address this, know very well, to be the true persuasive angle of incidence; . . . (122)

Later he again writes:

He stood,——for I repeat it, to take the picture of him in at one view, with his body sway'd, and somewhat bent forwards,——his right leg firm under him, sustaining seven-eighths of his whole weight,——the foot of his left leg, the defect of which was no disadvantage to his attitude, advanced a little,——not laterally, nor forwards, but in a line betwixt them; . . .

And so on. The whole description occupies more than a page. The sermon is interrupted by the story of Corporal Trim's brother. This is followed by the dissenting theological interpolations of the Catholic listener (125, 126, 128, 129, etc.) and by Uncle Toby's comment on fortifications (133, 134, etc.). In this way the reading of the manuscript in Sterne is far more closely linked to the novel than in Cervantes.

The found manuscript in *Sentimental Journey* became Sterne's favorite device. In it he discovers the manuscript of Rabelais, as he supposes. The manuscript breaks off, as is typical for Sterne, for a discussion about the art of wrapping merchandise. The unfinished story is canonical for Sterne, both in its motivated as well as unmotivated forms. When the manuscript is introduced into the novel, the break is motivated by the loss of its conclusion. The simple break which concludes *Tristram Shandy* is completely unmotivated:

L--d! said my mother, what is all this story about?——
A COCK and a BULL, said Yorick——And one of the best of its kind, I ever heard.

*Sentimental Journey* ends in the same way: ". . . So that when I stretch'd out my hand, I caught hold of the Fille de Chambre's—"

This is of course a definite stylistic device based on differential qualities. Sterne was writing against a background of the adventure novel with its extremely rigorous forms that demanded, among other things, that a novel end with a wedding or marriage. The forms most characteristic of Sterne are those which result from the displacement and violation of conventional forms. He acts no differently when it is time for him to conclude his novels. It is as if we fell upon them: on the staircase, for instance, in the very place where we expect to find a landing, we find instead a gaping hole. Gogol's "Ivan Fyodorovich Shponka and His Auntie" represents just such a method of ending a story, but with a motivation: the last page of the manuscript goes for the wrapping of baked pies. (Sterne, on the other hand, uses the ending of his manuscript to wrap black currant preserves.) The notes for Hoffmann's *Kater Murr* present much the same picture, with a motivated absence of the ending, but they are complicated by a temporal transposition (that is, they are motivated by the fact that the pages are in disarray) and by a parallel structure.

The tale of Le Fever is introduced by Sterne in a thoroughly traditional way. Tristram's birth occasions a discussion concerning the choice of a tutor. Uncle Toby proposes for the role the poor son of Le Fever, and thus begins an inset tale, *which is carried on in the name of the author:*

Then, brother Shandy, answered my uncle Toby, raising himself off the chair, and laying down his pipe to take hold of my father's other hand,——I humbly beg I may recommend poor Le Fever's son to you;——a tear of joy of the first water sparkled in my uncle Toby's eye,——and another, the fellow to it, in the corporal's as the proposition was made;——you will see why when you read Le Fever's story:—— fool that I was! nor can I recollect, (nor perhaps you) without turning back to the place, what it was that hindred me from letting the corporal tell it in his own words; ——but the occasion is lost,——I must tell it now in my own. (415-16)

The tale of Le Fever now commences. It covers pages 379-95. A description of Tristram's journeys also represents a separate unit. It occupies pages

436-93. This episode was later deployed step for step and motif for motif in Sterne's *Sentimental Journey*. In the description of the journey Sterne has interpolated the story of the Abbess of Andoüillets (459-65).

This heterogeneous material, weighed down as it is with long extracts from the works of a variety of pedants, would no doubt have broken the back of this novel, were it not that the novel is held together tightly by leitmotivs. A specific motif is neither developed nor realized; it is merely mentioned from time to time. Its fulfillment is deferred to a point in time which seems to be receding further and further away from us. Yet, its very presence throughout the length and breadth of the novel serves to link the episodes.

There are several such motifs. One is the motif of the knots. It appears in the following way: a sack containing Dr. Slop's obstetrical instruments is tied in several knots:

'Tis God's mercy, quoth he [Dr. Slop], (to himself) that Mrs. Shandy has had so bad a time of it,——else she might have been brought to bed seven times told, before one half of these knots could have got untied. (167)

In the case of *knots,* ——by which, in the first place, I would not be understood to mean slip-knots,——because in the course of my life and opinions,——my opinions concerning them will come in more properly when I mention. . . . (next chapter)

A discussion concerning knots and loops and bows continues ad nauseam. Meanwhile, Dr. Slop reaches for his knife and cuts the knots. Due to his carelessness, he wounds his hand. He then begins to swear, whereupon the elder Shandy, with Cervantesque seriousness, suggests that instead of carrying on in vain, he should curse in accordance with the rules of art. In his capacity as the leader, Shandy then proposes the Catholic formula of excommunication. Slop picks up the text and starts reading. The formula occupies two full pages. It is curious to observe here the motivation for the appearance of material considered necessary by Sterne for further development. This material is usually represented by works of medieval learning, which by Sterne's time had already acquired a comical tinge. (As is true also of words pronounced by foreigners in their peculiar dialects.) This material is interspersed in Tristram's father's speech, and its appearance is motivated by his manias. Here, though, the motivation is more complex. Apart from the father's role, we encounter also material concerning the infant's baptism before his birth and the lawyers' comical argument concerning the question of whether the mother was a relative of her own son.

The "knots" and "chambermaids" motif appears again on page 363. But then the author dismisses the idea of writing a chapter on them, proposing instead another chapter on chambermaids, green coats, and old hats. However the matter of the knots is not yet exhausted. It resurfaces at the very end on page 617 in the form of a promise to write a special chapter on them.

Similarly, the repeated mention of Jenny also constitutes a running motif throughout the novel. Jenny appears in the novel in the following way:

... it is no more than a week from this very day, in which I am now writing this book for the edification of the world,——which is March 9, 1759,——that my dear, dear Jenny observing I look'd a little grave, as she stood cheapening a silk of five-and-twenty shillings a yard,——told the mercer, she was sorry she had given him so much trouble;——and immediately went and bought herself a yard-wide stuff of ten-pence a yard. (44)

On page 48 Sterne plays with the reader's desire to know what role Jenny plays in his life:

I own the tender appellation of my dear, dear Jenny,——with some other strokes of conjugal knowledge, interspersed here and there, might, naturally enough, have misled the most candid judge in the world into such a determination against me. ——All I plead for, in this case, Madam, is strict justice, and that you do so much of it, to me as well as to yourself,——as not to prejudge or receive such an impression of me, till you have better evidence, than I am positive, at present, can be produced against me:——Not that I can be so vain or unreasonable, Madam, as to desire you should therefore think, that my dear, dear Jenny is my kept mistress; ——no,——that would be flattering my character in the other extream, and giving it an air of freedom, which, perhaps, it has no kind of right to. All I contend for, is the utter impossibility for some volumes, that you, or the most penetrating spirit upon earth, should know how this matter really stands.——It is not impossible, but that my dear, dear Jenny! tender as the appellation is, may be my child.—— Consider,——I was born in the year eighteen.——Nor is there any thing unnatural or extravagant in the supposition, that my dear Jenny may be my friend.——Friend! ——My friend. Surely, Madam, a friendship between the two sexes may subsist, and be supported without——Fy! Mr. Shandy:——Without any thing, Madam, but that tender and delicious sentiment, which ever mixes in friendship, where there is a difference of sex.

The Jenny motif appears again on page 337:

I shall never get all through in five minutes, that I fear——and the thing I *hope* is, that your worships and reverences are not offended——if you are, depend upon't I'll give you something, my good gentry, next year, to be offended at——that's my dear Jenny's way——but who my Jenny is——and which is the right and which the wrong end of a woman, is the thing to be *concealed*——it will be told you the next chapter but one, to my chapter of button-holes,——and not one chapter before.

And on page 493 we have the following passage: "I love the Pythagoreans (much more than ever I dare to tell my dear Jenny)."

We encounter another reminder on page 550 and on page 610. The latter one (I have passed over several others) is quite sentimental, a genuine rarity in Sterne:

I will not argue the matter: Time wastes too fast: every letter I trace tells me with what rapidity Life follows my pen; the days and hours of it, more precious, my dear

Jenny! than the rubies about thy neck, are flying over our heads like light clouds of a windy day, never to return more——every thing presses on——whilst thou art twisting that lock,——see! it grows grey; and every time I kiss thy hand to bid adieu, and every absence which follows it, are preludes to that eternal separation which we are shortly to make.——

——Heaven have mercy upon us both!

## Chapter 9

Now, for what the world thinks of that ejaculation——I would not give a groat.

This is all of chapter 9, volume 9.

It would be interesting to take up for a moment the subject of sentimentality in general. Sentimentality cannot constitute the content of art, if only for the reason that art does not have a separate content. The depiction of things from a "sentimental point of view" is a special method of depiction, very much, for example, as these things might be from the point of view of a horse (Tolstoi's "Kholstomer") or of a giant (Swift).

By its very essence, art is without emotion. Recall, if you will, that in fairy tales people are shoved into a barrel bristling with nails, only to be rolled down into the sea. In our version of "Tom Thumb," a cannibal cuts off the heads of his daughters, and the children who listen rapturously to every detail of this legend never let you skip over these details during the telling and retelling of the story. This isn't cruelty. It's fable.

In *Spring Ritual Song,* Professor Anichkov presents examples of folkloric dance songs. These songs speak of a bad-tempered, querulous husband, of death, and of worms. This is tragic, yes, but only in the world of song.

In art, blood is not bloody. No, it just rhymes with "flood." It is material either for a structure of sounds or for a structure of images. For this reason, art is pitiless or rather without pity, apart from those cases where the feeling of sympathy forms the material for the artistic structure. But even in that case, we must consider it from the point of view of the composition. Similarly, if we want to understand how a certain machine works, we examine its drive belt first. That is, we consider this detail from the standpoint of a machinist and not, for instance, from the standpoint of a vegetarian.

Of course, Sterne is also without pity. Let me offer an example. The elder Shandy's son, Bobby, dies at precisely the moment when the father is vacillating over whether to use the money that had fallen into his hands by chance in order to send his son abroad or else to use it for improvements on the estate:

. . . my uncle Toby hummed over the letter.

—— —— —— —— —— —— ——
—— —— —— —— —— —— ——
—— —— —— —— —— —— ——he's

gone! said my uncle Toby.——Where——Who? cried my father.——My nephew, said my uncle Toby. ——What——without leave——without money——without governor? cried my father in amazement. No:——he is dead, my dear brother, quoth my uncle Toby. (350)

Death is here used by Sterne for the purpose of creating a "misunderstanding," very common in a work of art when two characters are speaking at cross-purposes about, apparently, the same thing. Let us consider another example: the first conversation between the mayor and Khlestakov in Gogol's *The Inspector General.*

*Mayor:* Excuse me.
*Kh.:* Oh, it's nothing.
*Mayor:* It is my duty, as mayor of this city, to protect all passersby and highborn folk from fleecers like you . . .
*Kh.* (stammering at first, then speaking loud towards the latter part of his speech): What can I–I . . . do? . . . It's not my fault . . . I'll pay for it, really! I'm expecting a check from home any day now. (Bobchinsky peeps from behind the door.) It's his fault! He is to blame! You should see the beef he's selling, as hard as a log. And that soup of his, ugh! Who knows where he dredged it up. I dumped it out of the window. Couldn't help it. He keeps me on the very edge of starvation for days at a time . . . And while you are at it, why not get a whiff of his—ugh!—tea. Smells more like rotten fish than tea. Why the hell should I . . . It's unheard of!
*Mayor* (timidly): Excuse me, sir, I'm really not to blame. The beef I sell on the market is always first class, brought into town by merchants from Kholmogorsk, sober, respectable people, if ever such existed, I assure you, sir. If only I knew where he's been picking up such . . . But if anything is amiss, sir, . . . Permit me to transfer you to other quarters.
*Kh.:* No, I won't go! I know what you mean by "other quarters"! Prison! that's what you mean, isn't that right! By what right? How dare you? . . . Why, I . . . I am in the employ of . . . in Petersburg. Do you hear? (with vigor) I, I, I . . .
*Mayor* (aside): Oh, my God! He is in a rage! He's found me out. It's those damned busybody merchants. They must have told him everything.
*Kh.* (bravely): I won't go! Not even if you bring the whole police force with you! I'm going straight to the top. Yes, right up to the Prime Minister! (He pounds his fist on the table) How dare you?! How dare you?!
*Mayor* (trembling all over): Have mercy, please spare me, kind sir! I have a wife and little ones . . . Don't bring me to ruin!
*Kh.:* No, I won't! No way! And what's more! What do I care if you have a wife and kids. So I have to go to prison for their sake? Just splendid! (Bobchinsky, peeking through the door, hides in fear.) No, sirree! Thanks but no thanks!
*Mayor* (trembling): It's not my fault, sir. It's my inexperience, my God, that's all, just plain inexperience. And, you know, I am really anything but rich. Judge for yourself: The salary of a civil servant will hardly cover tea and sugar. Well, maybe I did take some bribes, Your Excellency, but, mind you, sir, just a ruble here and there, and only o-nnce or t-wwice, if you know what I mean . . . Just something for the table or maybe a dress or two. As for that NCO's widow, who runs a shop . . . I assure, sir, I never, I assure you, Your Excellency, never stooped so low as to flog her, as some people have been saying. It's slander, nothing but slander, fabricated

by scoundrels with evil in their hearts! They would stoop to anything to do me in! I assure you, Your Noble Excellency, sir! . . .

*Kh.:* So what? What does all this have to do with me? . . . (reflecting) I can't imagine why you are dragging in these scoundrels or the widow of a noncommissioned officer. . . . The NCO's wife is one thing, but don't you dare try to flog me. You'll never get away with it . . . And, besides, . . . just look here! I'll pay the bill, I assure you, sir, I'll get the money if it kills me, but not just now. That's why I am sitting here, because I am broke. Really, sir. I am clean broke.

Here is another example from Griboedov's *Woe from Wit:*

*Zagorestsky:* So Chatsky is responsible for the hubbub?
*Countess Dowager:* What? Chatsky has been horribly clubbed?
*Zagorestsky:* Went mad in the mountains from a wound in the head.
*Countess Dowager:* How is that? He wound up with a bounty on his head?

We see the same device used (with the same motivation of deafness) in Russian folk drama. However, because of the looser plot structure, this device is used there for the purpose of constructing a whole pattern of puns.

The old grave-diggers are summoned before King Maximilian:

*Max.:* Go and bring me the old grave-diggers.
*Footman:* Yes, Your Majesty, I shall go and fetch them.

(Footman and Grave-diggers)
*Footman:* Are the grave-diggers home, sir?
*1st Grave-digger:* What do you want?
*Footman:* Your presence is requested by His Majesty.
*1st Grave-digger:* By whom? His Modesty?
*Footman:* No, His Majesty!
*1st Grave-digger:* Tell him that no one is home. Today is a holiday. We are celebrating.
*Footman:* Vasily Ivanovich, His Majesty wishes to reward you for your services.
*1st Grave-digger:* Reward me for my verses? What verses?
*Footman:* No! Not verses, services!
*1st Grave-digger* (to 2nd grave-digger): Moky!
*2nd Grave-digger:* What, Patrak?
*1st Grave-digger:* Let's go see the king.
*2nd Grave-digger:* What for?
*1st Grave-digger:* For the reward.
*2nd Grave-digger:* For what gourd? It's winter. Where in the world will you find a gourd in winter?
*1st Grave-digger:* No, not gourd, reward!
*2nd Grave-digger:* And I thought you were talking about a gourd. If it's reward you've in mind, then by all means, let's go!
*1st Grave-digger:* Well, let's go.
*2nd Grave-digger:* Tell me, what kind of reward?
*1st Grave-digger:* Let's just go. I'll tell you when we get there.
*2nd Grave-digger:* No! Tell me now!
*1st Grave-digger:* Let's go. I'll tell you on the way.
*2nd Grave-digger:* Absolutely not! If you won't tell me now, I won't go.

*1st Grave-digger:* All right. Do you remember how we distinguished ourselves in the Battle of Sevastopol?

*2nd Grave-digger:* Yes. I remember very well.

*1st Grave-digger:* Well, there you are! That's what His Majesty probably has in mind. It's probably the fortieth anniversary of the Crimean War.

*2nd Grave-digger:* I see. Well, in that case, let's get going. . . . (Onchukov, *Folk Drama of the North*)

This device, canonical for folk drama, completely supplants, at times, novelistic plot structures. This subject has been analyzed by Roman Jakobson and Pyotr Bogatyrev in their studies of the Russian folk theater.

However, Sterne's own pun on death (see above) does not surprise us half so much (or does not surprise us at all) as do the father's puns. Bobby Shandy's death serves for Sterne, above all, as a motivation for development: "Will your worships give me leave to squeeze in a story between these two pages?" (351).

Sterne interposes an excerpt from a letter of condolence written by Servius Sulpicius to Cicero. Its incorporation into the text is motivated by the fact that it is delivered by Mr. Shandy himself. This is followed by a selection of anecdotes from the classics on the subject of contempt for death. It is worth noting what Sterne himself has to say concerning Mr. Shandy's eloquence:

My father was as proud of his eloquence as MARCUS TULLIUS CICERO could be for his life, and for aught I am convinced of to the contrary at present, with as much reason: it was indeed his strength——and his weakness too.——His strength——for he was by nature eloquent,——and his weakness——for he was hourly a dupe to it; and provided an occasion in life would but permit him to shew his talents, or say either a wise thing, a witty, or a shrewd one——(bating the case of a systematick misfortune)——he had all he wanted.——A blessing which tied up my father's tongue, and a misfortune which set it loose with good grace, were pretty equal: sometimes, indeed, the misfortune was the better of the two; for instance, where the pleasure of the harangue was as *ten,* and the pain of the misfortune but as *five*——my father gained half in half, and consequently was as well again off, as it never had befallen him. (352)

The difference between human (i.e., actual) "happiness" or "unhappiness" on the one hand, and "happiness" and "unhappiness" as material for art is underscored here with extraordinary clarity.

It remains for the mother to learn of her son's death. This is accomplished by having Mrs. Shandy eavesdrop by the door, as a parallel action unfolds in the kitchen. In doing this, Sterne asked himself the solemn question: How long can a poor mother stand in such an uncomfortable pose?

A conversation is taking place at this moment in the study about the son's death. This death has already become woven into the discussions concerning death in general. After the deliberations concerning the possible ways of disseminating knowledge of the classics (369), it is imperceptibly woven into Socrates' speech at his trial.

... though my mother was a woman of no deep reading, yet the abstract of Socrates' oration, which my father was giving my uncle Toby, was not altogether new to her.
——She listened to it with composed intelligence, and would have done so to the end of the chapter, had not my father plunged (which he had no occasion to have done) into that part of the pleading where the great philosopher reckons up his connections, his alliances, and children; but renounces a security to be so won by working upon the passions of his judges.——"I have friends——I have relations,——I have three desolate children,"——says Socrates.——
——Then, cried my mother, opening the door,——you have one more, Mr. Shandy, than I know of.
By heaven! I have one less,——said my father, getting up and walking out of the room. (370)

A very important source for development in Sterne is represented by erotic enstrangement, taking the form, for the most part, of euphemisms. I have already discussed this phenomenon in chapter 1. In Sterne we encounter an extraordinary variety of such cases of erotic enstrangement. There are numerous examples to draw from. Here are a few of them.

Let us begin with the identification of types of character:

I am not ignorant that the Italians pretend to a mathematical exactness in their designations of one particular sort of character among them, from the *forte* or *piano* of a certain wind instrument they use,——which they say is infallible.——I dare not mention the name of the instrument in this place;——'tis sufficient we have it amongst us,——but never think of making a drawing by it;——this is ænigmatical, and intended to be so, at least, *ad populum:*——And therefore I beg, Madam, when you come here, that you read on as fast as you can, and never stop to make any inquiry about it. (75-76)

Or, for example:

Now whether it was physically impossible, with half a dozen hands all thrust into the napkin at a time——but that some one chestnut, of more life and rotundity than the rest, must be put in motion——it so fell out, however, that one was actually sent rolling off the table; and as Phutatorius sat straddling under——it fell perpendicularly into that particular aperture of Phutatorius's breeches, for which, to the shame and indelicacy of our language be it spoke, there is no chaste word throughout all Johnson's dictionary——let it suffice to say——it was that particular aperture, which in all good societies, the laws of decorum do strictly require, like the temple of Janus (in peace at least) to be universally shut up. (320)

Very typical of this erotic enstrangement and the play provoked by it are two episodes in *Tristram Shandy* that very much resemble each other. Yet, while one episode is really no more than an episode, the other is developed into a plot line and forms one of the criss-crossing plot lines of the novel.

Chief among these plot lines is Uncle Toby's wound. Uncle Toby had suffered a severe wound in the groin. He is being wooed by a widow, who would very much like to know whether or not he had in fact been castrated by that wound. Yet, at this time she cannot bring herself to ask the fateful question. This greatly complicates the novel:

There is not a greater difference between a single-horse chair and madam Pompadour's *vis-à-vis,* than betwixt a single amour, and an amour thus nobly doubled, and going upon all fours, prancing throughout a grand drama. (209)

The novel is continually interrupted and takes on the form of innuendos and allusions. Finally, these allusions begin to consolidate (i.e., around volume 6, chapter 34).

At this point, though, we encounter an intrusion of the "travel" motif. This new material seems to have reached a dead end at the conclusion of volume 7:

I danced it along through Narbonne, Carcasson, and Castle Naudairy, till at last I danced myself into Perdrillo's pavillion, where pulling a paper of black lines, that I might go on straight forwards, without digression or parenthesis, in my uncle Toby's amours—— (538)

And so the groin wound, with the widow's reluctance to confront this issue directly, is introduced into the text as a device for the purpose of impeding the Toby–widow romance.

I shall now demonstrate in several excerpts just how Sterne brings about this retarding of the action.

After a solemn promise to tell the story of Toby's amorous adventures without digression, Sterne brakes the action by introducing digressions into digressions, which are then linked to each other by the repetition of one and the same phrase: "It is with love as with Cuckoldom" (540, 542).

This is followed by metaphors of love. Love is a warm hat, love is a pie (504-5). Then follows a history of the widow Wadman's attacks on Uncle Toby. Yet, this description is again interrupted by a long, "importunate story," told by Trim, called "The Story of the King of Bohemia and His Seven Castles."

This tale is similar to the one told by Sancho Panza to his lord, Don Quixote, on the night of his adventure with the textile mill, when he tied up Rocinante by its legs. It is continually interrupted by Uncle Toby's comments on military affairs, technology and literary style. I've already analyzed this device of Cervantes' in *Don Quixote.* Like every "importunate story," it is based on its conscious use as a braking device and must therefore be interrupted by a listener. In this particular case, its role is to impede the main plot line of the novel. A little later, Trim abandons the story of the King of Bohemia and takes up the story of his love (568-75). Finally, the widow Wadman makes her appearance once again. This is occasioned by the wound motif:

I am terribly afraid, said widow Wadman, in case I should marry him, Bridget ——that the poor captain will not enjoy his health, with the monstrous wound upon his groin——

It may not, Madam, be so very large, replied Bridget, as you think——and I believe besides, added she——that 'tis dried up——

——I would like to know——merely for his sake, said Mrs. Wadman——

——We'll know the long and the broad of it, in ten days——answered Mrs. Bridget, for whilst the captain is paying his addresses to you——I'm confident Mr. Trim will be for making love to me——and I'll let him as much as he will——added Bridget——to get it all out of him—— (581-82)

Once again, the author introduces new material, in this case, in the form of a realized metaphor (which, generally speaking, is quite common in Sterne): (a) he realizes the lexical (linguistic) metaphor "hobbyhorse" (in the sense of "whim, caprice") and speaks of it as if it were a real horse; and (b) he realizes the metaphor "ass" (in the sense of the buttocks). The source for this metaphor may well be St. Francis of Assisi's characterization of his body as "my brother, the ass." The ass metaphor is also developed. Besides, it is also the basis for a misunderstanding.

When Shandy Senior asks Uncle Toby about the ass, the latter thinks that the posterior part of the body is euphemistically meant (539). A detail from the development that follows is of some interest. Shandy Senior's speech to Uncle Toby is nothing less than a parody of Don Quixote's speech to Sancho Panza on governorship.

I shall not parody them in turn by quoting these two speeches in parallel texts, all the more so since we'd thereby be keeping the widow Wadman waiting. Uncle Toby and Trim are going to see her. Shandy Senior and his wife are also on their way there. They are observing the first pair from the corners of their eyes, meanwhile chatting about the forthcoming marriage.

Again, we encounter the leitmotiv of the impotent husband, who sleeps with his wife only on the first Sunday of every month. This motif, appearing first in the very opening of the novel, now emerges once again (vol. 9, chap. 11):

Unless she should happen to have a child——said my mother——
——But she must persuade my brother Toby first to get her one——
——To be sure, Mr. Shandy, quoth my mother.
——Though if it comes to persuasion——said my father——Lord have mercy upon them.
Amen: said my mother, *piano.*
Amen: cried my father, *fortissimè.*
Amen: said my mother again——but with such a sighing cadence of personal pity at the end of it, as discomfited every fibre about my father——he instantly took out his almanack; but before he could untie it, Yorick's congregation coming out of church, became a full answer to one half of his business with it——and my mother telling him it was a sacrament day——left him as little in doubt, as to the other part ——He put his almanack into his pocket.
The first Lord of the Treasury thinking of *ways and means,* could not have returned home, with a more embarrassed look. (613-14)

I've permitted myself this lengthy excerpt in order to show that Sterne's inset material does not play a merely peripheral role in the novel. On the contrary, every passage belongs to one of the novel's compositional lines.

Once again, we encounter digressions from other plot lines, e.g., the knot motif (617). Finally, the wound motif takes the stage. It is presented, as is usual in Sterne, in medias res:

```
    ___*    *    *    *    *    *    *    *    *         *
*    *    *    *    *    *    *    *    *    *    *         *
*    *    *    *    *    *    *    *

     *    *    *    *    *    *    *    *    *    *         *
*    *    *    *    *    *    *    *    *    *    *         *
*    *    *    *    *    *    *    *    *    *    *         *
*    *    *    *    *    *    *  ___
```

—You shall see the very place, Madam; said my uncle Toby.

Mrs. Wadman blush'd——look'd towards the door——turn'd pale——blush'd slightly again——recovered her natural colour——blush'd worse than ever; which for the sake of the unlearned reader, I translate thus——

*"L--d! I cannot look at it——*
*What would the world say if I look'd at it?*
*I should drop down, if I look'd at it——*
*I wish I could look at it——*
*There can be no sin in looking at it.*
*——I will look at it."* (623)

Yet, something quite different takes place.

Uncle Toby thinks that the widow wants to know the place where he was wounded (i.e., the geographical locality) when, in fact, she seems to have in mind the anatomical place on his body. By the way, neither is the reader quite sure at this juncture what is meant. The whole point of this shift in the plot, however, is clearly to impede the action.

Well, so Trim brings the disappointed widow a map of Namur (the locality where Uncle Toby was in fact wounded). Once again, we are witnessing a play on Uncle Toby's wound. This time Sterne himself picks up the theme in his digressions (625-29). Then comes the famous transposition of time. Chapter 25 (of volume 9) is succeeded by the previously missing chapters 18 and 19. The action resumes only with chapter 26:

It was just as natural for Mrs. Wadman, whose first husband was all his time afflicted with a Sciatica, to wish to know how far from the hip to the groin; and how far she was likely to suffer more or less in her feelings, in the one case than in the other.

She accordingly read Drake's anatomy from one end to the other. She had peeped into Wharton upon the brain, and borrowed Graaf upon the bones and muscles; but could make nothing of it. . . .

To clear up all, she had twice asked Doctor Slop, "if poor captain Shandy was ever likely to recover of his wound——?"

——He is recovered, Doctor Slop would say——

What! quite?

——Quite: madam——

But what do you mean by a recovery? Mrs. Wadman would say.

Doctor Slop was the worst man alive at definitions. (636-37)

Mrs. Wadman interrogates Captain Shandy himself about the wound:

"——Was it without remission?——
——Was it more tolerable in bed?
——Could he lie on both sides alike with it?
——Was he able to mount a horse?" (637)

Finally, the matter is resolved in the following manner: Trim is speaking to the widow's servant girl (Bridget) concerning Captain Shandy's wound:

. . . and in this cursed trench, Mrs. Bridget, quoth the Corporal, taking her by the hand, did he receive the wound which crush'd him so miserably *here*——In pronouncing which he slightly press'd the back of her hand towards the part he felt for——and let it fall.

We thought, Mr. Trim, it had been more in the middle——said Mrs. Bridget——
That would have undone us for ever——said the Corporal.
——And left my poor mistress undone too——said Bridget. . . .
Come——come——said Bridget——holding the palm of her left-hand parallel to the plane of the horizon, and sliding the fingers of the other over it, in a way which could not have been done, had there been the least wart or protuberance——'Tis every syllable of it false, cried the Corporal, before she had half finished the sentence—— (639)

It is worth comparing this hand symbolism with the same device of euphemistic eroticism found elsewhere in *Tristram Shandy.*

A brief, preliminary comment.

For the protagonists of this novel, this euphemistic manner of speaking represents proper speech. For Sterne though—when this same phenomenon is considered from an artistic point of view—this becomes material for enstrangement.

It is a curious point that this same device of hand symbolism is encountered in the specifically masculine, "obscene" anecdotes of folklore, where, as is well known, there are no rules of decency, other than, of course, the desire to speak as obscenely as possible. Yet, even here we encounter material of a euphemistic character, in particular hand symbolism, though employed as a device of enstrangement.

Let us now return to Sterne. I must again quote nearly an entire chapter. Fortunately, it is rather short:

——'Twas nothing,——I did not lose two drops of blood by it——'twas not worth calling in a surgeon, had he lived next door to us. . . . The chamber-maid had left no ******* *** under the bed:——Cannot you contrive, master, quoth Susannah, lifting up the sash with one hand, as she spoke, and helping me up into the window seat with the other,——cannot you manage, my dear, for a single time to **** *** ** *** ******?

I was five years old.——Susannah did not consider that nothing was well hung in our family,——so slap came the sash down like lightening upon us;——Nothing is left,——cried Susannah,——nothing is left——for me, but to run my country. (376)

She flees to Uncle Toby's house and he takes the blame, for his servant

Trim had removed the sash weights from the window to make some model cannons.

Once again we encounter a device typical of Sterne: the effects are presented prior to the causes. The description of this cause occupies pages 377-78. The incident is related with the aid of the hand symbolism:

> Trim, by the help of his forefinger, laid flat upon the table, and the edge of his hand striking a-cross it at right angles, made a shift to tell his story so, that priests and virgins might have listened to it;——and the story being told, the dialogue went on as follows. (379)

This is followed by a development of the rumors concerning the incident, then by digressions and by discussions concerning digressions, etc.

Interestingly enough, Shandy Senior runs to see his son the moment he finds out about the incident—with a book in his hands, whereupon begins a discussion concerning circumcision in general. It is worth noting at this point how Sterne parodies the motivation for interpolated passages:

> —was Obadiah enabled to give him a particular account of it, just as it had happened.——I thought as much, said my father, tucking up his night-gown;——and so walked up stairs.
>
> One would imagine from this——(though for my own part I somewhat question it)——that my father before that time, had actually wrote that remarkable chapter in the *Tristrapædia,* which to me is the most original and entertaining one in the whole book;——and that is the *chapter upon sash-windows,* with a bitter Philippick at the end of it, upon the forgetfulness of chamber-maids.——I have but two reasons for thinking otherwise.
>
> First, Had the matter been taken into consideration, before the event happened, my father certainly would have nailed up the sash-window for good an' all;——which, considering with what difficulty he composed books,——he might have done with ten times less trouble, than he could have wrote the chapter: this argument I foresee holds good against his writing the chapter, even after the event; but 'tis obviated under the second reason, which I have the honour to offer to the world in support of my opinion, that my father did not write the chapter upon sash-windows and chamber-pots, at the time supposed,——and it is this.
>
> ——That, in order to render the *Tristrapædia* complete,——I wrote the chapter myself. (383-84)

I have not the slightest desire to continue this study of Sterne's novel to the very end. This is so because I am far less interested in the novel itself than in the theory of plot structure.

I shall now say a few words concerning the abundance of citations in my book. Naturally, I could have made fuller use of every passage and excerpt in this book, since there is hardly a device that appears anywhere in its pure form. However, this would have transformed my work into a "pony," which, by obstructing the text with grammatical annotations, would have hindered the reader from interpreting it on his own.

Nonetheless, in analyzing this novel, I consider it my duty to demonstrate its thoroughgoing "lack of consistency." It is precisely the unusual order of even common, traditional elements that is characteristic of Sterne.

As an end-piece and at the same time as proof of Sterne's conscious manipulation and violation of traditional plot schemata, I'd like to cite his own graphic illustration of the story line in *Tristram Shandy:*

I am now beginning to get fairly into my work; and by the help of a vegitable diet, with a few of the cold seeds, I make no doubt but I shall be able to go on with my uncle Toby's story, and my own, in a tolerable straight line. Now,

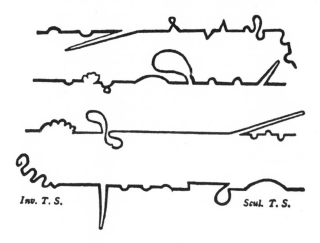

*Inv. T. S.*        *Scul. T. S.*

These were the four lines I moved in through my first, second, third, and fourth volumes.——In the fifth volume I have been very good,——the precise line I have described in it being this:

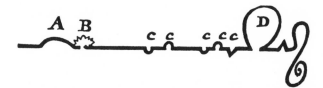

By which it appears, that except at the curve, marked A. where I took a trip to Navarre,——and the indented curve B. which is the short airing when I was there with the Lady Baussiere and her page,——I have not taken the least frisk of a digression, till John de la Casse's devils led me the round you see marked D.——for as for c c c c c they are nothing but parentheses, and the common *ins* and *outs* incident to the lives of the greatest ministers of state; and when compared with what men have done,——or with my own transgressions at the letters A B D——they vanish into nothing. (473-74)

Sterne's schemata are more or less accurate, but he fails to take into account the interruption of the motifs.

*

The concept of plot (*syuzhet*) is too often confused with a description of the events in the novel, with what I'd tentatively call the story line (*fabula*).

As a matter of fact, though, the story line is nothing more than material for plot formation.

In this way, the plot of *Eugene Onegin* is not the love between Eugene and Tatiana but the appropriation of that story line in the form of digressions that interrupt the text. One sharp-witted artist, Vladimir Milashevsky, has proposed to illustrate this novel in verse by focusing chiefly on the digressions (the "little feet," for instance) and, from a purely compositional point of view, this would be quite appropriate.

The forms of art are explained by the artistic laws that govern them and not by comparisons with actual life. In order to impede the action of the novel, the artist resorts not to witches and magic potions but to a simple transposition of its parts. He thereby reveals to us the aesthetic laws that underlie both of these compositional devices.

It is common practice to assert that *Tristram Shandy* is not a novel. Those who speak in this way regard opera alone as true music, while a symphony for them is mere chaos.

*Tristram Shandy* is the most typical novel in world literature.

# *Chapter 8*

# Bely and Ornamental Prose

## 1

The particular elements constituting literary form are more likely to clash than to work in concert. The decline or decay of one device brings in its train the growth and development of another device.

The celebrated progression in literary history from the epic to the lyric and, finally, to the drama is not so much a succession of organic forms as a succession of canonizations and displacements.

A writer's philosophical worldview is his working hypothesis. However, if we address the issue more precisely, we might wish to add that a writer's consciousness is nonetheless determined by literary form. The crises of a writer coincide with the crises of literary genres. A writer moves within the orbit of his art.

When an ideology, lying as it must outside the boundaries of the work of art, invades the writer's domain without that craftsmanship which alone can justify it, then the results cannot be considered art.

Such was the case when Andrei Bely set out to create his anthroposophical epopee, or epic. The attempt to create a literary work which would correspond to some extrinsic worldview can succeed only with much difficulty, if at all. This is so because a work of art distorts such a correspondence in accordance with its own laws.

Not surprisingly, the author himself may have a hard time recognizing his own work.

Blok, on the other hand, began *The Twelve* with street talk and racy doggerel and ended up with the figure of Christ. Unacceptable to many, this Christ was for Blok rich in content. Though taken aback himself, Blok insisted to the end of his days that *The Twelve* came off exactly as it was supposed to.

The "Christ" finale serves as a kind of closing epigraph, in which the riddle of the poem is unexpectedly solved.

"I don't like the ending of *The Twelve* either," said Blok. "I wanted a different ending. After finishing it, I was myself astonished and wondered: Why Christ, after all? Do I really need Christ here? Yet, the more I looked at it, the more clearly I saw Christ. And so I jotted down in my notebook: Looks like I'll have to go with Christ. With Christ and none other."

Is this an ideological Christ?

Here is an excerpt from a letter by Blok to Yury Annenkov:

Concerning Christ: He is no small, cowering figure bringing up the rear of a parade like a dog. He is not the kind to carry a flag at the back of a parade and then to be seen no more. "Christ Carrying a Flag"—that both is and isn't the Christ I have in mind. Do you know that when a flag is whipped about by the wind, we inevitably imagine someone huge and enormous standing in some relationship to it. That is, he doesn't just hold the flag or carry it. (Oh, how words fail me!)

In other words, we may understand the Christ theme in the following way: Wind. The wind rips the banners. The wind in turn calls forth the flag, and the flag, finally, calls forth someone enormous bearing a certain relationship to it. It is precisely at this point that Christ appears on the scene.

Of course, there is no denying that "he is Christ and none other" by virtue of the poet's stock of imagery, but the fact remains that he was called forth by the compositional pattern of these images (i.e., by the wind and by the flag).

It is hard, indeed, to write any piece of literature that corresponds to anything as such, whatever it be. This is so because art is not the shadow of a thing but the thing itself. A work of art makes for a poor accompanist.

One of the peculiar features of the anthroposophic theory to which Bely subscribed is its teaching of the multilayered nature of all phenomena. For example, a group of five anthroposophs (any five will do) headed by Steiner is not only a group. It is, in addition, a rose. A rose that corresponds in all its parts to a real rose. And so the world turns out, after all, to be multileveled, replicating itself in each of its parts. In its anthroposophic version, it resembles a series of shadows cast by one object placed before several sources of light.

In his epopee, Andrei Bely undertook the task of creating a multileveled structure that would vindicate the teachings of anthroposophy. The "swarm" and the "form" in *Kotik Letaev,* the crucifixion serving as a secondary level in *The Baptized Chinaman*—all of this fulfills the anthroposophic program.

Bely's works turned out well enough (though only in part), but the anthroposophic business, on the other hand, fared quite poorly. Feeling a need for secondary motivation, Bely uses linguistic techniques and the consciousness of a child to connect the two planes of swarm and form, world and consciousness, in *Kotik Letaev.* Overpowered by the literary material, the anthroposophical theory only served to intensify and consolidate the metaphor leitmotivs.

Instead of a multileveled anthroposophic work, what results is ornamental prose. The relationship between the two planes becomes thoroughly complicated, and a "realistic resolution" is therefore introduced. (See the case of "Lion" below.) At times Bely himself takes a rather humorous view of the collision of these two planes.

In the example later, where Aunt Dottie represents both herself and "Eternity," she is depicted with a carpet-beater in her hand. Eternity, therefore, is represented by this carpet-beater, too. In doing this, Bely does not give meaning to eternity nor does he symbolize it. Instead, he transfers the attributes from one metaphor leitmotiv to another. By means of this device he establishes a semantic disparity. In the struggle between anthroposophy and the device called forth by it, the device has devoured the theory. The ornamental prose of Andrei Bely has taken its place beside similar works by Leskov, Remizov, et al., that arose out of circumstances unique to them.

Andrei Bely is the most fascinating writer of our times. All of contemporary Russian fiction bears the stamp of his work. If we were to compare Bely to smoke, then we could go one step further and compare Boris Pilnyak to the shadow of smoke.

Andrei Bely was a prolific author who wrote in a wide variety of genres. He is the author of *The Silver Dove, Petersburg* and *Kotik Letaev,* the first volume of his epopee. I don't think that he himself knows just what this epopee consists of. Sometimes he says that the *Symphonies, Petersburg, The Silver Dove* and *Notes of an Eccentric* are all "medallions of an immense tale." He adds that *Notes of an Eccentric* is merely a preface to this epic. Now Andrei Bely tells us that he, Andrei Bely, wants to write like a simple cobbler. Having renounced the novel, he asks himself the following question in the name of the reader: Just what is this thing that you are offering us? It's neither a tale nor a diary, but disconnected bits of memories and "leaps."

Nonetheless, there is no need to exaggerate the validity of an author's pronouncements concerning himself. Often on such occasions, a writer addresses not his craftsmanship but the ideological position to which he is sympathetic. For example, in discussing his literary influences, an author will often point not to his own teacher but to some other writer, someone, you guessed it, who resembles him the least. Pilnyak, for instance, dedicates his work not to Andrei Bely but to Alexei Remizov.

## 2

Dresden, my friends, is absolutely gorgeous.

High atop a mountain overlooking the fields of Saxony, cherry trees blossom each spring. The trees are blue, as blue in the brilliant sunshine as forest scenery in the theater. Such stage sets are usually painted blue instead of green. And the blue fields of Germany are also blue in the spring air. Or, rather, they appear blue, while the viewer remembers them green. Leaping off from the mountain's wall of limestone below, the Elba River rushes on to Hamburg, dull as a kitchen knife.

And on that very mountain, which goes by the name of Cherry Mountain, or, then again, perhaps Deer Mountain (be sure to look it up, if you are ever in Dresden), there is a garden.

Every tree in this garden rests against a form fashioned out of iron rods. The tree is bound firmly to this form by its branches. The forms in question depict either a woman in a skirt or a soldier saluting in a peakless cap. The tree too is saluting, attached as it is to the iron form. A man might scream from the sheer horror of it all. At times this recalls Andrei Bely, who, like the saluting tree, is bound to the theory of anthroposophy. Bely feels duty-bound to write about Rudolf Steiner, his mentor, to discard his own mask and point out all of the anthroposophic hues in Blok.

Bely felt compelled to bind Blok to the iron trellis too. And yet Blok was a free man. Beginning his poetic career by quoting from Solovyov, Blok in due course came to write *The Fair Show Booth,* where he took an ironic view of his own mysticism.

For Blok, mysticism and sunrises, satirical doggerel and gypsy revelry— all of these are fair game for art.

Bely, though, reproaches Blok severely for his betrayal and laments the fact that he, Bely, a stranger to anthroposophy at the time, had been unable to show Blok how to live and write.

And yet Bely himself wrote his *Symphonies* from an ironic point of view. And even as we speak, Bely is adapting certain parts of his *Petersburg* for the vaudeville stage.

Lev Trotsky said somewhere that when engaging in polemics a man should maintain his emotional distance. He should know. He has been polemicizing for a long time.

An artist must maintain an emotional distance. He must not allow himself to be arm-twisted. He must adopt an ironic attitude toward his material and not let it get to him. Same as in boxing or fencing.

In my opinion, the reason for Andrei Bely's current failure lies in his unironic, incoherent exclamations on behalf of Rudolf Steiner. People are saying that Steiner's Johannes Building, whose columns were carved by Andrei Bely himself, has burned to the ground, and that the Jesuits are to blame. It is also rumored that Steiner is rebuilding this Johannes Building on a foundation of concrete. If it were up to me, I'd roll about four hundred pounds of dynamite into the basement of the building, cover the explosives with stone, run a Bickford fuse from it and show Steiner how to blow a building to smithereens. Why? Because a writer should never be yoked to a trellis and forced to salute.

Let Steiner have his Johannes Building. Still, art itself does not admit any tethers, and Andrei Bely simply wasted his time in Dornach.

Of course, if Steiner has recovered, then long live Dornach!

The art of the novel refuses to swallow the bait of anthroposophy. Bely's work represents an attempt on the part of anthroposophy to devour crafts-manship. Well, it was craftsmanship instead that devoured anthroposophy and continues to feed off it as if it were dung.

From his point of view, Andrei Bely wants to discard his mask, to make a clean break with the device itself, to renounce form, even while writing his epopee. A more objective assessment, though (and he himself has suggested it), would call for him to renounce his *Notes of an Eccentric* and to return to the novel form.

Still, don't fall for theatrical posturings. Beneath an actor's mask you'll find greasepaint.

Andrei Bely was no simple cobbler when he wrote *Notes of an Eccentric.* No sirree!

On the contrary, he even

> played
> such
> tricks
> as
> depicting
> a
> German
> mine

about to explode against the side of the ship on which he was traveling home. A cobbler is hardly capable of such art.

*Notes of an Eccentric* contains one of Bely's most complex structures. The compositors who set this "cobbler's" angular patterns, columns, and zigzags in type said that they had never faced such a complex task of composing in their life and demanded overtime pay.

In *Notes of an Eccentric* we observe a complex structure. Based on autobiographical materials with time shifts, this tale involves whole series of comparisons—metaphor leitmotivs connected to the original metaphor by means of puns.

For example, it turns out that Andrei Bely had never crossed "the frontiers of Switzerland." No, he had only crossed the "frontiers of his own self":

Clattering along and knocking against each other, the train cars rushed along the French landscape. The wind blew into the window, and my head spun as it struck the seat before me. The gleams of electric lamps flew in and out of the car, and my waking consciousness fell apart: The boundary of my consciousness shifted. I had crossed the frontiers of Switzerland, that is, the frontiers of my consciousness.

The metaphor leitmotivs, we may affirm, exist prior to their realization in the world.

Not infrequently, this is motivated by having recourse to a device that has become a tradition in the history of novels—the dream. As a novelistic device, it serves two functions: as a form of *premonition* and as a form of *prediction.* Often a dream may lead to a definite perception of future events. Sometimes, too, a dream may simply motivate the fantastic. I shall not bother with examples. Just look in Dostoevsky.

There is no point in becoming enamored of the biography of an artist. He writes first and looks for motivations later. And least of all should one be enamored of psychoanalysis. Psychoanalysis studies the psychological traumas of *one* person, while in truth, an author never writes *alone*. A school of writers writes through him. A whole age.

Let us try to formulate what it is that we see in Bely's works of the past six or seven years.

These works are autobiographic in origin or, rather, they are written as autobiographies. Plot development is rudimentary. In fact, you could say that, in reality, there is no plot at all. There is only the story line of a man who lives, reaches maturity, and grows old.

On this foundation the author has erected metaphor leitmotivs that serve as superstructures, as high-rise buildings. These structures—let's imagine them as buildings—are connected to each other by means of little suspension bridges. As the story moves along, it creates pretexts for the creation of new metaphorical leitmotivs which are connected, the moment they come into being, with the leitmotivs already in place. This is true of *Notes of an Eccentric, Kotik Letaev,* and *The Baptized Chinaman.*

The departures from this fundamental structure are effected somewhat differently in the case of Bely's *Recollections of Blok.*

The fragmentary "Arbat" (published in *Novaya Rossiya*) is constructed along simpler lines. Yet, Bely's touch is evident here, too, in the way he standardizes his imagery. So much so that in the latter part of the work Bely treats these images as if they were a kind of terminology.

The most consistent development of the two-tiered structure is to be found in *Kotik Letaev.*

### 3

*Kotik Letaev* was completed by Bely in 1917 and was evidently intended to form a part of the epopee. This epopee consists, first and foremost, of memoirs. This memoirist aspect of Bely's work has risen in prominence with each new work.

*Recollections of Blok* illustrates this memoiristic genre in its pure form. In special chapters devoted to an anthroposophic exegesis, Bely applies the devices used by interpreters of the church fathers to passages from Blok.

"Arbat" is pure memoir. What distinguishes this memoir, for example, from that of Koni, is Bely's peculiar use of images. Even in those passages where he most earnestly pursues his anthroposophic program, Bely fails to create an anthroposophic artifact. He succeeds only in creating a special imagistic structure.

In *Kotik Letaev,* which is almost entirely devoid of plot, the image holds complete sway. For this reason, the autobiographical works of Bely stand in sharp contrast to Dickens's equally autobiographical *David Copperfield.* In the latter we find a definite plot that involves two secrets: Grandmother's secret (i.e., that her husband is alive) and Uriah Heep's secret (the forging of documents). Em'ly's destiny is predicted by the use of premonitions. *David Copperfield* is very well-plotted. Of course, traditional novelistic techniques of plot formation do appear in *Kotik Letaev* and in *The Baptized Chinaman.* But, like the customs of the British Parliament—where a certain Lord of the Exchequer sits on a leather bag lined with fur—literary forms may outlive their usefulness. And what's the reason for these holdovers from the past? There is only one way to find out: Consult a reference book!

*Kotik Letaev* is a story about a little boy. Though told in the first person, it begins before the boy's birth. For that reason Bely has selected a passage from Tolstoi as his epigraph for this work. It may serve as a kind of caveat:

"You know," said Natasha in a whisper, "I think that when you start remembering, you really remember, you remember everything, even that which took place before you were born." (*War and Peace*)

These remembrances of the prenatal past are carried out in the following manner: A series of images is first presented. Then its point of departure from and contact with the story line is indicated. Finally, the formation of the boy's consciousness is expressed as the ravings of an infant in the throes of growth.

And now for some examples:

Each of our thoughts is like a vortex: the ocean of existence, moving in each thought, pours into the body like a cosmic storm. Leaping up, a child's thought brings to mind a comet. There it goes, bloodying its tail as it falls into a body and then pouring itself out in a rain of blood-red carbuncles into the ocean of sensations. Between the body and the thought, the watery vortex and the fire, someone has flung a baby. And the baby is terrified.

"Help!"
"It can't be helped!"
"Save me!"

"Madam, he's growing up."

There it is: the first episode of existence. The author fixes it firmly in his memory and describes it with precision. If it is as described (and it is), then we have been allowed a fleeting glimpse of pre-corporeal life through memory.

In the excerpt above, the device of "illumination" (see below) is only hinted at.

Let me quote further from the middle of the chapter entitled "On Fire." This title contains the motivation for images of delirium:

At first there were no images to speak of, though a place had been set for them suspended before me. Soon thereafter a child's nursery opened up before me. Behind me, a gaping hole was coalescing. It then turned into the mouth of a stove (the stove was a memory of something that had perished long before, of something old. Look there! The wind is whistling through the pipe of pre-temporal consciousness). . . . An exceptionally long reptile, Uncle Vasya, was crawling towards me from behind: a mustachioed young snake, he later split in two. One half of him would drop in to have dinner with us, while the other half I encountered later on the cover of a very useful book called *Extinct Monsters.* He was the dinosaur. They say that dinosaurs are extinct. Well, I saw them in the very first moments of consciousness.

My mother's voice forced its way into my ears: "He is on fire!" Much later they told me that I had been ill with dysentery, scarlet fever and measles precisely at the time my mother uttered that phrase.

Such also is the image of the "Lion" which Bely saw one day on Dog Square:

Among the strange images flashing before me from the haze of early childhood the oldest by far is that of the looming figure of the shaggy mug of a lion. The noisy hour had already struck. Around me I saw yellow mouths of sand. From them the shaggy mug and jaws are observing me calmly. A shout: "Here comes Lion!"

The "yellow mouths of sand" is the first detail to be "illuminated": "Much later I discovered the yellow circle of sand between Arbat and Dog Square."

Then follows the "illumination" of the Lion, a St. Bernard nicknamed "Lion" who used to hang around the square. This "illumination" took place twenty years later:

Twenty years later the fragments of my strange dreams became waking reality. Perhaps the labyrinth of our rooms was the original waking reality, while Uncle Vasya was the reptilian monster. And, perhaps, too, that altercation with Aphrosynia the cook was in reality the incident with the old woman. And the hurricanes of the red world were the stove in the kitchen, while the whirling torches were only sparks. I really don't know. Perhaps.

Later, though, in a chapter entitled "Nevertheless," Bely rejected this particular resolution. He asserted unequivocally that no such dog ever existed. All he had ever heard then was the cry: "Here comes Lion!"

And "Lion came."

Further on, he affirms the reality of the fantastical in the person of the "old woman and her rooms."

This game should not surprise us. It is customary in works of fantasy to leave behind an unresolved detail capable of spurring on the flagging mystery line.

So in Turgenev's "Clara Milich" the hero is cured of his nocturnal visions, which are attributed to an obvious case of delirium. Yet, on his deathbed, we find him holding a lock of hair in his hand, and this lock is introduced by the author without any resolution.

It is important for a writer to create a wide range of interpretations for his work, to introduce the possibility for "obscurity" (the very thing Blok was reproached for: i.e., his work was both this *and* that). For this reason the fantastic nature of a literary work is simultaneously affirmed and denied by the author.

Andrei Bely arrived at this device by way of anthroposophy. Yet, the regular appearance of Anna Pavlovna Sherer's salon in *War and Peace* plays much the same role of introducing an interpretation of the issue of war and peace that is at odds with that of the author. Unlike Bely, Tolstoi arrived at this device through considerations of a moral nature. But this business reminds me a lot of love affairs. Each case is unique. One man loves a woman for her blue eyes, while another man loves a woman for her grey eyes. The end result is one and the same: The earth is never short of children.

The world comes into being for Kotik Letaev. Dreams which until then had stretched out to infinity now cling like wallpaper to the walls of his room. Out of the sounds "Ti-da-do-di-ton-ty" emerges the name of "Aunt Dottie."

A little later Kotik hears Dottie play the piano. She taps melodically at the resonant, cold white keyboard:

Ton-ti
Ton-ti    To-tin-ton-ti-to.

Subsequently, "Aunt Dottie" was constructed out of a wave of sound. This is the way things are fashioned from sounds.

The real story line is indicated only by means of a dotted line. People and things are connected once again by sound waves.

And if Aunt Dottie is a sound wave, then Kotik's father, Prof. Letaev, is a "rumbling wave." He is connected to Aunt Dottie by sound.

Meanwhile, Aunt Dottie crystallizes into layers of being. This process of stratification began considerably earlier:

And Aunt Dottie dwindled before my eyes. She was not yet fully formed. She was not yet fully in the flesh, fully real. Rather, she rose silently before me like a mist from amongst the mirrors and slipcovers. She hovered over me . . .

And she was taking shape before me in severe majesty and in utter, empty calmness, moving forward with a carpet-beater raised high in her hand and with a familiar reflection in the mirrors and a no less familiar pensive look on her face: the thin, mute, tall, wretched, unsteady figure of my relative, Aunt Dottie, or, rather, Yevdokaya Yegorovna . . . that is, Eternity.

And that is how a relative of Kotik came to represent eternity. Somewhat later, Bely pulls the word from under the image and concludes with a pun: "I have a relative in Eternity."

Even as she assumes her real identity, Aunt Dottie, it turns out, is still associated in Kotik's mind with a drop of water in the washstand. She continues to be Hegel's "Bad Infinity."

## 4

It is my firm belief that a literary work, especially a long one, is not brought into being by fulfilling its task.

Yes, a task exists all right, but this task is completely altered by the technical means at the author's disposal.

The unity of a work of literature is more likely than not a myth. At least that is how I see it. And, as you know, I have written a piece of fiction or two in my time and have observed others of my generation at their craft.

Set pieces prepared in advance enter easily and conveniently into the composition of a poem. This explains the inclusion of certain set pieces in Pushkin's *Eugene Onegin.*

A monolithic literary work is perhaps possible in isolated cases. It seems to me that Bely came to understand his device of materializing the image while engaged in the creative process itself. He interpreted it in the following way: At first, he simply jotted down at the end of each chapter a note to the effect that he had been ill or that he was growing at the time. Then he consolidated the device by introducing the concepts of "swarm" and "form."

Objectively speaking, "swarm" designates a leitmotiv of metaphors, while "form" stands for an object inhering in a leitmotiv secured to the story line.

Subjectively speaking, form stands for the world already formed, while swarm designates the coming into being of the world. Swarm always precedes form.

The swarm is motivated by Kotik's infantile consciousness, by his illness, etc. It is also motivated by anthroposophy, which serves to replace the "spurious" motivation of childhood.

The appearance of the swarm, the loosening of plot structure, and a shift in favor of the image have brought into being a school of writers known as the Ornamentalists.

Contemporary Russian prose is to a large extent ornamental in character. That is, the imagery prevails over the plot. Certain Ornamentalists like Zamyatin or Pilnyak show Bely's direct influence, while others like Vsevolod Ivanov show no influence at all. Still others show the influence of Pilnyak and Zamyatin. Yet, this Ornamentalism has emerged on the literary scene less as a result of literary influences than in response to the general feeling that the old form has lost its resilience.

Social pressures and ideologies may be beneficial to the artist by spurring him on to change his form and to give it artistic expression in his subsequent work.

And now concerning the swarm and form in Bely:

The very first moments of my existence were a "swarm." "Swarm, swarm every-where—the whole world is a swarm" became my first philosophy. I was swept up in a swarm first and only later did I begin describing wheels with the old woman. The wheel and the sphere were the first to crystallize out of the swarm.

That which had crystallized had become for me form: Wheeling round and round I came out eventually through a hole leading into a pipe, and so on.

While Papa is emerging out of the swarm, the bullheaded man turns into Doctor Dornovov and Aunt Dottie arises out of her sound wave.

Objects arise out of words. Sometimes the swarm is presented as a pun motivated by a child's perception. For instance:

Mama kept repeating: "Yezheshikhinsky."
"What's that?"
"He's ended up in the gutter."

This is confirmed by someone's voice: " 'Yezheshikhinsky is spilling his guts.' "

The misfortunes of Yezheshikhinsky, who had wandered off into some tunnels and was still wandering through them to this day, occasioned Bely's first reflection on the vicissitudes of fate:

Explanation is the recollection of euphony. Understanding is their dance. Education is the ability to fly on words. The harmony of words is a siren.

As always, we are dealing here with one of Bely's puns. The word *obrazovanie,* for example, has two meanings: (a) education (the acquisition of knowledge), and (b) the formation (of something).

Bely is astounded by the sound of the word *Kre-ml* (Kremlin):

The "Kremlin"? What's that? I remember that I had once tasted a sweet creme-brûle. It was served in the form of a cookie mold with projecting ledges. I also remember that someone once showed me a "Kremlin" at Sevostjanov's Pastry Shop. These were projecting ledges of pink turrets made of fruit-drop. And I suddenly realized that the *kre* stood for the strength of the projecting ledges in the Kremlin [*Kreml'*] in cream [*krem*] and fortress [*krepost'*], while the *m* and *ml* stood for softness [*mjagkost'*] and sweetness [*sladost'*] and only then did they show me in the distant blue sky the rosy, firm, sweet towers of the Kremlin.

At times Bely uses the realized metaphor or the literal meaning of the word:

"Valerian Valerianovich Bleshchensky . . ."
"What's that?"
"He's a burned-out drunk!"
And Valerian Valerianovich Bleshchensky stands before me . . . consumed in flames. He is no better than a log, a puppet made of wood: the wooden puppet staring out of the barbershop window.

The swarm dominates the first two chapters of *Kotik Letaev.* Once the leitmotivs are firmly established, the author turns to the story line. The images here do not appear out of nothing. Rather, each protagonist— Papa, Doctor Pfeffer, the nanny—has its own leitmotiv. Kotik's habits— squinting, the sensation aroused in him by the gruel and even his sitting on a special baby armchair—are each furnished with its own leitmotiv. The moment they are mentioned in the text, they call forth their leit-motivs. As events in the domain of form, they are merely hooks to which the swarm is secured. The moment a new detail becomes swarm, it extends through the entire novel. Accompanying the leitmotivs in the story line, the swarm supports the literary work like a lining:

> I know how to squint my eyes, to look at my nose. And the patterns slip away.
>
> I look out from my bed at the bouquets of flowers on the wallpaper. I know how to squint my eyes, and the walls, flying over to my nose, slip away.
>
> I know how to squint my eyes, to look at my nose. The walls slip away.

Squinting is no frivolous game. Rather, it is a displacement of things, an overthrowing of form, a transition, a return to swarm. At times, the relationship between swarm and form is intentionally paradoxical. The infant on the chamberpot is really an ancient Orphist. His meal has betrayed him, and so he contemplates the ancient serpents and beholds the metamorphoses of the universe.

Bely is concerned here with the second motivation for his work (the first one being anthroposophy), but he fails to sustain its verisimilitude. His little boy sees, in great detail, the inner structure of a human skull. He sees hemispheres and constructs leitmotivs that, instead of realizing the metaphor, deprive the word of substance.

The general structure of a literary work allows one and only one of its tasks to gain dominance. The anthroposophic work written by Bely at the very height of his anthroposophic obsession turned more and more into autobiography.

## 5

*The Baptized Chinaman* continues *Kotik Letaev* and partly duplicates it. If we look at the story line, then the beginning of one work seems to overlap with the end of the other. From this point of view *The Baptized Chinaman* may be considered a second edition of *Kotik Letaev.* Andrei Bely's feelings concerning this work were, in fact, quite ambivalent.

*The Baptized Chinaman,* according to Bely, is a form of spiritual milk, of "food for the neophyte." But don't believe a writer. His worldview is quite separate from his literary work and should be considered as no more than an appendix to it. A poet often renounces verse in verse, while a novelist renounces fiction in fiction. Even in the cinema a hero will reply on the screen (I myself have seen this), "How beautiful! Just like in the movies." The creation of an illusion, its consolidation, and its dismantling are all devices of art. Objectively speaking, we may suppose that *The Baptized Chinaman* partially replaced *Notes of an Eccentric* and partially displaced *Kotik Letaev* in the author's inner struggle. One thing is certain: *The Baptized Chinaman* concedes nothing to the "neophyte."

By its structure, *The Baptized Chinaman* captures our attention by the fact that its memoirist character is even more pronounced than before: it is richer in events. Kotik's parents, developed apart from and existing independently of their son, now dominate the stage. The swarm has been dispersed. Perhaps it is in connection with this that the language of this work has changed its character: the imagistic difficulties associated with *Kotik Letaev* yield place here to difficulties associated merely with the use of dialect. It is no longer the image but the word that is enstranged.

In order to bring out this density, let me offer some examples taken from two different pages:

> Beyond the window, where the fog is, a pewter haze fell like a flurry of snowflakes, welded into drops, and a drizzle fell: Yes, a drizzle. A thaw is whirling down from the water-drinking gutters.

> And he would hurl obscenities, grin from ear to ear and show his gums (of course Grandma called them by a different name). He would cackle, gurgle, cough and utter a wild indecency.

Bely himself understands the dictionary meaning of his language perfectly well. For example, consider the following:

> I once overheard Grandma say: "He wore a barley cap!"
> And just what is a "barley cap"? Well, you can scratch your head all you want, but you'll never find it there. Try an unabridged!

It is curious how seriously the author relates to the word and with what specificity he uses it.

Kotik is being crucified. The quarrel raging between father and mother assumes cosmic proportions. Still, the word is brought into relief because it is part of the game of craftsmanship, that is, it is taken seriously. And here no miracle will help.

The swarm is gone, replaced by the world that has come into being. Yet, as an artist intent on maintaining the disparity of things, Bely needed a different version of our world. This different world is presented in this work by a generalizing of phenomena.

In *Kotik Letaev* the father grows to become a Socrates, a Moses, and the quarrel between papa and mama becomes an eternal quarrel. The tragedy of the protagonists is that each is struggling over "something uniquely his or her own." This at first seems a joke but, much later, it turns out to be quite fundamental. Bugaev (Bely's father) is presented in his ordinary, comic state, and therefore so much the more convincingly does the "something uniquely his own" in him lag behind the leitmotiv of Socrates and Confucius with whom he is associated.

Nonetheless, this "something uniquely one's own" was first spoken by Henrietta Martinova, the backward German nanny, in reference to a certain German.

This nonsensical phrase seemed, like a sign, to contain some hidden meaning. In fact, though, it has no meaning. Its alleged secret turns out not to exist at all, even though it is applied to Kotik's father and mother and to Aphrosim (who has a tendency to turn into Immortality). To complete the leitmotiv and deepen the mystery, it is even applied, finally, to two griffins on someone's doorway.

The mechanical application of an expression to a leitmotiv or concept by means of griffins is bound up with traditional mysteries. Here the mystery is given under the guise of nonsense or "obscurity" (i.e., a purely verbal confusion), for which Blok was reproached (by Bely himself). This confusion was, perhaps, necessary for art, but it did not lead to anthroposophy.

The canonization of the image leitmotivs and epithets running throughout Bely's works already begins in *The Baptized Chinaman.* The protagonists are persecuted by their corresponding leitmotivs. Often an image is comically realized and not once but several times, changing each time through the use of puns:

Uncle Vasya owns a medal and a cockade conferred upon him for bravery in battle. He has been nominated for a medal. Instead, for five years now he has been screaming and hollering, and to this day he is still trying to get his foot in the front door of the Imperial Treasury Department.

"How is that?" Well, it's not so simple if you are a rock, but quite easy if you are a strip of felt.

"How is that? You mean bent over like a hunchback?"

Bely then proceeds to realize the metaphor "bent over" by describing how Uncle Vasya bent over three times, shoved his head between his legs and pulled his handkerchief from under his coattails with his teeth. In order to complete the realization of this metaphor, this entire excerpt is set by Bely in an angular column in the middle of the page. The column bends like a hunchback.

Uncle Vasya's revolt and drunkenness is depicted by denying this second leitmotiv, by a repudiation of the realized image:

And Mama played—

And the events of life, dislodged and swept away, fluttered in the nothingness of the sounds. Once again a tall man comes towards us across the years. It's Uncle. He rises on his thin stilts, on his legs and walks forever away from us along the white roofs. He disappears into the sky and from there he begins railing at us from heaven: "Yes, I am tired of bending over like a hunchback. Enough is enough!"

"I am tired of trying to get my foot in the front door of the Treasury Department!"

"Here is the strip of felt and here are some stones. Let others try to shove their way in!"

"I'm tired of wearing out my life as a clerk. It's a useless profession!"

"I'm leaving you!"

I've deliberately extended this excerpt in order to show the relationship that exists between the images: the playing of Kotik's mother is associated with her "roulade" leitmotiv, while the final phrase generalizes "Uncle Vasya."

The playing itself is presented later in the form of a little girl, but still later she turns into Understanding.

In the conventional novel the protagonists' association with objects in the story line takes the limelight. If the hero was accompanied by anything, it was usually by an object, and at times this object played a role in the plot, serving as one of the connecting threads in the plot.

In Andrei Bely, though, it is not objects but images that are connected. The epopee is an enterprise of major scope.

6

*Recollections of Blok* may not be an epopee, but it is not far off. Most likely, it is material for an epopee.

This work evolves by means of both individual episodes as well as by the introduction of separate chapters devoted to Bely's anthroposophic interpretation of Blok. The latter chapters, consisting exclusively of passages quoted out of context, fail to take into consideration the changes in the meaning of words effected by their relationships with other words in the poem. These chapters purport, for example, to explain Blok's evolution in terms of the color modulations in his verse. This idea seems to be self-evident, but just the same it is wrong. One ought never to construe the works of a poet as a series of personal confessions held together by a kind of scouts' honor. Even a writer as given to the confessional mode as Bely is cannot succeed in unburdening his soul. That which Bely claims as a personal utterance is, in the final analysis, a new literary genre.

Even less so should we believe in the documentary character of a poet's confessions and in the earnestness of his worldview.

A poet's worldview is distorted—when the poet is indeed a professional one—by the fact that it serves as a source of material for his poems.

For that reason there is much irony in a poet's beliefs. They are, after all, full of mischief. The boundaries separating the serious from the humorous are blurred in a poet partly by the fact that the humorous form, being the least canonized and at the same time the most open to semantic disparities, lays the ground for new forms of serious art. The relationship between, on the one hand, the forms of the journal *Satirikon* and Mayakovsky's forms, and, on the other hand, between the doggerel of Russian vaudeville and the verse of Nekrasov has been brought out on numerous occasions by Formalistic critics (Osip Brik, Boris Eikhenbaum, Yury Tynyanov). Examples from Andrei Bely are less well known. His *Symphonies* border on humor, that is, the serious interpretation came later. Just the same, the new Russian literature is inconceivable without the *Symphonies*. Even those who scold Bely do so under the influence of his less than fully conscious style. As a matter of fact, Bely himself (if memory serves me right) once assured me of the "humorous" character of his *Symphonies*. He had the look of a man who had suddenly come across an astonishing illustration in the 1893 edition of *Niva*.

Apart from the anthroposophic chapters with their passages devoted to the lilac and gold color scheme, *Recollections of Blok* reverberates with the quarrels between Blok and Bely. These quarrels were most likely quite real and could not be reduced to a mere matter of style. Yet, we must make certain concrete reservations. In the good old days a writer would not have washed his dirty linen in public (Lvov-Rogachevsky believes that this is because writers in the old days would never have stooped that low). From the facts available to him, each writer decides for himself which ones he'll use in his novel and which ones he'll forego. For example, Chekhov never published his notebooks during his lifetime, and yet for us they are interesting in and of themselves. Gorky, on the other hand, is publishing his notebooks, while Chekhov's tales now seem rather stale. There is a tale about a peasant and a bear who worked as a team. Splitting their yield fifty-fifty, they agreed that one of them would get the roots, while the other took the green leaves. Well, the cunning peasant outsmarted the bear: When he sowed rye, he offered the bear the roots, and when he sowed turnips, he offered the suspicious bear the green leaves. Literature, too, has its root-lovers as well as its leaves-lovers, and the focus of the literary moment shifts continually from one camp to the next. Nowadays writers are sowing their turnips, as memoir literature; "the raw material of writers' notebooks" is riding high in the public's esteem.

This quarrel between Blok and Bely (apart from certain factors unknown to us that have not been elucidated in this book) is described in these *Recollections* in a way that implies that Bely was always a Dresden tree, while Blok never was. True, Bely, Aleksandr and Lyubov Blok and S. M. Solovyov formed a community that claimed the right to install a "Mama" on the throne of Orthodoxy as a counterpart to the Catholic "Papa" in Rome. The charter of this society, however, was meant as a kind of joke, as a parody. It is also true that Bely considered the wedding of Aleksandr and Lyubov Blok an event of epochal significance, with controversy raging as to whom Lyubov really represented: Some said Beatrice; others said Sophia. Meanwhile, the very formation of this coterie, which Bely views anthroposophically, was a deliberate act of parody.

The sessions of this coterie were repeatedly interrupted by jokes, improvisational skits and pure caricature:

We could have used the *Golden Carpet* of Apollo: We played the fool as we acted out what we would probably have looked like to the uninitiated. S. M. Solovyov would usually begin the buffoonery. And we would appear in these parodies performed in our presence like a sect of "Blok acolytes," under the searching eye of the conscientious Professor of Culture from the thirteenth century. Given the name of Lapan by Solovyov, this fictitious professor raised the abstruse question of whether a sect such as ours had ever really existed at all.*

*Bely may be playing on po*krov* (root meaning: "to cover"), the Symbolist image for the cover or veil (suggested by J. Hellie). "Appolonov" may refer not only to Apollo but also to the Apollonian hedonistic sect (suggested by J. Winston). The Fink reprint of Bely's works has *nuzhem* for *muzhem*. "Thirteenth" may be typo for "twenty-second." [Trans. note]

And so the philosophical idea existed in this milieu in a form bordering on parody. Blok's retreat from Lapan's commandments, as depicted by Bely, never took place in reality but rather between the covers of these *Recollections*. For the Bely of 1922, Lapan was the fountainhead of truth.

Blok's ironic, playful treatment of mysticism in *The Fair Show Booth* was interpreted by Bely as an act of betrayal. Blok used his raw material much more freely than Bely (that is, until the writing of *The Twelve*). He simply couldn't bear Bely's friends (such as Ellis, for instance), not to mention the whole anthroposophical business itself. Turning away from the book to address the public directly, Bely reproaches fate in tragic tones:

> Later I told Blok: Through anthroposophy I discovered the very thing which had been closed to us during those years. But it was too late. Blok had been singed because he stood before the Gates earlier than anyone else.

Sometime later, Bely said:

> We gave ourselves over to the ray of light. We reached out and grasped the light like children, but the light turned out to be a flame. And we were burned by it. . . . Blok is now asleep forever, while I hobble along like a cripple along a path of redemption that has opened up too late for me.

Bely's habit of using nearly every word as a springboard for the Infinite appears to the contemporary reader to belong to the generation of 1901. It could be read as a new interpretation of swarm, but in the dosages presented here it is intolerable. How many times is it necessary for Bely to mention that "humanity" comes from "humus"?

A far more interesting compositional device is employed by Bely throughout the *Recollections of Blok:* Objects are presented from two points of view, that of Bely and that of Blok. This proves especially effective in the passage in which Bely, after describing his meeting with Blok in great detail, follows it with a hypothetical description of the selfsame scene by Blok.

In addition, the device of an image leitmotiv has experienced a renewal, compositionally speaking, and especially so in the chapters devoted to D. S. Merezhkovsky. It is here that we meet with Merezhkovsky's celebrated "pompom" slippers as well as with Priozhkov (the publisher with whom Merezhkovsky was carrying on negotiations at the time). Pirozhkov is first described, then confirmed, then simply mentioned, and suddenly he has become "an image": "Kind and ever so worldly, Merezhkovsky makes his entrance. You would have thought it was Pirozhkov who has just arrived." The work is far from perfect. Bely keeps looking for "fantastical landscapes heard silently from behind the word." However, it is the memoirs that are most successful, and among them it is the humorous pages bristling with occasional caricature that are most accessible.

I cannot say for sure what relationship "Arbat" bears to *Recollections of Blok.* In appearance a sequel to *Recollections,* this work nevertheless evinces a totally different tone: It is clearly documentary in its orientation. And yet "Arbat" cannot easily be relegated to the genre of memoirs. It is artistically conceived from beginning to end. Proper names are utilized to create a difficult form. The work seems to have been written in dialect, a dialect with solid motivation behind it. Moreover, written in periods that roll on for two pages at a time, it teems with references to facts that turn into image leitmotivs.

The higher level of the work is presented by interpreting the happenings on Arbat Avenue as a microcosm of the world.

Thus, "the light from Vygodchik" refers to the light in the Vygodchik store. Seeing this light, Bugaev (Bely's original name) utters his first word: "Fire." Yet, "the light from Vygodchik" represents at the same time "light in general," while the proper names on the Arbat are nothing less than a peculiar form of substitution for the image leitmotivs.

Like a race of people divided into those with long heads and those with short heads, the Symbolist movement was split down the middle by an old controversy. Essentially, it involved the following question: Was Symbolism merely an aesthetic method or was it something more?

All of his life, Bely championed the second alternative (i.e., that Symbolism is much more than just art).

This controversy is apparently being laid to rest. We hear little in this latest work by Bely about anthroposophy. Anthroposophy has played itself out after creating a new attitude to the image and after introducing an original two-tiered conception of a literary work.

Poincaré, I believe, once said that mathematicians routinely remove the scaffolding which enables them to build their structures in the first place. Well, Bely has begun to remove his scaffolding. His prose today is not simpler than yesterday's, but its new form is now conceived along thoroughly aesthetic lines. It will take its honored place in the Russian prose of today.

Bely's attempt to live in accordance with the principles of anthroposophy shall forever cast a shadow over his personal life. Yet, it sometimes happens that human culture has need of such misfortunes in the same way that a novel may need to separate its heroes in order to brake the action of its plot.

# Chapter 9

# Literature without a Plot: Rozanov

## 1

In Goethe's *Wilhelm Meister* we come across "A Confession of a Beautiful Soul." The heroine of this work says that there was a time when the beauty of an artist's work would affect her in the same way that the beauty of a book's type affects others: "A beautifully printed book is positively gorgeous, but who reads a book for its type?"

Both the heroine and Goethe knew that anyone who spoke this way understood nothing about art. And yet such an attitude is as characteristic of the majority of contemporary art scholars as slanted eyes are for the Chinese.

This view, already laughed off the musical stage and recognized as provincial in the fine arts, still causes quite a stir in the literary world.

In considering the so-called form of a literary work as a kind of covering which we must penetrate, the contemporary theoretician of literature reminds us of the man who tried to mount a horse but ended up overshooting it.

A literary work is pure form. It is neither thing nor material, but a relationship of materials. And, like every relationship, this one too has little to do with length or width or any other dimension. It's the arithmetic significance of its numerator and denominator (i.e., their relationship) that is important.

Humorous works, tragic works, world-encompassing or intimate works, confrontations of worlds or of cats and stones—are all equal in the eyes of literature.

It is from this that comes the inoffensive character of art, its sense of being shut up within itself, its freedom from external coercion. The history of literature progresses along a broken path. If we were to arrange all of the literary saints canonized since the seventeenth century along one line, we would still fail to produce a single line of descent that might allow us to trace the history of literary form. On the one hand, what Pushkin wrote about Derzhavin [that he "thought in Tartar," not Russian—Trans.] is neither witty nor true. On the other hand, Nekrasov does not take the Pushkin tradition as his point of departure. Among prose writers Tolstoi quite obviously did not take his cue from Turgenev or from Gogol, while Chekhov, most certainly, did not have his origin in Tolstoi. These ruptures in literary history take place for reasons that have nothing to do with chronology.

No, the real point is that the legacy that is passed on from one literary generation to the next moves not from father to son but from uncle to nephew. Let us at first develop this formula. In each literary epoch there exists not one but several literary schools. They exist in literature in a state of simultaneity. However, one of them represents a canonized crest in its evolution, while the other schools coexist without such canonization in a state of obscurity. At the time of Pushkin, for example, the tradition of Derzhavin lived on in the verse of Kyukhelbeker, and similarly, the tradition of Griboedov existed alongside the tradition of Russian vaudeville verse and other such traditions as that of the adventure novel in Bulgarin.

Pushkin's tradition did not survive him. Instead, his example was followed by the disappearance of highly gifted children and geniuses from the literary scene.

At this very same time, however, new literary forms are emerging out of the lower stratum of society to replace the old ones. The old forms, no more consciously felt than grammatical forms are in speech, have lost their artistic character to assume an official status that precludes sensation. The new line of development breaks in on the old and the vaudeville showman Belopyatkin becomes Nekrasov (work of Osip Brik), Tolstoi, a direct descendant of the eighteenth century, creates a new novel (Boris Eikhenbaum), Blok canonizes the themes and the rhythms of the "gypsy song," while Chekhov introduces the alarm clock into Russian literature. Finally, Dostoevsky raises the devices of the cheap novel to the level of a literary norm. Each new literary school is a new revolution, something in the nature of a new class.

Of course, this is only an analogy. The defeated "line" is not annihilated, it does not cease to exist. It is only dethroned, pushed aside from its dominant position on the crest and submerged beneath it. Still, it continues to move forward, always poised for a resurrection as the eternal claimant to the throne. In reality, the matter is made much more complex by the fact that the new ruler does not usually represent a pure restoration of the previous form but rather includes features of other younger schools as well as the features inherited from its predecessor on the throne. But now in an official capacity.

Now let us turn to Vasily Rozanov for more digressions.

In my earlier essay on Rozanov I touched only upon his three latest books: *Solitaria* and the two volumes of *Fallen Leaves* (first and second "bundles").

Intimate to the point of offense, these works naturally reflect the soul of their author. But I shall endeavor to prove that the soul of a literary work is none other than its structure or form. Using my formula to the effect that the "content" (the soul is meant here) of a literary work is equal to the sum of its stylistic devices, permit me to turn to a passage from Rozanov:

> Everyone imagines the soul is a kind of being. But why couldn't it be music? And so they look for its "properties" (the properties of an object). But why couldn't it just have form? . . . (*Fallen Leaves*)

An artifact has a soul that is very much like a form, like the geometric relationship of masses. The choice of material for a work of art is also accomplished along formal lines. This material is chosen for its significant, felt dimensions. Every epoch has its own Index, its own list of themes forbidden because of their obsolescence. For example, Tolstoi imposes his own Index, which forbids him to write about the romantic Caucasus or about the moonlight. Here we meet with a typical banning of Romantic themes. In Chekhov we see something quite different. In his juvenile work entitled "What We Encounter Most Often in Novels and in Tales and so on," Chekhov enumerates stereotypical venues:

> Rich uncle, liberal or conservative depending upon circumstances:
> His exhortations are not quite as useful for the hero as death.
> Auntie is in Tambov.
> A doctor with a worried face offering hope in a crisis often carries a cane with a knob and is also often bald.
> The dachas on the edge of Moscow and the mortgaged estate in the south.

As you can see, a prohibition is imposed on certain typical, everyday "situations." This prohibition is made, not because there is a shortage of doctors to announce that the crisis has passed, but because this situation has become stereotypical.

It is possible to renew a cliché by emphasizing its conventionality. And here success is possible by playing with banality. But such success is unique. Let me illustrate from Heine:

> The rose, the lily, the sun
> all of whom I once loved in love's ecstasy

(There is further a play on rhymes: alleine-eine-kleine-seine-reine = krof'-lyubof', radost'-mladost'.)

But the outlawed themes continue to exist outside the literary canon in the same way that the erotic anecdote exists to this very day or in the way that repressed desires exist in the psyche, revealing themselves unexpectedly in dreams. Domesticity as a theme, the domestic attitude toward things, and the theme of infidelity were never or almost never brought up in "high society" literature. Still, it existed elsewhere, such as in the genre of letters: "I'm kissing you in the children's room behind the screen. You are wearing a grey bonnet—" Tolstoi writes his wife (29 November 1864). In another passage he says:

> And so Seroyosha put his face on the oilcloth and cried "agu?" I shall go and see. You astonished me by saying that you sleep on the floor. But Lyubof' Alexandra said that she too "slept on the floor," and I understood. I like it and then again I don't like it when you imitate her. I would like for you to be essentially as good a person as she is.
>
> Day after tomorrow on the nursery oilcloth floor, I shall embrace you, my slender, prompt, sweet wife. (December 10, 1864)

As time passed, Tolstoi's material and device lost their luster and degenerated into a cliché. Being a genius, Tolstoi had no disciples. And without posting a new list of forbidden themes, his art went out of use. At that moment ensued what happens in marital life when the feeling of distinction between husband and wife is blurred. In the words of Rozanov:

> The cogs rub against each other without engaging. The shaft stops, and the work grinds to a halt, because the machine as a system of reciprocating units has ceased to exist.
> This love, which has, of course, died, can never be resurrected. From this it follows that before the midnight hour has tolled, acts of infidelity flare up as in a final attempt to revive love. Nothing so differentiates, estranges lovers as betrayal. The other cog, not yet effaced, comes to life and engages with a cog lying opposite it. (*Fallen Leaves*)

The shifting movements represent just such a betrayal in literature.

It is a well-known fact that the greatest works of literature (I'm speaking here only of prose) do not fit into the framework of a particular genre. It is difficult to determine precisely what *Dead Souls* represents (i.e., what category to classify it under). *War and Peace* and *Tristram Shandy,* in spite of their nearly total lack of a framing story, may be called novels for the very reason that they violate the laws of a novel. The purity of a genre (for example, of the genre of "pseudo-classical tragedy") is understood only in opposition to a genre that has not yet been canonized. But the canonized novel lends itself to self-parody and modification perhaps more than any other genre. In accordance with the canon of the eighteenth-century novel, I would like to permit myself a digression.

Concerning digressions. There is a chapter in Fielding's *Joseph Andrews* that is placed by the author after a description of a fight. In it Fielding describes a conversation between himself and an actor. This chapter is announced as being "of no other use in this history, but to divert the reader" (book 3, chap. 10).

Generally speaking, digressions play three roles:

The first role consists of permitting the introduction of new material into the novel. So, for example, the speeches of Don Quixote permit Cervantes to introduce into the novel a variety of critical and philosophical materials.

Of far greater significance is the second role played by digressions, that is, of braking the action, of holding it back. This device is widely used by Sterne. In Sterne's hands this device consists essentially of a plot motif developed by either one of the characters or by the introduction of a new theme (as for example the story of the hero's aunt and her coachman).

Toying with the reader's impatience, the author repeatedly reminds him of the deserted hero. Nonetheless, he does not return to him after the digression, and reminding the reader serves only to renew the reader's expectation.

In a novel involving parallel intrigues, as in Victor Hugo's *Les Misérables* or in the novels of Dostoevsky, the interruption of one action by another is utilized as material for digression.

Thirdly, digressions in literature also serve the function of creating contrast.

This is what Fielding has to say about it:

And here we shall of Necessity be led to open a new Vein of Knowledge, which, if it hath been discovered, hath not, to our Remembrance, been wrought on by any antient or modern Writer. This Vein is no other than that of Contrast, which runs through all the Works of the Creation, and may, probably, have a large Share in constituting in us the Idea of all Beauty, as well natural as artificial: For what demonstrates the Beauty and Excellence of any Thing but its Reverse? Thus the Beauty of Day, and that of Summer, is set off by the Horrors of Night and Winter. And, I believe, if it was possible for a Man to have seen only the two former, he would have a very imperfect Idea of their Beauty. (*Tom Jones,* book 5, chap. 1)

I believe that the above passage sufficiently elucidates the third role performed by digressions, that is, the creation of contrasts.

In gathering his book, Heine selected his chapters with great care, changing their order when necessary, in order to create just such a contrast.

## 2

Let us now return to Rozanov.

The three volumes by Rozanov examined here represent a totally new genre, an extraordinary act of betrayal. Social and topical essays, presented as autonomous fragments, contradict each other at every point. A biography of Rozanov and scenes from his life as well as photographs, etc., have also been included.

These books are not entirely formless, since we see in them a certain constancy in the device used in their formation. For me these books represent a new genre, a genre that resembles, above all, the parodistic novel, that is, with the weakly expressed framing story (the main plot) and without a comic tinge.

Rozanov's work represents a heroic attempt to go beyond the confines of literature, "to speak without words, without form," and the work has turned out splendidly, because it has given birth to a new literature, a new form.

Rozanov introduces culinary themes into literature for the very first time. Such domestic themes had, admittedly, made their appearance earlier: the sight of Lotte cutting bread in *Werther* was for its time a revolutionary phenomenon, just as the name "Tatiana" was in Pushkin's novel. But the family hearth, the quilt, the kitchen and its smells (i.e., aside from satire) had never appeared in literature before.

Rozanov introduces these themes without reservation, for example, in an entire series of fragments:

My kitchen account-book rivals Turgenev's letters to Viardot. This book, of course, is a very different kind of thing, but the axis of the world runs through this book just as much as through Turgenev's, and, basically, it is just as poetical.

What effort and what care has gone into this kitchen ledger! And with what trepidation has the writer made his entries, lest the pen step over the lines! And what a sense of satisfaction when all of the columns tally perfectly.

And here is another passage:

I love tea, and I love to mend a cigarette (where it has been torn). I love my wife and my garden on my dacha. (*Fallen Leaves*)

Or consider, for example, the following passage motivated by nostalgia:

Just the same I shake out the cigarette butts. Not always, but if one half of the cigarette or even less has been left unsmoked, I will shake them. "You have to make use of them, you have to use the leftover tobacco." But I earn twelve thousand rubles a year and so naturally I don't need this. So why do I smoke? Maybe it's my old sloppy way of using my hands (as a child), or maybe it has something to do with my boyhood years. Why do I love my childhood so much? My tormented and disgraced childhood. (While collecting cigarette butts from my ashtray, shaking out the tobacco, and then mixing it with fresh tobacco.) (*Fallen Leaves,* bundle 2)

Among the things created in the new way we witness a new image of the poet: "Licking my lips I stare at the world with goggled eyes. That's me. Isn't that pretty? Oh well, what is one to do?" Or again: "These are golden fish playing in the sun but they are placed in an aquarium filled with slimy dung. And yet I'm not suffocating. This may not seem true to life. And yet it is" (*Solitaria*).

Rozanov introduces new themes. But why? Not because he was a special person, although he was a man of genius and therefore special. With the death of the old forms and in accordance with the dialectical generation of new forms and acquisition of new materials, Rozanov was faced with a vacuum. The artist in him yearned for new themes.

Rozanov found his theme. A whole category of themes, themes of everyday life and of family life. Objects stage periodic uprisings. In Leskov, for example, a "great, powerful, truthful" language emerged, a thoroughly new Russian, the fanciful language of the petty bourgeois and hangers-on. Rozanov's revolt was broader in nature. The objects demanded a halo. Rozanov gave them a halo and glory to boot:

Of course there had never been an example of this before . . . and I think it inconceivable for it to ever recur in the history of the universe. So that at the very instant when tears rolled down my cheeks and my soul was rent asunder, I perceived with the unmistakable ear of a listener that they roll in a literary way, musically. Go ahead and record them, I thought, and so for that reason only I recorded them. (*Solitaria*)

I would like to elaborate on two related passages:

If you give something, but come up short, you feel depressed. Even if it is a gift. (Spoken to the little girl at the railroad station in Kiev, whom I wanted to honor with a gift of a pencil. I waited too long and the little girl and her grandma left.) But the little girl did return and I gave her a pencil, which she had never seen before, as a gift. And I could hardly explain to her that this was in exchange for the "miracle." I felt so good and so did she. (*Solitaria*)

The ventilator in the little corridor whistled tediously, if not crudely. I almost broke down in tears. Yes, I want to go on living just so I can hear it. What really matters is for someone, a friend, to live. And the thought occurred to me: Is it really true that he [a friend] will not be able to hear the ventilator in the next world? And the longing for immortality seized me so violently by my hair that I nearly fell on the floor. (*Solitaria*)

It is the very concreteness of his horror that constitutes Rozanov's literary device.

In order to demonstrate the conscious use of domesticity as a literary device in Rozanov, I shall call your attention to one graphic detail from his books. Surely you remember the family photos inserted in the two volumes of Rozanov's *Fallen Leaves*. These pictures produce a strange, unusual impression on the reader.

If we look closely at these pictures, it will become clear to us why this is so: the photos are printed without any border, unlike the custom in book illustrations of the past. The grey background of the photos extends to the very edge of the page without any inscription above or below the picture. Taken together, all this produces the impression not so much of a book illustration as of a genuine photograph placed in a book. That this reproduction was arrived at consciously is proven by the fact that only certain family photographs have been reproduced by this special means. On the other hand, illustrations of an official character are printed in the usual way with margins.

It is true that the photograph depicting the author's children is printed with margins. However, we find here a curious inscription:

Mama and Tayna (standing on her knees) in the front garden on Pavlov's street in St. Petersburg (Peter's side). Next to them stands little Nesvetevich, a neighbor. Yfemov's house, apartment two.

What is characteristic of this inscription is the precise, documentary nature of the family's address, in the manner of the police. This, too, represents a definite stylistic device.

Under no circumstances should the reader infer from my comments on Rozanov's domesticity that Rozanov was "pouring out" his soul to the reader. No, he had assumed the "confessional mode" as a device.

## 3

In *The Dark Face, The People of the Moonlight* and in *The Family Question in Russia,* Rozanov came out as a social journalist on the offensive, as an enemy of Christ.

Such were his political views. True, he wrote in one newspaper as a black man and in another newspaper as a red one. But this was done under two different surnames, and each type of article was strong-willed and dynamic and demanded its own special energy. The coexistence of these two types in one soul was known to him alone and represented a purely biographical fact.

In his three latest books, Rozanov has undergone a major change. In fact, he has changed thoroughly from top to bottom.

"Yes" and "No" coexist simultaneously on the same page. A purely biographical fact is raised to a matter of style. Black and red Rozanov(s) create an artistic contrast similar to that of dirty and divine Rozanov(s). His very "prophecy" has changed its tone, has lost its proclamatory character. Now his prophesy has taken on a domestic tone going nowhere:

My prophecy is not meant for the Russians, and my domestic affairs concern me and no one else. Besides, they are of no significance to anyone, being in fact nothing more than a detail for my biography. December 14, 1911.

From this (its literary character), the "I do not want to" represents an absence of will to action on the part of Rozanov. The physical dimensions have become part of his artistic material, good and evil have become the numerator and denominator of a fraction, and the value of this fraction is zero.

I would like to offer a number of examples from *Fallen Leaves* to illustrate this "I do not want to" of Rozanov:

I have no interest in self-realization. I feel an absence of any and all external energy, of the "will to live." I am the least self-realizing person in the world.

Do I want to play a role? Not in the slightest.

Do I want my teachings to be widely disseminated? No. It would provoke a great deal of agitation, and I love peace and quiet so much . . . and sunset and the silent evening chimes.

I could fill the world with crimson puffs of smoke . . . but I don't want to. [*People of the Moonlight—if you insist!*] March 22nd, 1912. And everything would go up in flames . . . but I do not want to. May my grave be peaceful and away from everybody else's. (*People of the Moonlight,* same date)

There was one thing he felt like doing, one thing he never doubted in all of this, and that was to "record it"!

Every movement of my soul is accompanied by an *utterance.* And every utterance I want to unfailingly *record.* That is an instinct. Is it not just such an instinct that literature sprang from?

All of these "I do not want to"s are written in a special book, in a book placing itself on an equal footing with the Holy Scriptures. I would like to call attention to the fact that the alphabetical index to *Solitaria* and *Fallen Leaves* (both volumes) is compiled in the manner of the *Symphony,* an anthology of passages from the Old and New Testaments arranged in alphabetical order:

*Ab*raham was called forth by God, but I myself called forth God. (*Solitaria,* p. 129)
*An*d I could not shake the petty shopkeeper from my soul. (*Fallen Leaves,* p. 40)
*Au*tonomy of the university. (*Fallen Leaves,* bundle 1, pp. 240 ff.)

I have taken pains to show that these three books of Rozanov constitute a literary work. I have also indicated the nature of one of its predominant themes (i.e., the theme of the everyday world, of ordinary life, the hymn to private life). This theme is not used in its pure form, but rather it is utilized to create contrasts.

The great Rozanov, dashing off his holy scripture like a firebrand enveloped by flames, also loves to smoke a cigarette after a bath and to write a chapter on the theme of "One Ruble, Fifty Kopeks." Here we enter into the domain of a complex literary device.

"Just look, she delights in sorrow, being so elegantly naked," writes Anna Akhmatova. In this passage it is important to note the contradiction between the words "delights" and "sorrow" and again "elegantly" and "naked" (not elegantly dressed but elegantly naked).

In Mayakovsky, we find whole works constructed on this device, as for example, "The Four, Heavy as a Blow." Here are a few fragments:

If I were poor as a billionaire
If I were as little as the great ocean.

This device is known as an oxymoron. We may attribute to it a broader range of meaning.

The title of one of Dostoevsky's tales, "The Honest Thief," is undoubtedly an oxymoron, but the *content* of this tale is also an oxymoron as it is *deployed in the plot.*

In this way we arrive at an understanding of the oxymoron in the plot. Aristotle says (though I'm not quoting him as Holy Writ):

But the poet should seek a plot which involves the sufferings that arise among family or friends, for example, when a brother kills a brother or a son a father, or when a mother kills a son or a son a mother, or when he intends to kill, or does something else of that along these lines.

The oxymoronic character of this passage lies in the paradoxical opposition of kinship and enmity.

Many plots are constructed on the basis of an oxymoron, for example: the tailor kills the giant, David kills Goliath, a frog kills an elephant. The plot in these cases plays the role of justifying, motivating and developing the oxymoron.

This role of "justifying life" appears also in Dostoevsky. I have in mind Marmeladov's prophecy concerning the drunkards at the strange trial.

The creative work and peaceful words spoken by Rozanov against the background of "One Ruble, Fifty Kopeks" and his opinion on how to shut the damper represent one of the most beautiful examples of an oxymoron.

This effect is augmented by yet another device. In this case, contrasts are achieved not only by a change of theme but also by *an incongruity between a thought or experience and the place which serves as its background.* There are two fundamental ways of creating a literary landscape: a landscape that is attuned to the action of the plot or a landscape that conflicts with it.

Examples of landscapes in harmony with the plot are legion among the Romantics. A good example of a conflicting landscape may be found in the description of nature in "Valerik" by Lermontov or in the description of the sky above Austerlitz by Tolstoi. Gogol's landscape (in his later works) represents a somewhat different phenomenon: Plyushkin's garden doesn't conflict directly with Plyushkin himself. Rather it enters as an element into the lyrical and lofty aspect of the work, and this entire lyrical aspect serves as a counterpoint to the "satirical" aspect of the work. Besides, Gogol's landscapes are "phonetic," that is, they serve as a motivation for phonetic structures.

Rozanov's "landscape" belongs to the second, conflicting type. I'm speaking of those notes located at the end of his entries, where Rozanov informs us of their place of composition.

Some of these passages were written in a bathroom. Thoughts of prostitutes would come into his head as he walked behind Suvorin's coffin, the article on Gogol was thought out in the garden experiencing stomach pains, while many other entries were either "written" in a coach, or else were ascribed by Rozanov to such a time.

This is what Rozanov himself has to say about this matter:

The place and circumstances concerning the newly given thought are indicated everywhere with absolute precision in order to refute the fundamental idea of sensualism that *nihil est in intellectu, quod non fuerat in sensu* ["there is nothing in the intellect that was not first known through the senses"]. On the contrary, I have observed in my life that what takes place in the intellect is in stark, complete contrast with what is experienced through the senses. Furthermore, I have observed in general that the mind and the flow of sensations do naturally collide, repel, and work against each other. Although they coincide and flow parallel to each other at times, this happens only occasionally. As a matter of fact, the life of the mind has its own channel, its own independent channel, and chiefly, it has its own source, its own impetus unique to itself.

And where does this impetus come from?

From God and from birth.

The discrepancy between the inner and outer life is known of course to everyone, but, in the final analysis, I have felt this discrepancy from my earliest years (thirteen-fourteen) with such force (and distressingly, and insofar as my "work" and "career" are concerned, so utterly harmful and destructive) that I remained in a state of perpetual astonishment in the face of this phenomenon (the extent of this phenomenon). And being in the habit, at that point in my life, of writing down pretty much everything that "struck and astonished me," as well as everything that I liked or didn't like, I proceeded to record this one, too.

Have made no changes whatsoever concerning the time or circumstances of these recordings that might have gone against the "nature of things."

So much for the intellectual view of the matter. These recordings of time and place, however, also have a moral motivation behind them. Of this, later.

All of this commentary is printed in *Fallen Leaves after* the list of errata. Here we see a device commonly used by Rozanov: the placing of material in an unusual place.

What interests me here is Rozanov's view of the possible contradiction between the place of action and the action itself. His instructions regarding the authenticity of place are less interesting, because it was he who made the decision concerning indications of locality in the first place (not all fragments have been thus documented; rather, only the majority). The mere affirmation of the documentary character of something, already used by Abbé Prévost in *Manon Lescaut,* is another device frequently used by Rozanov. It is given its most popular form in the following comment: "If I had written a novel, then the hero would have done this and that, but since I'm not writing a novel . . ." and the novel moves forward. I suggest a comparison with Mayakovsky:

> It is impossible to say in verse
> Whether we can lick the fiery pans
> with the well-groomed tongue of a poet.

And so on and so on.

Generally speaking, when an author suggests that he is abandoning literature, he is actually introducing a motivation for a new literary device.

# 4

Now I shall endeavor briefly to delineate the plot schemata of Rozanov's *Solitaria* and of the two volumes of *Fallen Leaves.*

Several themes are presented. Of these the most important are: (1) the theme of "the friend" (concerning his wife), (2) the theme of cosmic sex, (3) the theme of the opposition newspaper and of the revolution, (4) a literary theme with articles on Gogol, (5) biography, (6) positivism, (7) Judaism, and (8) a major introductory episode containing letters and other things.

Such a wealth of themes is not unique. We know of novels with quadruple and even quintuple intrigues. The mere device of breaking up a plot into a number of interweaving themes had been used as early as the eighteenth century by Sterne.

Of the three books, *Solitaria* represents a perfection entirely unto itself.

The introduction of new themes is carried out as follows: A fragment of a given situation is presented without any explanation whatsoever. We do not understand what is going on before our eyes. Then follows its unfolding, as if we were watching the solution to a riddle. The theme of "the friend" (concerning Rozanov's wife) is very characteristic of this procedure. At first mentioned only in passing, it is subsequently woven into the heart of the work by nuances of various sorts. A human being emerges before us piece by familiar piece, but only much later do these fragments coalesce to bring forth a coherent biography of Rozanov's wife. This biography may be reconstructed by copying out all of the notes concerning her in the theme of "the wife." The unsuccessful diagnosis by Bekhterev also appears first as a simple reference to the surname "Karpinsky":

Why didn't I call Karpinsky.
Why didn't I call Karpinsky.
Why didn't I call Karpinsky. . .

Only later are we given an explanation for this in the story of the neurological diagnosis that failed to take into account the "reflex of the pupils." So also with "Byzov." First we're given his surname; then his image is fully developed. By resorting to this device, Rozanov introduces a theme not out of a vacuum, as in a collection of aphorisms, but by a gradual preparation or build-up, and the character or his situation *runs like a thread through the entire plot.*

These interweaving themes constitute those threads that, appearing and then disappearing, create the warp and woof of this literary work. In developing the second part of *Don Quixote,* Cervantes uses the names of people mentioned in the first part, for example, Ricote the Moor, a neighbor of Sancho.

We observe in certain themes a curious accumulation of fragments. For example, in the literature theme there is, in addition to some fragments, a fully developed essay on Gogol. And so at the end of the second part all of Rozanov's juxtaposed allusions are concentrated in one full entry. It is written in journalese and set against the book's cosmic finale concerning the universal breast.

In general, the fragments in Rozanov follow each other in accordance with the principle of juxtaposition (i.e., playing off one theme against another, setting off one plane against another). More specifically, this means that everyday existence alternates with the theme of the cosmic. Thus, for example, the theme of the "wife" alternates with the theme of Apis.

We thus see that the three books of Rozanov represent a certain compositional unity of the novelistic type, but without the connecting part played by motivations. Let me offer an example. Novelists frequently introduce poems into their works, as, for instance, in Cervantes, in *A Thousand and One Nights,* in Ann Radcliffe and occasionally in Gorky. These poems represent specific material that bears a certain relationship to the prose of the work. In order to introduce them into the text, different kinds of motivation are employed: they are either epigraphs, or else they are the creations of the leading or secondary protagonists of the novel. The first one lays bare the device, while the second one represents a plot motivation. In essence, however, it is one and the same device.

We know, for example, that Pushkin's "The Upas Tree" and "There once lived a wretched knight" could have served as epigraphs to individual chapters of Dostoevsky's *Idiot.* When we encounter these poems in the body of the work, we find them recited by characters of the novel. In one of Mark Twain's novels we discover epigraphs taken from the sayings of the leading character of the work, *Pudd'nhead Wilson's Calendar.* So too in Vladimir Solovyov's *Three Conversations,* where it is stressed that the epigraph on Pan-Mongolism was written by the author himself (as brought out in a certain gentleman's answer to a question posed by a certain lady).

In precisely the same way, the genealogical relationships among the characters of the novel, often poorly established and utterly capricious (see Werther's patrimony or Mignon's family ties in *Wilhelm Meister*), are merely a motivation for the construction of the novel, for the device of its compositional juxtaposition. At times, what is to be motivated is established only with great difficulty, such as a dream. And at times it is established humorously. The dream motivation is typical for Remizov. In Hoffmann's *Kater Murr* the plot-shifts and the entanglement of the parodistic story of the cat with the story of the man are motivated by the fact that the cat pissed on its master's papers.

*Solitaria* and *Fallen Leaves* may be called novels without motivations.

And so, what is characteristic of them, thematically, is the canonization of new themes, while, compositionally, they are characterized by a laying bare of the device.

### 5

Let us consider the sources for these new themes in Rozanov and new tone. On the first level, as I have already said, we find the genre of letters. This relationship is emphasized by Rozanov himself in his individual instructions:

Instead of nonsense in the form of tales it would be better to discard from the journal this latest form of fiction and instead . . . Well, it would be better to publish some *deed or cause:* a work of science, deliberations (of some society) or philosophy. However, it is often better to reproduce a suitcase of old letters in individual books. Tsvetkov and Gershenzon would have found them good fishing. And a reader, at least a few serious people, would have read it deeply and thoughtfully. (*Fallen Leaves*)

Rozanov did in fact make an attempt at introducing letters "in the raw" into literature by publishing the letters of his schoolmates in the second part. They represent the most impressive section in the book and go on for forty pages.

The second source for the themes is the newspaper, and, in spite of Rozanov's convention of intimacy, we come across newspaper articles quoted in their entirety. His very approach to politics is journalistic. These little feuilletons feature the typical feuilleton device of expanding an individual fact into a fact of universal significance. This expansion is presented by the author in its completed form.

But the chief feature attesting to Rozanov's dependence on newspaper style is the fact that half of his book is taken up with social journalistic material.

Perhaps the very abruptness of transition in Rozanov, the lack of motivation for the relationship of the parts, occurred first as a result of newspaper technique and only later was appreciated for its stylistic possibilities. Apart from the canonization of the newspaper as such, it is interesting to observe in Rozanov a strong awareness of himself as a successor to a younger generation of Russian writers.

If Leskov's genealogy has its source in Dal and Veltman, then Rozanov's genealogy is even more complex.

First of all, he makes a complete break with the official tradition of Russian social journalism and spurns the legacy of the 1870s. And yet, at the same time, Rozanov is a deeply literary man. In his three books he mentions one hundred and twenty-three writers. Still, the fact remains that he is constantly drawn to younger, lesser-known writers, to Rtsy, to Shperk, to Gavarukhe-Otrok. He even says that fame interests him mainly because it gives him the opportunity to bring fame to these obscure writers:

How vast is my literary activity in comparison with Rtsy and Shperk! How many books indeed have I not already published!

But no laudatory reviews in the press, no words of praise in the newspapers have ever given me the kind of quiet, good sense of pride as friendship has (and I felt it) of these three men (and from Shperk I received love).

But how fickle is the destiny of literature: Why are they so unknown, rejected, forgotten? Having a premonition of his fate, Shperk used to say: "So have you read (apparently) Gruber? No? I would desperately love to find something by him. *I am in general drawn* to writers who are obscure, who have remained unnoticed. What sort of people were they? And you're overjoyed when you encounter in them an unusual idea ahead of its time." How simple and deep and true this is.

There is no doubt about Rozanov's relationship with this younger off-shoot of writers. The very title of his book *Fallen Leaves* recalls Rtsy's *The Falling of the Leaves*.

Rozanov was the Pushkin of this movement, but, instead of coming before them, he came after them (Pushkin, too, in the opinion of Stasov and Rozanov, followed rather than preceded his school):

Pushkin's connection with the literature that succeeded him was in general problematic. There is one little-noticed feature in Pushkin, and that is that by the nature of his spirit his face was turned to the past and not to the future. The great harmony of his soul and precocious intellect, which had already shown its clarity in his earliest works, came from the fact that he essentially represented the culmination in himself of a gigantic intellectual and spiritual movement beginning with Peter the Great and ending with himself . . .

In his splendid *Notes on Pushkin* Strakhov demonstrates by an analysis of the great poet's style that, for the most part, no "new forms" make their appearance in Pushkin. He attributes this to Pushkin's modesty and "humility," to his refusal to seek originality in matters of form.

Pushkin built anew. There was as yet no need to overthrow a canon, since there was as yet no canon strong enough to be overthrown. This is proven by the literature dominant in Russia in his time and in the generation immediately before him.

The same holds true for Sterne. No one understood the English novelist's way of complicating the plot structure nor the way he playfully undermined it. Karamzin "imitated" Sterne by writing works whose structure was simple, indeed downright infantile. *Sterne was appreciated in Russia only thematically,* while Germany saw a strong affinity between his principles of composition and its own Romantic movement; that is, it discovered that its new Romantic literature, however independent, "rhymed" with Sterne's achievement.

Rozanov became the canonizer of the younger school of writers at a time when the older school was still mighty. In short he represents an uprising.

It is worth noting that not all the features of this older art, which had been playing a pitiful, uncanonized role before Rosanov, were raised by him to artistic prominence. Rozanov borrowed from everywhere, even from the argot of thieves:

I have not disturbed Your Excellency, Sir, precisely because I wanted to catch them red-handed. I really like this folklore. I believe there is something artistic in the language of thieves and policemen.

Rozanov is rapturous over jargon like "brandlyas." Finally, he introduces the theme of the detective novel, speaking lovingly and in great detail about the Pinkertons. On the basis of this material he builds the themes of "The People of the Moonlight" and *Fallen Leaves:*

There are terribly interesting and lovely details. In one little book the matter concerns "the first thief of Italy." The author evidently brought his manuscript to the publisher. But the publisher, finding that *The King of Thieves* was not sufficiently enticing and fascinating for purposes of sale, crossed it out and wrote over it his publisher's title *The Queen of Thieves.* And so I read and read in anticipation, wondering when the *Queen* would make her appearance in *The Queen of Thieves.* Nowhere in the book is there any mention of her. The only thing we have is a reference to a "gentleman thief."

Here the publisher's trick is taken for an artistic detail.

There are many comments concerning Sherlock Holmes, especially in the second volume:

My children, it is harmful for you to read Sherlock Holmes. And, removing the bundle clandestinely, I set about to greedily devour Sherlock Holmes myself. Each volume comes in forty-eight little pages. Now the Syversky–Petersburg Express is flying past like a dream. Still, I can't help feeling that I am sinning as I read these tales of the great sleuth till three or four in the morning. Horrifying stories!

As you can see, the theme here too is first named without being developed. It is developed in the second volume, where whole episodes are presented conceptually. There is an episode in the first part of *Fallen Leaves* that is very characteristic of Rozanov: here Sherlock Holmes is not so much presented as adumbrated. The whole meaning of this device lies in the heightening of the material and in the enstrangement of the marriage question.

For instance, consider the following passage:

"Wicked, envious witch, that keeps lovers apart. You horrible witch! And you dare to bless marriage?"

. . . a domestic story in Sherlock Holmes's "The Blue Tattoo" and "In the Subterranean Vein." A bride is under obligation to return to the hooligan who had cut her husband's throat, taken possession of his documents and abandoned her for America. By a stroke of ill luck, this hooligan also bears a striking resemblance to his victim. In accordance with Church law, the ruffian is forced to give up the bottle, while the aristocratic lady reluctantly becomes his wife.*

It is not the ideas that are important here but the device. Every man sees things differently.

But not all of the material has undergone, as I have already said, a transformation. Part of it has remained unprocessed. There are elements in Rozanov's works which echo the sentimental verses of Nadson, a decadent poet of an earlier generation. These elements do not lend themselves well to modification. Such, for example, are the following half-verses:

> Silent, dark nights,
> The fear of a crime,
> The anguish of loneliness
> The tears of despair, fear and the sweat of work.
> It is you, oh Religion . . .
> Who are a help to the hunchbacked, help to the weary,
> The faith of the sick man.
> These are your roots, oh Religion,
> Eternal, miraculous.

Or

---

*These stories are not by Arthur Conan Doyle but are pastiches of uncertain origin. Cf p. 98, note. [Trans. note]

> Dim little star, pale little star
> You burn before my eyes continually alone
> You are ill and you tremble,
> Soon you will turn into darkness utterly forever.

Here's an example from prose:

> What do you like?
> I like my nocturnal dreams, I love to whisper to the facing wind.

These themes, no less than the composition, are felt as banal. Evidently the time of their resurrection has not yet come. They are not yet "bad" enough to become good. We are dealing here with a continual change in perspective, with the presentation of things anew, against the backdrop of new material and a new setting. Rozanov's images are organized in precisely the same way.

6

The image-trope represents an unusual way of naming an object, that is, naming it with an unusual name. The purpose of this device is to place the object in a new semantic category, a category of concepts of a different order (e.g., a star is an eye or a woman is a grey duck). Thus, the image is expanded by a description of the object under comparison.

We may compare the image with a syncretistic epithet (i.e., an epithet defining, for instance, sound concepts by means of auditory concepts and vice versa—for example, the mellow chime, the brilliant sounds). This device is often found in the works of the Romantics.

Auditory sensations are mixed up with visual ones. Yet I do not think that there is any real confusion here. What we have instead is a device that places an object in a new category by expelling it from an old one. It is interesting to examine Rozanov's imagery from this point of view. Here, for example, is what he has to say concerning this phenomenon. Rozanov's brief comment follows Shperk's analysis:

> Children are distinguished from us by the fact that they perceive everything with a kind of powerful realism which is inaccessible to adults. For us "chair" is a piece of "furniture" but a child knows nothing of the category "furniture," and "chair" is such a huge and living object for him as it cannot be for us. From this it follows that children delight in the world infinitely more than we do.

Much the same can be said for the writer who violates the category by withdrawing the "chair" from the "furniture."

# Chapter 10

# Essay and Anecdote

Greece has not left us a theory of the novel, although it has left us both novels and novelistic schemata, part of which is still alive to this very day. Still, little respect was paid to this genre. Although in existence for centuries before, the novel was deemed outside the scope of theory.

The same was true of Russian literature, where the only theory of the novel available, perhaps, was to be found in the translator's preface. The novel and tale were long considered to be a genre outside the scope of theory.

This is the position in which plotless prose finds itself today. Its specific gravity today and its historic significance are very great. Nearly the entire work of the Encyclopedists, of Russian social journalism, of the essay and of a whole array of works by the so-called Russian belletrists lies outside the scope of the plotted genre.

Nevertheless, even without a genealogy, this genre exists. True, quantitatively speaking, the purely aesthetic part predominates over its novelistic part. Still, this genre calls for new discoveries.

A plot is a picklock, not a key. Plot schemata conform closely to the social reality that they put into shape. The plot distorts the material by the very fact that it selects it, and on the basis of rather arbitrary criteria. This is especially noticeable in the history of Greek literature, whose themes focus on the conflicts obtaining in a specific number of families. The formal causes for this focus were already pointed out by Aristotle. The anecdotes which we shall now relate concerning our contemporaries have their origins in the depths of the ages.

When Count von Rantzau died, *Izvestiya* recalled one of his successful repartees. Someone had apparently alleged that his family had descended from an illegitimate line of the Bourbons. Parrying this charge, he replied simply that it was his father, and not his mother, who had carried on a friendly liaison with the Bourbons (i.e., implying that his accusers are, in actual fact, his illegitimate relatives). This schema repeats with precision the elegant conversation which the immortal George, the English Milord, had carried on at the home of "Elizabeth's mother."

The anecdotes that friends tell each other are of a similarly honorable origin. The anecdotes recorded by Pushkin came out later under the title of "Ukrainian Anecdotes," while the famous anecdote about the Jew who had obligated himself to teach the elephant how to speak—hoping that either the elephant will die, or the shah will die, or the Jew himself will die—was told, according to Bolotov, by Catherine the Great, who, however, did without the Jew.

A plot schema with a resolution is a rare thing in anecdotes. This is an accidental affliction of the material itself, which connects with the schema only at one point. Such a resolution is as rare as goldfish with transparent tails and telescopic eyes.

Sometimes a historic fact has nothing whatsoever to substantiate it and immediately becomes an anecdote. There is, for example, the story by Leo Tolstoi called "What For?" concerning the Pole who fled from Siberia in a coffin, in which the bones of his children allegedly were found. Connoisseurs of Tolstoi point to Maksimov's *Siberia and Forced Labor* as the source of that story. As a matter of fact on page 356 of that book you will find an account of that story indicating the surname of the woman who was the subject of this story, Migurskaya. There is also a reference to the fact that the story is told in greater detail by Dal in his story "The Fantastic in the Real and the Real in the Fantastic."

Such stories do exist in the complete works of Dal. The incident concerning the Pole is printed in the second volume (it was published beforehand in *Patriotic Notes* in 1846). You will find it on page 94. The schema for this anecdote is exactly the same as in Tolstoi (i.e., the couple is betrayed by the cossack). The hero has no surname and the entire conversation ends in the following way: "So you are saying that you witnessed that incident . . ." This is remarkable not only because this incident is strange, but also because it involves someone else's speculation. Who has read the little book by Kotzebue, *The Most Remarkable Year of My Life?* Kotzebue tells all this in the form of speculation as to how his wife should cart him back with her.

If you look in Kotzebue's little book, you will find this entire story in it, but in the form of speculation, in the guise of a dream of flight:

I wanted to build a wooden partition in my big room and to set up a makeshift wardrobe in the corner behind it. I then wanted to live quietly and contentedly with my wife. After about two months of this apparent tranquility, I was to gradually feign illness and, at long last, madness. This too would have lasted several months. And I wanted one dark evening to put on my sheepskin coat and hat on the shore of Tubla, by an icehole, and then silently to steal away home and hide in the wardrobe which would be open at the top. My wife would raise the alarm. They would look for me. They would find my coat. Obviously he has drowned in an icehole, they would say. The letter I would leave behind would confirm this fact. My wife would be in despair. She would lie awake in bed by day and feed me at night. This incident would be reported to Tabalsk and from there to Petersburg. Once there, this report would be laid aside and they would forget about me. After a certain period of time my wife would recover a bit and ask for travel expenses for passage to Liflyandia, which could not be refused her. She would then buy a big rolling *kibitka* wagon in which a man could lie at leisure. And it's really true. This is the only vehicle which could accommodate this daring exploit.

This story by Kotzebue, which makes no mention of a coffin, has not yet been played out. When we consider certain details, though, such as the flight that takes place precisely in the winter, the sheepskin coat by the icehole and so forth, we realize that what we have before us is not the working over by the writer (Tolstoi) of extra-literary fact but rather the adapting of a literary invention (by Kotzebue, for instance) to a certain locality using a different surname, the recording of this legend and the renewal of its literary life.

This case is very typical. Even if we take into account the register of criminal acts, we see that the same incidents are worked over continually by writers. For example, I know of an anecdote from the eighteenth century concerning a jeweler who was brought to a psychiatrist. This anecdote makes the psychiatrist the customer and the jeweler the patient who rants and raves constantly about diamonds. Because it shapes and selects, the plot plays a deformational role. Similarly, in order to create a type, it is also necessary to assign existing facts to a specific hero in a different context. And again we deform these facts.

At the present time the inertia associated with the plot has been brought to light with special force while the deformation of the material has reached new extremes. Our notion of the class struggle takes the atypical form of a struggle within the bosom of a family, although, generally speaking, the family is more often than not homogeneous in our literature.

The schema of "Two Brothers," motivated by "White and Red" instead of "Good and Evil," perpetuates the rather worn-out anecdote about Cain.

But we simply cannot repudiate the plot, including the story line based on the circular pattern of the hero's fate. The hero plays the role of a godson in a photograph or as chips of wood floating on the river current. That is, he vastly simplifies the mechanism for focusing attention. In cinematography, for example, the feature movie plot uses its material more intensively than the documentary movie. Of course, we could also say in reverse that plot squeezes out material.

The question arises today: What should replace the role of plot in prose? A fundamental change would be brought about by shifting the point of narration, either spatially, as in the case of journeys, or temporally, as in the case of memoirs. There is in our literature, however, a pure interest in material and in the conventional method of moving from fact to fact.

Of course, we must stipulate that even memoirs have been subject to the powerful deformational influence of the devices of art. The beginning of Balaktovsky's memoirs shows more than a trace of *Gil Blas,* while Vinsky's memoirs with his direct reference to Shandyism show, of course, the influence of Sterne. The influence of the English writer on Zhikharev's memoirs is very great.

The contemporary feuilleton represents an attempt to integrate the material not by means of the hero but by means of the narrator. This is a form of denovelization of the material. The feuilletonist does this by transferring his work to a different plane, that is, not by manipulating his plot, but rather by comparing big things with little things, by locating the point of intersection between them in a certain word or by relating a certain incident that has happened in the West and comparing it with a similar incident here.

The feuilletonist does in his work what ought to be done by every ideal editor. Of course, not only by an ideal editor but also by a real one. When we say that the novel will be squeezed out by the newspaper, we are not speaking of individual articles in the newspaper as such. No, we mean the newspaper as a genre, so to speak. The journal represents a certain literary form already in evidence in the early days of English journalism, when the editor's authorship was clearly felt.

Today's journal has lost its literary form and this is especially true of the "thick" journals. An organic personality can, however, be felt in a newspaper, provided it is not overburdened with material of an informational nature. A newspaper such as the *Red Gazette* (during its first period of existence) can definitely be appreciated as literary form. In addition, the general orientation of a newspaper is to be found not only *in* its articles but also *between* them.

It is easier nowadays for a writer of documentary prose to work with excerpts than with whole works.

The essayist of today, unfortunately, has a habit of simply coloring his material in the manner of fiction (i.e., he includes a description of the color of the sky). Yet, this is done in a useless fashion, all the more so when we consider that this color is applied from memory without any real scientific understanding of what clouds are and what they designate. But the good essayist has his standard of comparison. So Goncharov describes the exotic against the touching though feebly expressed background of Nature and the everyday life of ordinary Russians. This discovery of a fundamental point of view that drives the material forward, enabling the reader to reassemble it once again, is a far more organic device for the essayist to use than comparisons that rarely hit the mark.

The development of a literature of fact should not attempt to emulate high literature but rather to part company with it. One of its chief conditions should include a struggle with the traditional anecdote, which carries in its own nucleus all of the virtues and all of the vices of the old aesthetic method.

# Works Cited

*Because of Shklovsky's erratic citations and the obscurity of some of his references, this list is by necessity incomplete.*

Afanasiev, Aleksandr. *Zavetnye skazki* [Indecent Tales]. Geneva, 1860s.

Anichkov, Evgeny. *Vesennaya obryadovaya pesnya* [Spring Ritual Song].

Attaya, Mikhail, trans. *Kniga Kalilah i Dimnah* [The Book of Kalilah and Dimnah]. Moscow: Lazarev Institute of Eastern Languages, 1889.

Beilin, Solomon. *Stranstvuyushchie ili vsyomirnye povesti i skazaniya v drevnei-ravvinskoi pis'mennosti* [Nomadic or Universal Tales and Legends in Ancient Rabbinical Literature]. Irkutsk, 1907.

Brik, Osip. "Zvukovye povtory" [Sound Repetitions]. 1917.

Brunetière, Ferdinand. *Manuel de l'histoire de la littérature française.* Paris, 1898.

Bücher. *Rabota i ritm* [Work and Rhythm]. St. Petersburg, 1899. Perhaps a translation of Bruno Bücher's *Die Kunst im Handwerk.* Vienna, 1872.

Buslaev, Fyodor. "Stranstvuyushchie povesti i rasskazy" [Nomadic Tales and Stories]. *Ruskii vestnik* [Russian Herald], May 1874.

Derzhavin, Nikolai. *Sbornik stat'ei posvyashchennykh V. N. Lamanskomy* [Collection of Essays in Honor of V. N. Lamansky]. Part 1. St. Petersburg, 1907.

Diez, Friedrich. *Leben und Werke der Troubadours.* Zwickau, 1829.

Dovnar-Zapolsky, Mitrofan. *Pesni Pinchukov* [Songs of the Pinchuks]. Kiev, 1895.

Eikhenbaum, Boris. *Molodoi Tolstoi* [The Young Tolstoi]. Petrograd, 1922.

Gilferding, Aleksandr. *Onezhskie byliny* [Olonetsian Folk Rhapsodies]. 1873.

Khristiansen, S. V. *Filosofiya isskustva* [Philosophy of Art]. St. Petersburg, 1911.

Khudyakov, Ivan. ["Russian Riddles," in:] *Etnograficheskie sborniki* [Ethnographic Collections]. Russian Imperial Geographical Society, 1864.

Kireevsky, Pyotr. *Pesni, sobrannye P. V. Kireevskim* [Songs Collected by P. V. Kireevsky]. Edited by Pyotr Bessonov. 8 vols. Moscow, 1860-74.

Kotzebue, August von. *Dostopamyatnyi god moei zhizni* [The Most Remarkable Year of My Life, trans. from the German *Das merkwürdigste Jahr Meines Lebens* (1801)]. 1879?

Maikov, Apollon. *Sbornik posvyashchenny V. N. Lamanskomy* [Collection in Honor of V. N. Lamansky]. 1908.

Maksimov, Sergei. *Sibir' i katorga* [Siberia and Forced Labor]. St. Petersburg, 1900.

Mandelshtam, Iosif. *O kharaktere gogolesvskogo stil'ya* [The Nature of Gogol's Style]. Helsinki, 1902.

Merezhkovsky, Dmitry. *Vechnye sputniki* [Eternal Companions]. St. Petersburg, 1897.

Miller, Vsevolod. "Vsyomirnaya skazka v kulturno-istoricheskom osveshchenii" [The Universal Legend in the Light of Culture and History]. *Russkaya mysl'* [Russian Thought], November 1894, 207-29.

Onchukov, Nikolai. *Severnye narodnye dramy* [Folk Drama of the North]. St. Petersburg, 1911.

———. *Severnye skazki* [Legends of the North]. St. Petersburg, 1909.

Østrup, Johannes. *Issledovanie o 1001 nochi* [A Study of *A Thousand and One Nights,* trans. from the Danish *Studier over "Tusind og en Nat"* (Copenhagen, 1891)]. Moscow: Lazarev Institute of Eastern Languages, 1904.

Ovsyaniko-Kulikovsky, Dmitry. *Yazyk i isskustvo* [Language and Art].

Peretts, Vladimir. *Istochnik skazki* [Origin of the Tale].

Pogodin, Aleksandr. *Yazyk kak tvorchestvo* [Language as Art]. Kharkov, 1913.

Potebnya, Aleksandr. *Iz lektsy po teorii slovesnosti* [Lectures on the Theory of Language]. Kharkov, 1914.

———. *Iz zapisok po teorii slovesnosti* [Notes on the Theory of Language]. Kharkov, 1905.

Pypin, Aleksandr. *Istoriya drevnei russkoi literaturi* [History of Early Russian Literature]. 2d ed. 1902-3.

Romanov, E. R. *Velikorusskie skazki* [Great Russian Tales]. *Zapiski Imperskovo Russkovo Geograficheskovo Obschestva* 42, no. 52: *Belorussky sbornik* [Belorussian Anthology], 1886-1912.

Rybnikov, Pavel. *Pesni, sobrannye P. N. Rybnikovym* [Songs Collected by P. N. Rynikov]. Edited by A. E. Gruzinsky. Moscow, 1909-10.

———. *Pis'ma* [Letters], vol. 3.

Savodnikov, Dmitry. *Zagadki russkogo naroda* [Riddles of the Russian People]. St. Petersburg, 1901.

Serapion Brothers. *Serapionovye Brat'ya: Zagranichnyi al'manakh* [Serapion Brothers: Almanac from Abroad]. Berlin, 1922.

Shklovsky, Viktor. *Voskreshenie slova* [Resurrection of the Word]. St. Petersburg, 1914.

Sokolov, Boris and Yuri. *Skazki i pesni Belozerskogo kraya* [Tales and Songs of the Belozero Region]. 1915.

Spencer, Herbert. *The Philosophy of Style.* New York: Appleton, 1873.

Speransky, Mikhail. *Russkaya ustnaya slovesnost'* [Russian Oral Literature]. Moscow: Mikhailov, 1917.

Strakhov, Nikolai. *Zametki o Pushkine* [Notes on Pushkin]. 1888.

Tseretely, Grigory. *Novootkrytye komedii Menandra* [The Newly Discovered Comedies of Menander]. St. Petersburg, 1908.

Veselovsky, Aleksandr. "Belletristika u drevnykh grekov" [Belles Lettres in Ancient Greece]. *Evropeisky vestnik* [European Herald], December 1876, 683.

———. *Sobranie sochinenii* [Complete Works]. Academy of Sciences, 1908 ff.

Yakubinsky, L. P. "O zvukakh poeticheskogo yazyka" [On the Sounds of Poetical Language]. *Sborniki* 1 (1916): 38 ff.

———. "Skopleniye odinakovykh plavnykh v prakticheskom i poeticheskom yazykakh" [The Accumulation of Identical Liquids in Practical and Poetic Language]. *Sborniki* 2 (1917): 13-21.

Yatsimirsky, A. P., trans. *Skazki sokr. zab. ugolka sobr. sk. i legend* [Tales from the Sokr. Zab. Ugol. Collection of Rumanian Tales and Legends]. Moscow: Sytin, 1902.

Zelenin, Dmitry. *Velikorusskie skazki permskoi gubernii* [Great Russian Tales of the Perm Province]. St. Petersburg, 1913.

Zelinsky, [Kornely?]. *Sofokl* [Sophocles]. 2 vols. Moscow: Sabashnikov, n.d.

# Index

# DALKEY ARCHIVE PAPERBACKS

Visit our website at www.cas.ilstu.edu/english/dalkey/dalkey.html

Dalkey Archive Press
ISU Campus Box 4241, Normal, IL 61790–4241
*fax* (309) 438–7422